STRIKES

D0989042

Also by Richard Hyman

DISPUTES PROCEDURE IN ACTION
*INDUSTRIAL RELATIONS: A MARXIST
  INTRODUCTION
MARXISM AND THE SOCIOLOGY OF TRADE
  UNIONISM
NEW TECHNOLOGY AND INDUSTRIAL RELATIONS
*THE NEW WORKING CLASS? (*editor with Robert Price*)
*THE POLITICAL ECONOMY OF INDUSTRIAL
  RELATIONS
SOCIAL VALUES AND INDUSTRIAL RELATIONS
THE WORKERS' UNION

Also published by Macmillan

Strikes

Richard Hyman

Professor of Industrial Relations
University of Warwick

Fourth Edition

MACMILLAN

UNIVERSITY
OF NEW BRUNSWICK

JUL 0 4 2016

LIBRARIES

© Richard Hyman 1972, 1977, 1984, 1989

All rights reserved. No reproduction, copy or transmission
of this publication may be made without written permission.

No paragraph of this publication may be reproduced, copied or
transmitted save with written permission or in accordance with
the provisions of the Copyright, Designs and Patents Act 1988,
or under the terms of any licence permitting limited copying
issued by the Copyright Licensing Agency, 33–4 Alfred Place,
London WC1E 7DP.

Any person who does any unauthorised act in relation to
this publication may be liable to criminal prosecution and
civil claims for damages.

First edition (Fontana) 1972
Second edition (Fontana) 1977
Third edition (Fontana) 1984
Fourth edition (Macmillan) 1989
Reprinted 1991

Published by
MACMILLAN ACADEMIC AND PROFESSIONAL LTD
Houndmills, Basingstoke, Hampshire RG21 2XS
and London
Companies and representatives
throughout the world

Printed in Great Britain by
Billing and Sons Ltd
Worcester

British Library Cataloguing in Publication Data
Hyman, Richard, *1942–*
Strikes.—4th ed.
1. Great Britain. Industrial relations.
Strikes
I. Title
331.89'2941
ISBN 0–333–47360–4 (hardcover)
ISBN 0–333–47361–2 (paperback)

Contents

Preface to the First Edition

This is a small book on a large subject. Those obliged to rely on the mass media for their knowledge of industrial relations might be forgiven the impression that the average British employee spends more time on strike than at work. Industrial conflict, it is clear, is widely viewed as one of the major social problems of our time. This popular preoccupation with strikes is reflected in the academic world: today there exists a substantial literature devoting at least partial attention to the subject from a variety of viewpoints.

It would require a considerable volume to deal comprehensively with this literature; my treatment is therefore deliberately selective. Since this study appears as part of a sociology series, most attention is devoted to the *sociology* of industrial conflict; I have made little attempt to explore the perspectives of the labour lawyer, economist, or historian. I have, however, been sufficiently free in my interpretation of the sociological approach to devote a fair amount of space to the industrial relations background of the current British strike situation.

In this respect, my treatment is regrettably insular. The nature and development of the strike in Britain are in many respects atypical of the industrial relations patterns of other countries. An exploration and explanation of the contrasts and affinities revealed by the uses and meanings of strike action in different cultures would be of great value. But while I do not make limited international comparisons, space prevents any detailed examination of industrial conflict as a world phenomenon.

Selectivity in the coverage of this book also reflects my own predilection for theoretical controversy. I have not attempted to add to the many valuable but somewhat arid works which provide complex statistical analyses of the various dimensions of strikes. Nor have I more than touched on the vexed question of assessing the consequences of stoppages of work. My focus has been rather on the causes of industrial disputes, and their meanings for those involved. If this emphasis is somewhat arbitrary, I hope nevertheless that the reader will find the treatment stimulating.

It is virtually obligatory for any academic writing on an acutely controversial topic to make ritual genuflections in the direction of objectivity. I am sceptical of such moralistics. As is urged in one of the most intelligent of recent works of sociological theory, 'objectivity is the way one comes to terms and makes peace with a world one does not like but will not oppose; it arises when one is detached from the *status quo* but reluctant to be identified with its critics'. I have attempted to indicate, and to present dispassionately, those theories and interpretations which conflict with my own; but I cannot claim to be detached. My commitment to the traditional humanistic goals of freedom and reason colours the treatment of my subject. Where people's efforts consciously to control their own destinies clash with social arrangements rooted in ignorance or manipulation, I cannot profess neutrality. And since I consider it more illuminating to view conflict as a natural response to specific social and institutional arrangements in industry, rather than as the outcome of human wilfulness and irrationality, my approach to strikes is scarcely orthodox.

I make little claim to originality in this book; my main purpose has been to present the views and theories of others. Since there exists a substantial literature in the field of industrial relations and industrial sociology, much of which is not readily accessible to the student or lay reader, I have made more liberal use of references than is normal in an introductory volume of this nature. Even so, there will be many authors whose ideas I have purloined with at best the minimum of acknowledgement. To these I offer my apologies. They also share, with those colleagues who have offered criticism and advice on drafts of this text, my thanks.

R. H.
University of Warwick, Coventry, October 1971

Preface to the Fourth Edition

The three previous editions of *Strikes* were published by Fontana Paperbacks; I am delighted that the book now appears, like many of my other works, under the imprint of Macmillan.

I wrote this book in an intense fortnight in the hot summer of 1971. Industrial turbulence raged across national frontiers, seemingly as part of a far broader social crisis; and I sought to capture and make comprehensible this turmoil. Five years later, when I prepared the second edition, the pattern of industrial struggle had altered significantly; but its level remained high. Today it is evident that the nature of British industrial relations has been radically transformed, and one reflection of the change is a diminution in strike activity. It is also obvious that both sociological theory and Marxist analysis have altered greatly during the past decade.

It is even clearer than in 1977 that if I were to rewrite the book fully today it would involve an effort of total reconstruction. I would, for example, locate strikes much more intimately within the routine processes of accommodation and conflict in everyday work relations; would attempt a fuller theoretical analysis of the notion of conflict; would pay greater attention to why strikes so *rarely* occur; and would relate British experience to overseas patterns. But this would make *Strikes* an altogether different text; whereas I still see value in the work as it stands; and if sales are any indication, many others agree.

In this new edition, the main text has been left largely unaltered, beyond updating the statistical tables and commentaries on trends. As before, this permits the reader to judge how far my assessments (and occasional predictions) have stood the test of time. The concluding chapter seeks to bring the argument up to date, and gives some attention to issues of theory and interpretation which are raised (or sometimes neglected) in the body of the book. The Guide to Further Reading has also been updated.

R. H.
January 1988

Acknowledgements

The author and publishers gratefully acknowledge the following for permission to quote from works in their copyright: Allen and Unwin Ltd; Basic Books Inc.; G. Bell and Sons Ltd; Cambridge University Press; Collier Macmillan Ltd; Columbia University Press; Doubleday and Co. Inc.; The Fabian Society; Harper and Row; Her Majesty's Stationery Office; Holt, Rinehart and Winston Inc.; Leeds University Press; McGraw-Hill Book Co.; Macmillan, London and Basingstoke; The Macmillan Company, New York; Merlin Press; *New Left Review; New Statesman*; Penguin Books Ltd; Pluto Press Ltd; *The Political Quarterly*; Prentice-Hall Inc.; Routledge and Kegan Paul Ltd; *The Sunday Times*; Tavistock Publications Ltd; *The Times*; Weidenfeld and Nicolson Ltd.

1. The Anatomy of the Strike

An unremarkable dispute

A strike at a British car factory is scarcely a remarkable event. The stoppage at the Halewood factory of the Ford Motor Company, in the week of 14 to 21 June 1971, possessed few intrinsically memorable features; it will indeed have been generally forgotten by the date that this book appears. It has been chosen to introduce the present study of strikes partly because it *was* unremarkable; but mainly because it was the first dispute after the commissioning of this volume to attract detailed press coverage. The account which follows is based wholly on these press reports.

The issue

On Monday, 14 June, a shop steward, John Dillon, was summarily dismissed by Ford management; the reason given was that he had held an unofficial meeting during working hours and had taken a leading part in an 'unruly demonstration' on company premises. Since Ford's account of this episode was challenged by union representatives, it is useful to cite the account given in the *Sunday Times* of 20 June 1971:

> Under Ford procedure agreements, embodied in a Blue Book, shop stewards may not hold meetings on company premises or during working hours; they may not leave their ordinary jobs to act as shop stewards in a dispute between workers and foreman unless the foreman has first had two shifts to sort it out; and they must accept a foreman's instructions, unless these are over-ruled at a higher level.

11

Mr Dillon has been suspended twice, and was ultimately dismissed for breaching these and other rules. According to union sources, the first suspension was for leaving his job in the paint shop when a group of men got him to represent them in an argument with a foreman, in spite of the fact that the foreman had told them that a shop steward should not be brought in at that stage.

The second suspension, again according to a union account, was for 'advising' a group of men to continue doing a job a particular way, although the foreman had said it should be done differently. Three men had been taking turns at using either hand or power-driven sanding equipment, but the foreman had said that each man should stick to the same piece of equipment. Dillon argued that it didn't seem to him to matter either way. The plant manager's letter said that the second suspension was for 'telling employees to disobey their supervisor who had instructed them in the way in which the job should be done, then telling them not to listen to the supervisor's advice'.

The third and final incident arose last Wednesday week [i.e. 9 June] over a manning dispute. One man, union sources say, was taken off a job usually done by five men (it involved manhandling car bodies from overhead to lower-level conveyor belts). The men objected, but Mr Dillon advised them to try it, which they did for two days and nights. The foreman complained about the way the job was being done and warned them that if it wasn't done properly, they would be dismissed. Rather than risk being dismissed for failure, the four men stopped work altogether. The foreman promptly suspended them.

About thirty other men also stopped work (union sources say they were laid off; the company says they struck). A shop steward takes up the story: 'On the way out, some of them got hold of Dillon and asked him what the hell was going on. He said: "Let's go outside and talk about it with the others." They said: "Come on, John. Tell us what it's all about." So he told them about the manning dispute.

'Some of the men said: "Let's go and get hold of the manager." Dillon said: "You can't do that." So he went to the shop manager's office instead and asked him if he would come out and talk to the men. Dillon came out of the office and said the manager wouldn't talk to them. But the men pushed him back and went into the shop manager's office. He followed them in to see what was going on. There was a bit of shouting, but not by Dillon. Eventually he persuaded them to go outside.'

For the next two days, the management carried out its own investigation of what happened. Last Sunday two senior Ford labour relations officials travelled to Liverpool and in the Adelphi Hotel heard the results of the investigation. District officials of Mr Dillon's union, the Transport and General Workers, were informed on Monday that he would be dismissed, and dismissed he was.

The background

At the end of January 1971, workers at a number of Ford factories stopped work in support of a pay claim. Within days the strike had spread to all Ford establishments in Britain, involving over 45,000 employees. It was not until nine weeks later, at the beginning of April, that a settlement was reached. The dispute was thus exceptionally large and protracted; with two million 'striker-days' registered it was indeed one of the half-dozen largest British stoppages since the 1930s, and perhaps the biggest British strike of all time involving a single private employer. The unions affected, notably the Transport and General Workers' Union and the Amalgamated Union of Engineering Workers, paid out roughly £2 million in dispute benefit – a massive sum in relation to the limited reserves of most British trade unions. Ford itself claimed to have suffered a loss of production worth £100 million. And the cost of the stoppage to the strikers themselves must have been substantial.

This last factor may well have influenced company thinking in the aftermath of the dispute. According to *The Times* (18 June), 'since that strike ended there have been clear signs of a hardening of attitudes by the management at Halewood on shop steward activities'. *The Times* reported (17 June) that 'behind the apparently simple issue of the dismissal of one shop steward for what the company calls "continued breaches of company agreements" lies the much more deep-rooted problem of a power struggle between the Halewood management and the shop stewards' organization at the plant'.

This underlying conflict was described in more detail by the *Guardian* (17 June):

The Ford plant on Merseyside appears to have been suffering from a disturbing sickness since the ten-week strike over pay which ended just over two months ago. Labour relations have deteriorated to such an extent that a leading union negotiator, Mr Moss Evans, of the Transport and General Workers, expressed his disquiet publicly two days ago. Shop stewards at Halewood have complained repeatedly in recent weeks that the plant management has tightened its shop floor discipline and was now 'playing everything according to the book'. The book in this instance is the 'Blue Book' agreed between unions and management at Fords for negotiating procedures. . . . In the normal course of events, procedures are interpreted to suit events and circumstances on the shop floor, but the Halewood stewards claim that since 8 April, when work resumed at Halewood after the big pay strike, the management has insisted on observing the letter. The result has been disciplinary measures – including suspensions – against shop stewards on eleven occasions. . . .

The company denies having any devious scheme up its sleeve and insists that it merely expects employees and stewards to observe agreements. But it seems obvious that the company has become meticulous about procedure since it agreed to pay a – by today's standards – modest increase in April. And the pressure is clearly on the Halewood shop stewards. . . .

Inevitably, therefore, the Halewood workers have reached the conclusion that Fords have decided to 'take on' the tightly-knit shop stewards' organization and are out to erode its strength.

The 'purge' of the Dagenham plant in 1962, when several militants lost their jobs, is being recalled and stewards are wondering if Fords are trying to help history to repeat itself. With a band of 'tame' shop stewards in its plants – so the argument runs – Fords would be in a position to change working arrangements – such as track speeds in the assembly shops.

Fords strongly refute such arguments, although the circumstances of Mr Dillon's dismissal raise some disturbing questions.

After a manning dispute in the Halewood paint shop last week, he believed he had satisfied the company's allegations. . . . On Monday he was sacked, and the rest of the stewards are now asking what connection there was between this change in attitudes and a conference, rumoured to have taken place in Liverpool during the weekend, between the Halewood management and Mr Bob Ramsey, Ford labour relations director.

Other press reports gave a similar story. The *Daily Telegraph* (21 June) quoted union allegations that on the return to work in April, 'stewards were summoned and warned that the "blue book" – the 93-page booklet detailing agreements, procedures, and conditions of employment for Ford workers – must now be strictly adhered to. Since these procedures, including those applying to shop stewards' activities, had fallen into a certain amount of disuse, friction was inevitable.' The *Financial Times* added its opinion that 'there seems little doubt that of late the company has been stricter over discipline' (22 June), and described Dillon's dismissal as 'an unusually severe step' (15 June). Another report interpreted this intensification of discipline as part of a concerted management strategy which impinged on conditions of work throughout Halewood. 'Day and night, local agreements on manning and conditions were ignored. Men were physically prevented from seeing their stewards' (*Socialist Worker*, 26 June). Allegedly, the reduction in manning which caused the paint shop dispute and led to Dillon's dismissal not only intensified the pressure of work on a physically taxing operation but also put workers' lives in jeopardy.

The stoppage

John Dillon was dismissed by the company on the morning of Monday, 14 June. Men at the assembly plant (Dillon's factory, one of three in the Ford Halewood complex) held a lunchtime meeting and voted to strike. By Wednesday, workers at the adjacent body and transmission plants had joined the stoppage, involving over 10,000 employees and bringing production at Halewood to a standstill.

On the Tuesday and Wednesday, meetings were held at national level between Bob Ramsey, Ford labour relations director, and Moss Evans, chief union negotiator. The union insisted that Dillon must be reinstated, but suggested that he could return to work as an ordinary employee pending a joint investigation of his activities as a shop steward. The company rejected this, refusing even to discuss Dillon's case until after the strikers returned to work. The talks thus ended in deadlock, with no date fixed for further discussions. This led senior shop stewards from nineteen Ford factories to meet in London on Friday, and the outcome was a call for the unions to declare a national strike of all Ford workers.

With all observers expecting a protracted stoppage, the strike ended as suddenly as it had begun. During Sunday the company approached union officials, and several hours of discussions were held that evening, ending with Ford's virtual acceptance of the union's previous peace plan. Dillon's dismissal would be withdrawn, and he would return to work in a different section of the factory – though not as a shop steward. (It was unclear whether any restoration of his steward's credentials could be made by the union alone or would require company approval: a possible source of future conflict.) This formula was put to a mass meeting on the Monday, a week after the strike began, and was accepted.

It is not easy to explain the company's sudden reversal of policy and, in effect, its surrender to the union's demands. However, the solidity of workers' response to Dillon's dismissal may well have come as a surprise; given the recent protracted stoppage and the proximity of the holidays, management might have hoped that a single sacking would not provoke a mass walk-out. But not only did strike action take place in Dillon's assembly plant; by spreading to the transmission plant it stopped production of gearboxes for Ford factories elsewhere in Britain. Whether or not the unions had agreed to the call for a company-wide strike, production throughout British Ford would have been rapidly paralysed.

Five points which may be made in conclusion are of relevance to the discussion later in this book. First, the 'quality' press was unanimous that the Halewood stoppage was provoked by management action. Second, the strike was 'unofficial' throughout, but the men enjoyed the obvious sympathy of national and local full-time officers. Third, Dillon's sacking had been agreed by Ford management at the highest level; only immediate 'wildcat' action could have achieved his reinstatement. Fourth, the strike cannot be understood as an isolated incident; it must be seen as part of an overall struggle for control over shop-floor conditions. And finally, this stoppage exemplifies – what can easily be forgotten in abstract discussions of strikes and strike statistics – that every dispute represents the working out of real human problems and involves real individuals like John Dillon.

Dimensions of the strike

A strike has been defined as 'a temporary stoppage of work by a group of employees in order to express a grievance or enforce a demand'. Each element in this definition is important. A strike is a *temporary* stoppage: the workers intend that at its conclusion they should return to the same jobs with the same employer, who himself normally views a stoppage in the same terms. It is a *stoppage of work*, and thus in principle at least distinct from such actions as an overtime ban or go-slow. It is a collective act, undertaken by a *group* of employees. The fact that the group is of *employees* is also crucial; refusal by tenants to pay rents or students to attend lectures are called strikes only by analogy. Finally, a strike is almost always a *calculative* act, designed 'to express a grievance or enforce a demand' (Griffin, 1939: 20–2).

Strike statistics

In Britain, and in most other countries, an official record of industrial disputes is provided by three main statistical series. The first gives the number of stoppages. British statistics exclude small strikes involving less than ten workers or lasting less than one day, unless 'working days lost' total at least 100. Since employers are not obliged to report stoppages, it is likely that a number of disputes large enough to meet this criterion escape the notice of the Department of Employment, which compiles the statistics. Because of differences in criteria and completeness, international comparison of strike numbers can easily be misleading.

British statistics once distinguished between strikes and lock-outs – stoppages initiated by the employer. This distinction is no longer officially made, because of the difficulty of applying it in practice.

'The only essential difference between a strike and a lockout is that the union takes the first overt step in one case and the employer in the other' (Ross, 1948: 106–7). In either situation, employees are willing to work on their terms, while the employer is willing that they should work on his. Which side takes the first identifiable initiative in stopping work may itself be a matter of dispute, and is in any case of secondary importance. To take the first step need not indicate special aggressiveness. In a period of falling prices, the employer will want to alter wage rates; when prices rise, workers will try to change them. So lock-outs are normally rare in periods of economic expansion. Another reason why strikes are far more common than lock-outs is that the employer has the formal right to alter working conditions unilaterally; workers who want changes, or object to changes introduced by management, have to take the initiative in stopping work. This is a point of fundamental importance, and will be considered in more detail later.

The second dimension of strikes is the number of workers involved. This may appear straightforward, but is not. Comparison of press reports of a dispute will often show how estimates of numbers vary. If a stoppage affects only part of an establishment, the strikers may wish to exaggerate the extent of their support, while management may understate the impact of the dispute. Even if the factory is forced to close – as at Halewood – there will be the problem of distinguishing those actively supporting the strike and those laid off in consequence. This distinction is impossible to apply accurately, short of interviewing every employee; and, even then, there is the difficulty that support is a question of degree rather than of all or nothing. British statistics do however separate workers 'directly' and 'indirectly' involved at each establishment, even if the estimates must on occasion be little more than guesses. Perhaps wisely, the Department of Employment does not even attempt to guess the number of workers in other factories made idle by stoppages.

The third index of disputes is the number of 'working days lost'. This figure can be calculated for each stoppage by multiplying its duration in days by the number of workers involved. The official title of this statistic has been criticized as a loaded term, since it assumes what is in fact questionable: that time spent in striking would otherwise have been spent working, and cannot be made up afterwards. A more neutral title would be 'striker-days' (Turner *et al.*, 1967: 54). This too is open to objection, since it labels as strikers those who may be only 'indirectly involved' in a dispute. Despite this it seems preferable, if only for its brevity, and will be used in this book.

Any inaccuracy in the assessment of number of strikers is necessarily reflected in statistics of striker-days. Moreover, the number of workers involved may alter as a dispute proceeds; and even its duration may be difficult to judge, particularly if there is delay in resuming production after a return to work is agreed. Nevertheless, this index does have the virtue of combining several dimensions of strike activity in one statistic. Since small, short stoppages which may escape or be ineligible for the official records would have little impact on the aggregate of striker-days, this is normally considered most appropriate for international comparisons.

Mechanics of the strike

This section outlines briefly the manner in which strikes typically are commenced, prosecuted and ended. Inevitably this involves oversimplification. Alvin Gouldner, in his well-known study of an American 'wildcat' strike, made a comment which is often quoted: 'a "strike" is a social phenomenon of enormous complexity which, in its totality, is never susceptible to complete description, let alone complete explanation' (1955: 65). A recent British author has added that 'one cannot sensibly speak of a strike as though it were a single category of social action. There are varieties of strikes and indeed, the very same social conditions which give rise to certain kinds of strikes may also lead to the diminution of other kinds of strikes' (Eldridge, 1968:3).

One important characteristic which may distinguish different types of strikes is their duration. An international comparative study has noted that stoppages in some countries normally last only a matter of days, while in others the typical dispute is of several weeks' duration; 'really it is misleading', the authors comment, 'to use the same word for such different phenomena' (Ross and Hartman, 1960: 24). This appears a valid argument, and in the discussion which follows a rough distinction is made between strikes which function as a genuine trial of strength, and those which are little more than a token demonstration.

The trial of strength

The trial of strength has become the classic stereotype of the industrial dispute – the only sort which is ever likely to make the history books. Trade unionists with any consciousness of the history of their movement have heard not only of the General Strike of 1926 but also of the London Dock Strike of 1889. The more serious student will be able to cite a series of massive confrontations: in mining, the fight against reductions in 1893, the Rhondda strike of 1910–11 and the national dispute of 1912, both involving the issue of a minimum wage, the stoppages of three months in 1921 and eight months in 1926, both against heavy wage cuts; in engineering, the national lock-outs of 1897–8 and 1922; in the docks, the bitter conflict of 1912 following the unions' successes of the previous year; in cotton, the resistance to reduced rates in 1892–3, the lock-out over union membership in 1911, the struggles against reductions in 1921, and in a series of major conflicts between 1929 and 1932. Precisely because, understandably, it is disputes of this nature which become famous, the impression is easily gained that they were typical of the past usage of the strike; though as will be seen, this is incorrect.

Since a protracted stoppage can be expected to involve substantial costs for the employer, the workers, and the union which pays them benefits, this is normally regarded as a weapon of last resort. The 'classic' strike is in many respects the industrial equivalent of war between nations. Like war, it is sometimes described as the conduct of industrial relations by 'other means', but is normally regarded by all concerned as sufficiently momentous an event to be planned with some care and launched only after intensive efforts at peaceful resolution of the question at issue.

A prolonged dispute has always involved serious deprivations for strikers and their families. An account of trade unionism in the early years of this century has noted that

> even when he got strike pay, the member needed great self-control and courage to see a long stoppage through, if only because that pay

was so much less than his wage. . . . He might have savings to draw on; after that there was the pawnshop; but sooner or later he would be getting hungry, and, what is worse, seeing his wife and children get hungry too. In practice she could get relief, but under penalty of appearing as a pauper before the relieving officer, with the threat of the workhouse in the background. He, being engaged in a trade dispute, could not (Phelps Brown, 1960: 159).

While the workhouse is a thing of the past, little else has changed. Some strikers are entitled to rebates on the income tax they paid before the dispute; their dependants can claim benefits from the modern equivalent of the relieving officer. (Moves are afoot at the time of writing to curb the striker's rights in both respects, on the grounds that his family ought to suffer for his 'sins'.) The predicament of the contemporary British worker engaged in a protracted dispute has been described as follows.

The severity of hardship varied according to whether other members of the strikers' households were working and whether other members of their families were eligible for social security benefits. But some hardship was involved for everyone. Standards of living had to be stripped to the bare essentials; many were obliged to go into arrears on rent and HP payments; savings were swallowed up; in some households durable goods had to be sold; some strikers were forced to rely on charity from relatives and friends (Lane and Roberts, 1971: 107).

In the past, elaborate arrangements were often made to reduce such hardship. Special strike committees would issue appeals for financial support to fellow trade unionists and the general public; street collections were sometimes held; shopkeepers were asked for donations of food and landlords for restraint in demanding rents. Such efforts permitted additional support for strikers in special need, the provision of soup kitchens, and other measures of this sort. All this helped maintain strikers' morale, and some activities were organized specifically to this end: regular mass meetings and demonstrations, mass pickets at the place of work, sometimes even sports and entertainments. Special meetings were sometimes held to ensure that strikers' wives understood and supported their actions, and efforts would also be made to win general public sympathy. In addition, where the employer was able to divert production from a strike-bound factory, attempts were usually made either to extend the stoppage or to persuade other trade unionists to 'black' the products involved.

It is normal for employers to counter strikers' propaganda efforts, and a far more forceful response was common in the past. Attempts might be made to keep the factory working by recruiting 'blackleg' or 'scab' labour, thus often provoking conflict with pickets who saw their jobs in jeopardy. Frequently the forces of 'law and order' have been used to intimidate strikers. And on occasion, particularly in the United States, employers have incited or organized violence against workers' leaders.

Strikes today may occasionally give rise to drama of this order; but most are far more passive affairs. The experience of the typical worker in the seven-week Pilkington dispute of 1970 has been described as 'the sheer tedium of being at home all day' (Lane and Roberts, 1971: 107). Even in the past, the same was probably true of the great majority of stoppages; but there has certainly been a significant decline in the proportion of dramatic confrontations. These normally occurred, however, when union organization was itself at issue: the union struggling to consolidate its membership and win recognition, the employer to break his workers' union allegiance or replace them by a more pliant labour force. Such questions only exceptionally underlie disputes today, and much of the heat has disappeared from industrial conflict.

'All disputes end at some point, and all strikes are concluded' (Kerr, 1964: 179) – this follows from the definition of a strike as a *temporary* stoppage of work. The only exceptions occur when an employer closes his factory or recruits a new labour force, rather than negotiating a settlement. Some strikes end in capitulation by one side or the other, but a form of compromise is far more usual. Having endured the losses which a strike entails, both sides are normally determined to end with something to show for their pains; even if unable convincingly to claim victory, employers and workers will often sacrifice a lot to avoid a humiliating surrender; and each side, knowing this, will normally offer at least token concessions to facilitate settlement of a dispute.

At first sight it might seem surprising that an agreement can be negotiated in the course of a stoppage when this proved impossible beforehand. One reason is that, though entrenched positions may at first be reinforced by the outbreak of a strike, the costs of its continuance eventually push both sides towards a settlement. Another is that the reality of the conflict demonstrates to each party the determination of the other – proving that the other side was not, as may have been assumed, bluffing. Also important is what one study has termed intra-organizational bargaining (Walton and McKersie, 1965). Company and union are not monolithic entities; conflict usually occurs within each as well as between them as to the acceptability of particular terms. After a time at least, the experience of a strike tends to bring to the fore the 'doves' on either side.

Settlements are often speeded by the involvement of 'third parties'. Government mediators (in Britain, the Advisory Conciliation and Arbitration Service) can often function as a face-saving mechanism for resuming negotiations and reaching agreement. (Government intervention, however, is often far from 'neutral' – as is argued later.) On occasion – though this is very rare in this country – both sides may end a strike by submitting the questions at issue to independent arbitration. In the case of major conflicts, the government may intervene, for example by appointing a Court of Inquiry. While this imposes no formal obligations on the disputants, work is almost always resumed and the eventual report and recommendations are usually accepted.

The demonstration stoppage

Protracted trials of strength have always been a small minority of stoppages; and not all of these have been large-scale disputes involving a major company or a whole industry. While relatively few in number, such major conflicts often dominate the statistics of striker-days. Though massive stoppages have become particularly rare in Britain since the war, they still occur and may well be increasing in frequency; the postal workers' strike of 1971 is a recent example. Within small firms, the particularly protracted strike has not disappeared entirely: the Roberts-Arundel dispute at Stockport, beginning at the end of 1966, lasted a year and a half; while in the summer of 1971 a stoppage at Fine Tubes in Plymouth entered its second year.

The great majority of contemporary strikes fall, however, into the category of 'demonstrations in force' (Knowles, 1952: xi). The decision to stop work is often virtually spontaneous – though the dispute will probably still centre around, or at least reflect, long-standing grievances which peaceful application has failed to remedy. In such cases, spontaneity need not imply unpredictability.

At other times, such conflicts may involve what have been termed 'perishable disputes' (Eldridge, 1968: 70): issues which management would win by default if workers did not act immediately. The Halewood strike came within this category: the only way that workers could obtain Dillon's reinstatement was to stop work on the spot. It is inherent in the employment relationship that if the employer provokes conflict by altering conditions of work in a manner which is considered objectionable, the *workers* must appear technically as the aggressors by stopping work.

Another variant of this type of stoppage occurs where workers are employed on piecework or some other form of payment by results. Whenever a new job is introduced (as happens daily in many engineering factories, for example) a piece-rate has to be agreed. If management insists that employees work to a price which they find unacceptable, a strike may be inevitable.

The spontaneous or demonstration strike is usually both small in scale and quickly settled. It is true that such strikes sometimes spread, as at Halewood; and occasionally they prove unexpectedly protracted – the seven-week Pilkington strike snowballed from a small dispute over an error in workers' pay packets. But these cases were very unusual. As an American author has noted,

the possible costs of a wildcat strike are a serious matter to the workers involved and should keep them from continuing the strike for long. They lose wages; they receive no compensatory pay from the union and they are subject to possibly severe disciplinary penalties from management and perhaps from the union. Management and union also suffer from a wildcat strike. The consequences should therefore spur both to act swiftly to get the parties back to work in the shortest time consonant with an appropriate resolution of the issue (Kuhn, 1961; 53–4).

Since the primary purpose of a demonstration stoppage is to call attention to the urgency of workers' feelings of grievance, such strikers are usually willing to return to work 'to permit negotiations to take place', even before concrete concessions have been offered. In some firms, workers may engage in very short stoppages – known as 'downers' – while remaining on factory premises, solely in order to direct immediate attention to a grievance (Clack, 1967: 61). There is considerable evidence that demonstration strikes regularly prove highly effective in speeding negotiations towards an acceptable outcome.

2. Strikes and British Industrial Relations

The hue and cry about strikes

'Britain as a whole', according to one recent study, 'has become accustomed to consuming strikes with its cornflakes' (Lane and Roberts, 1971: 232–3).

During the Labour Government's period of office between 1964 and 1970 the increasing rate of unofficial strikes was raised to the status of a 'serious economic problem'. Politicians, ably assisted by the mass media, successfully created the impression that if only strikes could be made to go away they would take with them most of Britain's economic ills. Where before this period strikes were mainly of interest to aficionados and industrial relations 'experts', they became a matter of widespread popular and political debate. The view that British industry was especially strike-prone became firmly embedded in popular consciousness.

Since these comments were written, the attitude described has formed the justification for anti-union legislation by a Conservative government: the 1971 Industrial Relations Act. So it is important to consider how far British industry really matches its strike-prone image, and what explains any peculiarities in British patterns of industrial conflict.

The trend of strikes

Because strike statistics are the one type of industrial relations data readily available in quantitative form, they are the subject of considerable and often exaggerated attention. As was suggested in the previous chapter, such statistics – however 'official' – contain built-in sources of inaccuracy. Some employers are more efficient or scrupulous than others in recording disputes. The precise criteria used to determine what is counted as a work stoppage will vary; as will be seen later, it is often difficult to decide whether or not a particular incident should be regarded as a strike. Situations may tempt companies to be liberal or restrictive in their recording: a firm wishing to give an impression of harmonious industrial relations may turn a blind eye to certain disputes; employers keen to provide evidence of a need for legal restrictions on the right to strike may record numerous minor incidents which would otherwise be ignored.

All this means that strike statistics must be used with caution. It must be remembered that they are an imperfect measure of work stoppages; and that work stoppages themselves are only a very partial indication of industrial conflict, let alone the general climate of industrial relations in a nation or an industry. With these qualifications, however, such statistics can provide a useful guide to trends in industrial disputes.

The trend of strikes since the beginning of the century is shown in Table 2.1; the periods into which the eighty years have been divided are ones in which strike patterns were reasonably homogeneous.

It is readily apparent that, even ignoring year-to-year fluctuations, the trend of British strikes has been anything but simple. Generalizing very crudely, however, it is possible to define the decade of the 1930s as something of a watershed in the history of British strikes. Since records were first compiled in the 1890s, in only five years before 1941 did the number of recorded stoppages reach 1,000; the annual average for this period was roughly 700. In every subsequent year there have been over 1,000 recorded strikes, and the annual average in this latter period is over 2,000. But the trend of striker-days has been in the opposite direction. In the years up to 1933, the annual average was nearly 15 million; even excluding 1926, with its record 162 million striker-days, the average was well over 10 million. But between 1933 and 1967 there were only three years with more than 4 million striker-days, and the annual average was well under 3 million. (It should be mentioned that the occupied population has risen from 16 million at the beginning of the century to 25 million today. Relative to the labour force, then, the long-run increase in the number of strikes is less than the absolute figures suggest, and the decline in striker-days is greater.)

Table 2.1
British strike statistics: annual averages 1900–87

	Number of strikes	Workers involved ('000)	Striker-days ('000)
1900–10	529	240	4,576
1911–13	1,074	1,034	20,908
1914–18	844	632	5,292
1919–21	1,241	2,108	49,053
1922–25	629	503	11,968
1926	323	2,734	162,233
1927–32	379	344	4,740
1933–39	735	295	1,694
1940–44	1,491	499	1,816
1945–54	1,791	545	2,073
1955–64	2,521	1,116	3,889
1965–69	2,397	1,215	3,929
1970–74	2,917	1,573	14,077
1975	2,332	809	6,012
1976	2,034	668	3,284
1977	2,737	1,166	10,142
1978	2,498	1,041	9,405
1979	2,125	4,608	29,474
1980	1,348	834	11,964
1981	1,344	1,513	4,266
1982	1,538	2,103	5,313
1983	1,364	574	3,754
1984	1,221	1,464	27,135
1985	903	791	6,402
1986	1,074	720	1,920
1987	1,016	887	3,546

Source: Employment Gazette.

The average size of strikes has shown no clear long-term trend: the 'average strike' (assuming that such an entity exists) involved some 600 workers in the 1960s. This was double the figure of the turn of the century and of the 1940s and 1950s, but less than half that of the decade of mass stoppages from the end of the First World War. The fact that striker-days have tended to fall while the

frequency of stoppages has risen is due to a substantial reduction in
their average duration: from several weeks throughout the period
before the 1930s, to less than one week thereafter. In the 1970s the
average length rose again, with peaks of 14 days in 1972 and 1980,
while in 1984 it was over 18 days.

Averages can be misleading; a few large or protracted stoppages
can dominate a year's figures. Two national one-day engineering
strikes in 1962 accounted for the bulk of that year's striker-days;
the statistical consequence was an 'average' dispute involving 2,000
workers and lasting little more than day. By contrast, the length of
the 'average' strike in 1972, 1980 and 1984 reflected the long national
disputes of miners and steelworkers.

To an important extent, the statistical pattern of British strikes
reflects the incidence of major industry-wide conflicts. Writing in
the 1950s, one writer commented:

> In earlier years in which losses from strikes were heavy, the great
> bulk of them were due to a few official disputes which tied up a
> whole industry. The coal strike of 1912, the railway strike of 1911,
> and the cotton spinners' strike of 1908 account for the bulk of the
> days lost between 1908 and 1914. From 1919 to 1925 nearly 150
> million out of 194 million working days were lost in seventeen
> official national disputes (out of a total of over 6 thousand disputes),
> 72 million of them in the coal lock-out of 1921. In 1926, 160
> million out of 162 million working days were lost in the General
> Strike and the coal lock-out; the remaining 321 disputes shared
> the odd 2 million working days. Of the 30 million days lost from
> 1927 to 1933, over 18 million are accounted for by five national
> textile strikes (Clegg, 1956: 32).

After 1933, however, there was not one single official national dispute
until December 1953.

Two main explanations are usually suggested for this change. First,
it can be said that there has been a growing accommodation between
employers and trade unions as the latter become 'established' and the
institutions of collective bargaining 'matured' – a thesis which will be
examined further in Chapter 4. A second argument treats economic
conditions as a key influence: 'whereas the number of strikes tends

to rise during periods of prosperity (that is, when prices are rising and unemployment is falling), the severity of strikes, measured in working days lost, tends to rise during periods of depression (when prices are falling, and unemployment is rising)'. It is suggested that when major strikes *do* occur in periods of economic expansion, 'their cause is usually not a straightforward disagreement over wages or hours of work. Instead of this, or besides this, such strikes have for the most part involved some principle of the system of relationships between employers and trade unions' (Clegg and Adams, 1957: 1–2). This latter point is relevant in considering the upsurge of official industry-wide stoppages from the late 1960s: government efforts to impose restraints on pay settlements introduced a new and contentious element into the established pattern of peacetime industrial relations. These developments are discussed in more detail in Chapter 7.

Strike-prone industries

Resort to strike action is not evenly distributed throughout the occupied population. Though strikes by non-union employees are not unknown, an effective stoppage normally presupposes collective organization. In consequence, strikes are most common among male manual workers, and tend to be particularly prevalent in occupations where unionism is strongest. Even among the strongholds of union organization, however, there are variations in the frequency of stoppages.

The 'strike-proneness' of an industrial or occupational group can be calculated by relating the number of stoppages or striker-days recorded to the size of its labour force. This measure is reliable only within limits: the compilation of labour force statistics, like those of strikes, involves a number of problems. Nevertheless, it provides a useful indication of relative propensities to strike.

Coal-mining ranks near the top of virtually every national table of strike-proneness, and Britain is no exception. The miners have featured in many of the most severe conflicts in labour history; while for two decades from the Second World War they provided over half the recorded stoppages in every year. In the mid-1950s, indeed, coal-mining was responsible for *three-quarters* of recorded stoppages. (In

Table 2.2
Some strike-prone British industries: annual averages

	Strikes per 100,000 employees				Striker-days per 100 employees			
	1966–70	1971–5	1976–9	1980–2	1966–70	1971–5	1976–9	1980–2
Docks	140	154	126	93	286	401	126	214
Coal-mining	67	67	100	124	109	1,056	38	94
Motor vehicles	51	44	41	36	206	359	1,812	166
Shipbuilding	50	41	23	19	110	320	96	119
Iron and steel	31	38	33	13	65	114	119	1,030
All industries and services	12	11	10	6	24	59	57	32

Source: Employment Gazette.

Note: the basis on which these statistics are published has altered since 1982.

part, this may have reflected the thoroughness with which the nationalized mining industry did record its disputes; it is in the private sector that smaller stoppages are most likely to escape the statistics.) After that date, however, there was a dramatic decline: from 2,224 mining strikes in 1957 to 135 in 1971. This change occurred partly because, with the Coal Board's drastic policy of pit closures, there were far fewer miners left to strike; and also because the abolition of piecework payment during the 1960s removed a major cause of sectional disputes. For most of the post-war period, strikes were almost invariably small and shorᵗ as well as unofficial, and striker-days were relatively low. But larger stoppages in 1969 and 1970 were followed by the great official confrontations of 1972 and 1974; Table 2.2 shows how mining came to dominate the striker-days 'league table' in the early 1970s.

By contrast, in virtually every other industry there has been, since the mid-1950s, a substantial increase in the number of stoppages; the total for all industries excluding mining rose from 600 at that time to 3,700 in 1970. This simultaneous shrinkage in mining strikes and growth elsewhere was responsible for a deceptive stability in Britain's overall strike figures until the end of the 1960s.

It is possible to indicate in more detail the industrial distribution of strike activity in Britain. Table 2.2 gives annual averages for the most strike-prone industries during the period 1966–82, relating the numbers of stoppages and striker-days to labour force size. The industries are ranked in terms of relative propensity to strike in 1966–70.

It is apparent that British strike statistics are dominated by the mining, transport, and metal-producing and using industries. At the other extreme are a group of industries with a very low strike propensity: these include agriculture, the distributive trades, financial, administrative and professional services, and clothing. The middle ground is occupied by the remaining manufacturing industries and by some public services whose strike-proneness has recently increased.

Strike statistics indicate the extent to which disputes are becoming common in industries which previously were relatively immune. This point has indeed been remarked in an earlier study by Goodman (1967): excluding mining from consideration, the five industries with the most stoppages in each year accounted for a majority of British strikes; but this proportion had fallen from 69 per cent in 1959 to 52 per cent in 1965. This trend has continued; in 1970 the five leading industries accounted for only 47 per cent of non-mining strikes, and by the early 1980s for only 40 per cent.

International comparisons

Considered in isolation, it is very difficult to assess the significance of British strike statistics. One way of placing the figures in perspective is by international comparisons. This can be hazardous; since each country has its own peculiarities in its compilation of statistics, there is ample room for controversy in the interpretation of relative strike-proneness (Turner, 1969; McCarthy, 1970).

The Royal Commission on Trade Unions and Employers' Associations (the Donovan Commission) compared the United Kingdom strike record with that of fifteen other major industrial countries. Its Report presented (p. 95) statistics of stoppages in these countries in the three years 1964–6 and these are shown in Table 2.3; in most cases the statistics relate to the mining, manufacturing, construction, and transport industries.

The Commission noted that in terms of striker-days in relation to size of labour force, 'the United Kingdom's recent record has been about average compared with other countries'. It went on to make the following points in respect of the relative *number* of stoppages in Britain:

While this country has a comparatively large number of stoppages, they are of fairly short duration and do not usually involve very large numbers of people. The pattern in Australia and New Zealand is similar, though both have more stoppages than ourselves in proportion to the workforce. Stoppages in Canada and the USA are less frequent than ours in proportion to the workforce, and involve comparable numbers of workers, but each one lasts more than four times as long as our own. Of the remaining countries, it may be remarked that France has a comparatively large number of stoppages involving many people but of very short duration, indicating the frequent use of 'token' strikes. Some countries are fortunate in having so few stoppages that no established strike pattern can be said to exist: this applies to the Netherlands, Norway, Sweden, and the Federal Republic of Germany (p. 96).

The main criticism to be made of this summary is that on the Donovan Report's own figures, the relative frequency of strikes in Britain is only marginally higher than in North America; and the small difference might be attributable to the different methods used in recording stoppages.

Table 2.3
Comparative international strike statistics 1964–6

	No. of stoppages per 100,000 employees	Average no. of persons involved per stoppage	Average duration of each stoppage in working days	No. of working days lost per 1,000 employees
United Kingdom	16·8	340	3·4	190
Australia	63·8	350	1·8	400
Belgium	7·0	680	9·2	200
Canada	15·8	430	14·0	970
Denmark	5·5	370	7·3	160
Finland	10·8	360	2·1	80
France	21·8	1,090	0·8	200
Federal Republic of Germany	Not available		3·6	10
Republic of Ireland	25·6	450	15·2	1,620
Italy	32·9	720	5·3	1,170
Japan	7·6	1,040	2·9	240
Netherlands	2·2	370	2·4	20
New Zealand	26·8	250	2·1	150
Norway	0·6	100	26·0	5
Sweden	0·5	570	15·4	40
United States	13·2	470	14·2	870

Source: **Royal Commission on Trade Unions and Employers' Associations, Report.**

The evidence suggests, then, that Britain is unusual not in the dimensions of its strike record but in the attention which the latter attracts. This has indeed been officially admitted: 'the UK's reputation abroad has probably suffered more than the time lost through strikes in comparison with other countries would warrant' (Ministry of Labour, 1965: 41). In effect, the direct consequences of strikes are no more serious in Britain than in other countries; it is not so much strikes as the hue and cry which they attract which is the real 'problem'. 'One is left to wonder', writes one author,

> why it is – in the light of the actual evidence – that strikes should apparently be so commonly thought as important and damaging as they are. One reason is undoubtedly a seeming public preference for the disastrous in its taste for reportage of any kind. British workers are thought to be remarkably strike-prone for much the same reason as (for example) British students are currently conceived of as generally revolting. From the point of view of the mass media, good news is no news, and the effect of the selection of the satisfyingly catastrophic is to project the abnormal in behaviour as the norm. Data chosen for its sensationalism, however, is an extremely poor basis for policy (Turner, 1969: 47–8).

Other reasons for the media's preoccupation with strikes will be considered in Chapter 6.

Other causes of 'lost production'

Contrary to popular imagination, then, 'striking is an exceptional habit' (Clegg, 1970: 318). This is underlined by the findings of a survey carried out for the Donovan Commission (Government Social Survey, 1968). Only one trade union member in three, and a slightly smaller proportion of managers, could recall a strike at their place of work since they had been there; and of this third, roughly a half were aware of only one stoppage. Since the trade unionists interviewed had been with their existing firm for an average of ten years, and works managers for nine, this indicates how rare strikes really are in most work situations.

Another way of putting strike statistics in perspective is to compare them with other eventualities which affect industrial production. In 1970, when striker-days reached a new post-war peak, the total was just over 10 million. By contrast, industrial accidents cost 20 million working days. An unemployment level near the million mark is the equivalent of well over 200 million working days. And in recent years, loss of time through certified sickness has accounted for over 300 million working days. An effective anti-influenza vaccine – or stricter control over unsafe working conditions – would be likely to save far more working time than the most draconian anti-strike laws. Knowles' conclusion is indisputable: 'it is clear that the loss of working time from other causes has hitherto been very much greater than the loss from strikes. Again, the loss of time and output through managerial inefficiency, for example, may sometimes be considerable; but while the time lost by workers is measurable, that lost by management is not' (1952: 271).

It can of course be replied that this argument misses the point. This was the contention of the Ministry of Labour (now the Department of Employment) in its evidence to the Donovan Commission.

As sickness and injury are spread throughout the year and throughout the whole labour force, their effects can often be absorbed by those remaining at work. Moreover, these effects are to a great extent predictable and can be allowed for in the scale of manning. Strikes, on the other hand, can hardly be allowed for in this way and can, therefore, disrupt production in a way in which sickness does not (1965: 40).

This contention deserves to be examined in detail.

The cost of strikes

Since statistics of striker-days cover only those workers directly or indirectly involved at the establishment(s) immediately concerned by a dispute, they understate the disturbance to production caused by stoppages which affect other establishments. This is likely to be an important factor in two distinct situations. First, the interdependence of numerous establishments in a complex production process – as in the British car industry – entails that any break in the chain may have extensive repercussions. Thus when transmission workers joined the Halewood strike, production throughout Ford was soon threatened. Second, certain industries – for example, transport and power supply – are vital to production throughout large sectors of the economy, and the consequences of stoppages here will be correspondingly magnified. Prolonged stoppages in industries with an important role in British exports may have serious effects on the balance of payments.

Yet if strike statistics may in some contexts understate the economic impact of disputes, in others they give an exaggerated impression. To refer automatically to 'loss' of working days through stoppages is misleading because, as the Donovan Report noted, 'it is possible for some of the loss of working days to be made good after a strike, either by overtime or by greater effort under incentive schemes' (1968: 111). Some sociologists have indeed suggested that participation in strike action can raise workers' 'morale', resulting in a spontaneous rise in productivity – presumably most likely to occur where the strike is successful. One example of 'lost' production being made up after a stoppage is cited by Clegg (1970: 341): 'the national coal strike of 1912 . . . cost the industry 11 per cent of its annual working time, but only 4 per cent of its expected annual output'.

To speak of 'working days lost' is also to imply that days spent striking would otherwise have been spent working. But as has long been noted, 'some strikes . . . are merely substitutes for curtailments of work which would otherwise take the form of layoffs' (Kornhauser *et al.*, 1954: 8). Recent confirmation of this point has come from a detailed analysis of strikes in Britain's car industry: striker-days tend to be highest in periods of recession, when the production 'lost' could not have been sold anyway.

In these circumstances, the strike becomes almost a form of 'work-spreading'. To have a strike is not perhaps the most rational way to fill in a slump, but it is more interesting and sociable than some other forms of idleness, and helps to keep workers from drifting away to other jobs (Turner *et al.*, 1967: 118–19).

The same authors add that 'the frequency with which managements themselves lay men off . . . makes it seem nothing abnormal for workers to withhold their labour' (p. 331).

Attempts by employers to quantify the losses occasioned by disputes typically ignore such factors. In addition, statements by motor manufacturers display surprising optimism in their calculation of the production which would have been achieved but for a stoppage; and in setting a cash value to this 'lost production' they tend to forget that they have been saved such costs as wages, materials, and components (Turner, 1969). A stoppage, then, may not be unwelcome in all situations. It has been argued that the Post Office made a profit out of the 1971 dispute: the strike closed down the letter and parcel service, which had been running at a loss; but there was a large increase in use of the profitable telephone service (Foot, 1971: 15). The cynic might suspect that in some circumstances a strike could even be provoked – when an employer is faced by production difficulties or dwindling order books. Certainly it has been argued that

the art of the sympathy strike, the secondary boycott, has been in this country not so developed as the bosses' sympathy lay-off, where a strike by 48 people in a car radiator factory automatically means within 48 hours that thousands of men elsewhere in the industry lose their jobs (*New Statesman*, 12 November 1965).

To the extent that this is true, many of the 'indirect effects' of sectional stoppages may reflect not the impossibility of continued production but a pressure tactic to force a speedy return to work.

In view of these complicating factors, it is evident that 'one cannot draw up an exact account of strike losses' (Knowles, 1952: 278). To do so would require knowledge of what would have occurred in the absence of each stoppage, and the ability to calculate and weigh the difference: an impossible enterprise. It is possible only to commend the verdict that 'the judgement of most specialists is that the economic consequences of strikes are overrated' (Kornhauser *et al.*, 1954: 8).

The case of the 'wildcat' strike

It is sometimes argued that it is not so much the frequency of British stoppages, or the number of striker-days, which is economically damaging; rather, that the harm results from their origins and status. What is emphasized is the fact that the typical British strike is both unofficial and unconstitutional.

An unofficial strike has been defined as 'one which is not recognized by the Executive Committee of a Union' (Knowles, 1952: 30). An unconstitutional strike is one in breach of an agreed disputes procedure: such procedures normally specify a series of meetings through which a grievance must be processed, in an attempt at peaceful resolution, before a stoppage of work becomes legitimate. The Department of Employment has estimated that some 95 per cent of recorded strikes are unofficial. If strikes which are not recorded were taken into account, the proportion would be higher still; evidence from the motor industry suggests that a majority of strikes last less than a day, and these by their very nature are unofficial. An overwhelming majority of British stoppages are also unconstitutional.

These figures are undisputed; their implications are more controversial. Four arguments are, however, commonly put forward, and these will be considered in turn. First, it is suggested that unconstitutional strikes are morally improper through being in breach of agreement. Second, that strikes without official union backing must for that reason be irresponsible. Third, that such stoppages, by virtue of their spontaneity, are particularly disruptive. Fourth, that these characteristics create a strike pattern unique to contemporary Britain.

Breach of agreement

The moral impropriety of action in breach of a collective agreement is regularly and colourfully asserted by employers, politicians, and the proprietors of newspapers; some academics have also joined in the chorus. A less naïve response to strikes in breach of procedure, however, might be to consider whether the procedure itself could be at fault. The disputes procedure which in 1971 applied to manual workers in federated engineering firms was imposed in a lock-out half a century earlier (when a quarter of the engineering labour force was unemployed), and its principles derived largely from the end of the earlier lock-out in 1898. A detailed analysis a decade ago showed that grievances (which might already have been subject to protracted domestic discussions) took on average three months to pass through all the stages of procedure, and might still remain unresolved. Where an issue is considered urgent, such delays are intolerable. This helps explain why many trade unionists in the industry have seen nothing unethical in acting unconstitutionally – at least in certain situations. 'Men are only committed to what they perceive themselves as committed to' (Fox, 1971: 151). Workers are unlikely to feel a moral obligation to a procedure which they consider discriminatory or obsolete. Normally, commitment presupposes consent; and workers' consent ought not to be taken for granted, by managers or by union officers.

A more fundamental reason for unconstitutional stoppages is inherent in the employment relationship itself.

Workmen are very often censured in the newspapers for striking in breach of agreement. But newspaper readers, before accepting these censures at their face value, should be very sure that they understand what lies behind these sudden strikes. Employers and workmen may be, in the eyes of the law, equal parties to a civil contract; but they are never equal parties in fact. The workman, under the contract, is bound to serve his employer: the employer is entitled to order the workman about. The relation between them is thus essentially unequal. The workman can do nothing to change the terms of employment without the employer's consent: the employer who wishes to change them needs only to give an order, which the workman is expected to obey. The employer, therefore, never needs to break a contract by locking out his workmen without notice. He issues an order, and they have either to obey it or go on strike in breach of contract, and thus put themselves legally in the wrong. It is easy for employers to talk about the 'sanctity of contracts', because they are seldom under any inducement to break them. But the workmen have sometimes to choose between breaking their contracts and breaking faith with their fellow-workers, in such a way as to allow the employer to worsen the conditions of employment. Under such conditions, workmen cannot be expected to keep their contracts: indeed, they would be wrong to do so, if it is in their power to resist (Cole, 1939: 86–7).

This argument is particularly cogent in the context of 'perishable' disputes – as with the dismissal which introduced this book. If workers

> merely call in the Trade Union official, and then wait with the grievance unremedied until all the elaborate processes of formal negotiation have been gone through, very often the mischief is done, and the solidarity of the men broken, before the negotiations have run their course. The time for effective action has gone by, and the cause is lost (Cole: 86).

Unconstitutional action is normally the only effective response to what is seen as the victimization of a workmate, or dangerous working conditions, or an attack on established work practices. Moral censure is inappropriate from those whose everyday occupations do not confront them with any such predicaments.

The unauthorized nature of the unofficial strike

The argument that strikes which lack official union sanction must therefore be 'irresponsible' would seem 'partly to rest on an unrealistic view of the way in which strikes in fact occur' (Turner, 1969: 21). As was seen in the last chapter, the common stereotype of the strike as a carefully planned confrontation between union and employer organizations is not characteristic of stoppages in general. Disputes have traditionally stemmed principally from the initiative of the union rank and file.

> Though union organization was a necessary condition of big stoppages, they seldom began at union headquarters. It was thinkable that the leader of a union should start a strike for reasons of long-run strategy or power politics, when the men left to themselves would not have moved; but that did not often happen,

if only because a leader needed to be extraordinarily trusted for the
men to follow him in cold blood into all the hardships of a strike.
Usually headquarters did not move until the men were raring to go,
and had in fact in one place or another already come out (Phelps
Brown, 1960: 158–9).

Today, as will be seen below, issues are normally the subject of
lengthy shop-floor negotiation before a union official is called in. It
follows that most strikes originate in the more or less spontaneous
action of workers at their place of employment, with official union
authorization following – if at all – only after several days have
elapsed.

Since most British strikes are very short, the large majority 'are
over before the unions which might have members involved have even
heard of them, the matters at issue having been settled by direct
negotiation between the management and workers concerned'
(Turner, 1969: 22). But when disputes do continue long enough for
the possibility of claiming union benefit to arise, they often do receive
retrospective official backing; the Donovan Commission found that
in 'a substantial proportion' of such cases dispute benefit was
eventually paid (1968: 109).

The minority of longer unofficial stoppages necessarily come to the
attention of the union leadership, which must decide what attitude
to take. The strikers often appeal for official backing for their action,
and are at times successful. Even if formal sanction is withheld – as
at Halewood – leadership sympathy may be obvious. Thus during the
Ford dispute the *Financial Times* noted (19 June 1971) that 'the
TGWU is, in fact, already supporting the strike in the sense that it
is fighting Mr Dillon's case and has made no attempt to instruct the
strikers to resume work'. For this reason, many 'unofficial' stoppages
might best be regarded as 'quasi-official': union leaders often give
tacit support but not formal backing – either because of rule-book
restrictions on their ability to pay dispute benefit, or to avoid
embarrassment in sanctioning a strike in breach of procedure. In such
circumstances, union executives have sometimes authorized the
payment to strikers of a 'hardship allowance' equivalent to the dispute
benefit. At other times, official support may be withheld from a
stoppage simply in order to save union money.

It is also true that some unofficial strikes are genuinely anti-official, being directed against some policy accepted by union leaders; the strikes against aspects of decasualization in the docks in 1967 are an example. Other unofficial stoppages are actively opposed by union leaders, who may order a return to work and perhaps threaten penalties against the strikers. Such instances, however, are not typical of unofficial strikes in general. And even in these cases, it would be rash automatically to assume that the strikers are either knaves or fools. Union officials, being human, are sometimes wrong; it is, after all, the rank-and-file members who have first-hand knowledge of the grievances which underlie their action.

The costs of spontaneity

'It is', according to the Donovan Report, 'characteristic of unofficial action that it is unpredictable' (1968: 112). This is not perhaps strictly true: in many cases a stoppage is, predictably, provoked by managerial action; at other times workers' discontent may be manifest long before they walk out. Nevertheless, management often has far less opportunity to plan its response to such stoppages than it has when formal notice is given of an official dispute. This factor was seen by the Donovan Commission as accentuating the economic significance of British industrial disputes.

It is in fact only when the impact on managements of unofficial strikes and other forms of unofficial action is taken into account that their gravity becomes apparent. Such action may face a manager with a sudden and acute dilemma. He may be under severe pressure from customers to produce goods or materials by a particular deadline, and in a competitive market such pressure is not easy to resist. . . . It is also necessary to take account of the effect on management of fear of the possibility of strikes even if they do not take place. If an employer forestalls a strike by making concessions in the face of threats which it might have been better to resist, or by refraining from introducing changes which he believes to be necessary in the interests of efficiency, then the economic consequences of his doing so may be more serious than those to which a strike would have given rise (1968: 111–12).

This is to argue that the spontaneity of strikes makes them damaging at second hand: it was the economic effects of their psychological effects on management that worried the Commission. Such an argument is difficult to evaluate critically. As the Commission's own Research Director put it:

It is, at base, a matter of impression or judgement. Personally I have always thought that the Donovan Report grossly oversold the psychological deterrent effect of strikes; it has always seemed to me a managerial excuse, the first refuge of the lazy and the last ditch of the cowardly. Good managers make much more use of the more sophisticated point that all change has to be paid for in one way or another, and sometimes it is just not worth the price (McCarthy, 1970: 236).

It might be added that it is usually the workers who pay the price of greater 'efficiency', in the form of redundancy for some and increased pressure of work for the others. Which leads to the essence of the Donovan critique: that unofficial strikes are *effective*, that they oblige managements to take account of the wishes and interests of their employees. This fact will be considered further in Chapter 6. Here it is worth noting the emphasis currently placed on (somewhat vague) notions of 'participation' or 'industrial democracy', on the need for production to be based on 'management by consent'. The Royal Commission itself asserted the importance 'of giving workers the right to representation in decisions affecting their working lives, a right which is or should be the prerogative of every worker in a democratic society' (1968: 54). In some circumstances the 'spontaneous' strike is perhaps the only effective means of translating this 'right' into a reality.

Is Britain unique?

The assumption is widespread that a pattern of strikes dominated by unofficial and unconstitutional stoppages is peculiarly British and peculiarly recent. Neither proposition is correct.

The spontaneous strike is internationally familiar: a multi-national survey concluded that 'the strike is no longer a sustained test of economic strength but a brief demonstration of protest' (Ross and Hartman, 1960: 6). The term 'wildcat strike' derives of course from American experience; and one study of industrial relations in the US has noted that 'unauthorized walkouts – or the threat of them – the most dramatic of disruptive tactics, are a familiar and even routine part of grievance negotiations in such industries as coal mining, city transit, construction, automobile, steel, metalworking, and longshoring' (Kuhn, 1961: 50–1). Recent statistics show that over a third of recorded stoppages in the USA take place during the currency of a (fixed-term) collective contract; these are therefore normally unconstitutional and almost invariably unofficial. In addition, some strikes during contract negotiations represent rank-and-file repudiation of terms negotiated by union officials; while as in Britain, many unauthorized walk-outs do not appear in the statistics. Experience in many European countries is similar. To cite a recent French commentator:

> The 'wildcat' strike that has recently been 'discovered' by industrial observers is, in fact, the norm in this country. While union officials may provide support and advice for a strike movement, and may attempt to give it a semblance of 'organization', it is increasingly the rank-and-file members who take the initiatives and the responsibilities (*Nouvel Observateur*, May 1970).

The popular assumption also reflects an ignorance of industrial relations history. That most British strikes have long been unofficial in origin is clear from the description by Phelps Brown which was quoted earlier. Another writer has commented that

> most strikes, in this century at least, have probably always been unofficial in the strict sense that the unions whose members were involved had not formally approved them by awarding strike benefit to the participants: in 1936 and 1937 a Ministry of Labour statement suggested that only a third of the stoppages reported to it were thus consecrated (Turner, 1963: 14).

The bulk of strikes have been unconstitutional also, at least since the existence of complex industry-wide procedures.

If the pattern of stoppages in Britain today is to be contrasted with that in many other countries or in earlier periods, the difference which emerges is thus only of degree.

Strikes and the British pattern of bargaining

Given that this difference of degree does exist, why are strikes in Britain today overwhelmingly short, small, and 'spontaneous'? To explain this it is necessary to examine the structure of collective bargaining in this country, and in particular the role of the shop steward.

Collective bargaining

'Britain', declared the Donovan Report, 'has two systems of industrial relations. The one is the formal system embodied in the official institutions. The other is the informal system created by the actual behaviour of trade unions and employers' associations, of managers, shop stewards, and workers' (1968: 12).

The official structure of collective bargaining has been established in most industries for at least half a century – with regular negotiations at national level between the union or unions concerned and the relevant federation or association of employers. The resulting national agreements specify rates of pay, hours of work, and other conditions of employment for the industry. In theory, this process of national negotiation determines all important aspects of the employment relationship: all that is left for discussion at local or factory level are questions of implementation of the national agreement, and minor problems of local or domestic concern. Decentralized bargaining is thus, in most industries, meant to provide only minor embellishments to the basic structure of the industry-wide agreement.

The reality is very different: in most well-organized industries it is the national agreements which are of minor significance, setting a bare minimum standard for wages and conditions; the worker relies primarily on shop-floor bargaining to win acceptable terms. The impact of this domestic bargaining is particularly apparent in the gap between officially negotiated wage rates and workers' actual earnings. The Donovan Report contrasted basic rates in engineering in October 1967 – £9·37 for a labourer and £11·08 for fitters – with actual average earnings of £21·39 for men in engineering and electrical goods and £24·42 in vehicle manufacturing. This 'earnings gap' stems from three main sources: payment by results, or piecework, which obliges workers to organize and bargain effectively if they are to achieve acceptable earnings; overtime work (paid for at an enhanced rate), the amount and allocation of which is often controlled by shop-floor bargaining; and straightforward negotiation at factory level for supplements to the nationally agreed rates.

Shop-floor bargaining has less obvious but important consequences in respect of control over the process of production. As was seen earlier, managements possess almost unlimited legal authority over the labour they employ. If workers wish for any control over their working lives they must achieve this through collective organization, particularly at the point of production; and where organization is strong workers do indeed have considerable say – usually wholly unofficially – over who shall be employed or dismissed, how machinery shall be manned, what shall be the rate of production, whether men shall be moved from one job to another. These limitations on the 'sacred rights of management' are no less real for the fact that few employers will publicly admit to their existence. And they mean that conflict is never far from the surface in industrial relationships.

The shop steward

Central to the process of domestic bargaining is the shop steward. Since the nineteenth century, unions have had shop-floor representatives to carry out such functions as checking that all workers are paid-up members, collecting subscriptions, and reporting about employment conditions within the factory. Such stewards came gradually to act as representatives of their fellow-workers when urgent issues arose within the workshop, and this function became particularly prominent during the First World War.

In the period of mass unemployment between the wars, when shop-floor union activists could easily be victimized, their importance as domestic negotiators waned. But from the 1940s there was a great expansion, first mainly in engineering, then in a wide range of industries and occupations.

By definition the steward is a shop-floor employee, typically chosen directly by fellow-workers because he (or increasingly she) enjoys their trust. Their negotiating authority does not derive from the union of which they are a member: until very recently, few union rule-books even mentioned the steward's bargaining functions. Nor, in the main, does it derive from formal procedure agreements: most of these define the steward's powers in an extremely restrictive manner. The Ford 'Blue Book' is a good example: stewards could not carry out their functions effectively by adhering to the letter of the agreement. Their authority stems essentially from the fact that they share the aspirations of the employees, are personally involved in their experiences and grievances at the point of production, and are expected to represent their interests in negotiation with management. Should they fail to do so adequately, it is relatively easy for the rank and file to reassert control, through shop-floor meetings or less formal pressures. In the last resort, workers can replace a steward whose competence or integrity they doubt by one in whom they have greater confidence.

Because of this relationship with rank-and-file union members, shop stewards often figure prominently in unofficial stoppages; and in consequence, the popular definition of the steward is as a 'troublemaker' or 'agitator'. As so often in such cases, reality is more complex. The 'militant' Halewood steward whose case introduced this book had advised his members *not* to strike over their manning dispute. Garfield Clack, who worked as a participant observer in another car factory, described stewards as usually counselling moderation; the typical dispute was 'unofficial-unofficial', taking place without the knowledge or against the advice not only of full-time officials but of shop stewards also. With his fellow-authors he has argued that 'in the motor industry, at any rate, this type of dispute appears to be becoming the norm' (Turner *et al.*, 1967: 223).

This does not mean that stewards normally disown such stoppages: 'often, a steward is forced to defend unofficial action he has not instigated' (Goodman and Whittingham, 1969: 180). Or rather than being 'forced', a steward may feel obliged to support his members even though they have acted against his advice. Anyone who has met and talked with shop stewards knows that few indeed deliberately seek to become involved in disputes; at the same time, as the representative of men whose work situation constantly generates grievances, the steward's role is always one of potential conflict. The remarks of the Donovan Report should however be quoted:

> It is often wide of the mark to describe shop stewards as 'troublemakers'. Trouble is thrust upon them. . . . Shop stewards are rarely agitators pushing workers towards unconstitutional action. In some instances they may be the mere mouthpiece of their work groups. But quite commonly they are supporters of order exercising a restraining influence on their members in conditions which promote disorder (1968: 28–9).

Domestic bargaining and unofficial action

One reason for the prevalence of the myth of the 'wildcat' shop steward is that it seems to offer a simple explanation of unofficial strikes. Such a simplistic interpretation is presupposed, for example, by such legislation as the Industrial Relations Act – which aims to prevent strikes through penal sanctions against 'strike leaders'. If such 'leaders' are typically spokesmen pushed forward after a dispute erupts, rather than engineering it in advance, such sanctions might be expected to accentuate rather than diminish conflict.

The Donovan Commission appreciated the need for a more sophisticated interpretation of industrial conflict. 'The underlying causes of unofficial strikes', it argued, lie 'in our present methods of collective bargaining and especially our methods of workshop bargaining' (1968: 128). Since the most important issues relating to workers' employment are settled at shop-floor level, it is natural that the decision to apply sanctions should be taken here when negotiations prove unsatisfactory. Since the 'constitutional' procedures for resolution of disputed issues are quite unsuited to the multiplicity of questions arising within the workplace, it is inevitable that they are often disregarded. Since the vast majority of stoppages are settled quickly, strikers rarely need the financial support available in an official strike – particularly since the level of strike pay is so miserly (in most unions around £5 a week). And since the role of the official union is for most members extremely limited, it is hardly surprising that in most cases they see no reason for seeking official approval before stopping work.

Unofficial strikes and official trade unionism

The prevalence of unofficial strikes is often seen as a reflection on official trade unionism. Such criticism can come from at least two directions.

The call for 'discipline'

On the one hand, it is widely argued that unofficial and unconstitutional action could be prevented or reduced if unions were to exercise more 'discipline': since unions are, jointly with the employers, custodians of national agreements, they should compel their members to adhere to these agreements; and since unofficial strikes are by definition unauthorized by the union, the latter should reassert its own authority. Presumably this means that unions should apply sanctions – in the last resort, expulsion – to members who engage in unofficial stoppages, and should withdraw credentials from stewards associated with such action.

Popular opinion on this question tends to reveal certain contradictions. It is widely held that unions should be more 'democratic': that union leaders should be more attuned and responsive to the wishes of their members. Union leaders, after all, often describe themselves as the servants of their members. It is scarcely consistent to accept this view yet also argue that union leaders should be less democratic, wielding disciplinary powers to compel members to remain at work against their will. It is also widely assumed that trade unions in Britain are 'too strong', that they are able to 'hold the country to ransom', that their powers should accordingly be reduced. The main premise of this argument, as will be seen later, is questionable. But in any case, internal and external union power cannot be dissociated. 'The present critics of the unions . . . cannot have it both ways. If they want the unions to be strong enough to maintain the peace by controlling members' behaviour, they should not complain of excessive union power' (Fox and Flanders, 1969: 154).

In any case, it is necessary to ask from where trade union officials are to derive enhanced disciplinary powers. Since strikes normally reflect a breakdown in domestic bargaining, and since the official union is largely detached from industrial relations at this level, it is unclear how it might be expected to intervene and prevent stoppages. This was indeed the conclusion of the Donovan Report:

> The great majority of unofficial strikes have nothing to do with industry-wide agreements. It is a mistake therefore to suppose that the shift of power to the work group could have been prevented by a more ready exercise of disciplinary powers by trade union leaders. Even if successful this could do little to halt the transfer of authority from management to the work group. And it is unlikely that it would be successful. Trade union leaders do exercise discipline from time to time, but they cannot be industry's policemen. They are democratic leaders in organizations in which the seat of power has almost always been close to the members (1968: 32).

Even the Royal Commission, however, was not immune from the naïve perspective underlying most public discussion. 'Unofficial strikes', it argued, 'will . . . persist so long as neither employers nor trade unions are willing adequately to recognize, define, and control the part played by shop stewards in our collective bargaining system' (p. 120). If trade unions should not be required to act as 'industry's policemen', it is not obvious how they can be expected to 'define and control' the actions of their shop stewards – and through them, presumably, the membership generally.

The question of trade union 'communications'

Those who call for greater 'discipline' are also prone to argue that union leaders are 'out of touch' with their members. The logical conclusion, though one that is rarely recognized, is that official union policy should be more militant. This has indeed been explicitly argued by Allen.

> The existence in Britain of a high proportion of unofficial strikes indicates an important defect in formal union activity. It is an indictment of unions not of employees. The way to reduce unofficial strikes is to adapt union organizations so that they are involved in strike moves, thus making them official. . . . Unofficial action is informal trade unionism, occurring because formal unions are incapable of fulfilling their functions satisfactorily and have, for this reason, lost some control over their members (1966: 115).

In America, also, it has been argued that 'wildcat' action by work groups may often 'indicate not so much the failure of these groups to abide by judicial grievance procedures as the unwillingness of management, and probably also the union, to satisfy the expectancies of the members' (Kuhn, 1961: 113).

While this analysis is plausible, the failure of official union action to satisfy members' expectations cannot be explained merely by the thesis that their leaders are 'out of touch'. For this implies that if only trade unions could devise better 'communications' between members and officials, the unofficial strike would become a thing of the past. This thesis may perhaps apply in the case of the 'anti-official' strike: the protest against an agreement signed in opposition to (or ignorance of) the wishes of the membership. But as has been seen, most unofficial strikes are not of this nature. Domestic bargaining attained its importance in part, no doubt, because of the failure of the formal union machinery to satisfy members' wishes and aspirations. But now that the primacy of workplace bargaining *has* become established, changes in union policy or official organization will not readily succeed in integrating the official machinery with shop-floor industrial relations.

Emphasis on 'communications' also ignores the extent to which the unofficial status of disputes reflects a conflict between the *roles* of union members and union officials. The official's job necessarily centres around compromise and accommodation. For him, workers' grievances are problems to be solved; and once a formula has been agreed with the employer, he feels an obligation to stand by it. He also comes to value the negotiating relationship with the employer as something to be protected in its own right, and for this reason is reluctant to act in a way which may jeopardize managerial goodwill. All this forms part of the pressure towards the institutionalization of industrial conflict which is discussed in a later chapter.

One consequence is that while the response of the shop-floor worker to his grievances and deprivations may be relatively volatile and spontaneous, the official is always conscious of the long-term bargaining relationship. When the temperature rises, it is therefore natural that the official will find himself exercising a restraining influence, urging his members to follow 'constitutional' procedures. This role-conflict does not merely affect the *full-time* official: the shop steward is subject to very similar pressures. Significantly, less than one manager in four considers stewards to be more militant than their members (Government Social Survey, 1968: 136; McCarthy and Parker, 1968: 31). This factor helps explain why stewards are more likely to restrain overt conflict than to provoke it.

The unofficial strike as a safeguard of democracy?

Given the existence within trade unionism of institutional tendencies towards the suppression of workers' grievances rather than their expression, the unofficial strike might well be described as an important counterbalance. 'Union members who feel that their leaders misrepresent them may resort to wildcat strikes' (Magrath, 1959: 523). This 'willingness of work groups to follow their unofficial leaders in defiance of their unions, by striking for what the unions will not demand, or against what the unions will accept' has been seen by Clegg as a significant restraint on the development of autocratic leadership (1970: 107).

In this respect, the implications of unofficial action are largely negative: preventing officials from acting in ways which diverge too far from their members' expectations. But since union leaders are sensitive to the charge that unofficial stoppages reflect adversely on their own leadership, such action can have important positive implications also. As was noted two decades ago, the post-war growth in unofficial stoppages, as union leaders embraced a policy of 'responsible' passivity, eventually forced a change of direction.

Attempts to suppress unofficial outbreaks having failed, 'union leaderships . . . finally reacted by an increased militancy: they began to declare strikes official; they even began to organize strikes themselves' (Turner, 1963: 15–16). More recently this process has become even more manifest: union leaders who for years were renowned for their 'statesmanship' and 'responsibility' have found themselves obliged, in the face of unwonted rank-and-file belligerence, to articulate their members' demands rather than lose all influence over the latter's actions. This development reached a peak in the early 1970s with a series of major stoppages conducted by union executives – particularly in the public sector – in the absence of any recent tradition of official militancy.

Only those who see the proper status of trade unions as junior partners in the application of managerial discipline can view this as an unhealthy development.

3. The Sociology of Industrial Conflict

Varieties of industrial conflict

As was seen in the first chapter, the strike is not a homogeneous phenomenon: it can vary from a massive and protracted confrontation to a half-hour protest by half a dozen workers. At the latter end of the scale it may be difficult to decide precisely what is to count as a strike. If a lunch-hour meeting of workers to discuss a grievance runs over into working time, are they technically on strike? Or if they refuse to start a new piecework job at the price offered, or disregard a disputed instruction, have they stopped work? Employers themselves differ in their classification of such instances: '"strikes" at one establishment may be "pauses for discussion" at another' (Turner *et al.*, 1967: 52–3).

This suggests that stoppages of work are in fact part of a continuum of behaviour.

Complete work stoppages and outbreaks of violence due to industrial disputes are certainly the most dramatic expressions of industrial conflict. For the general public they are also the most disturbing. In the minds of many industrial conflict has come to *mean* strikes. . . . But a true understanding of industrial strife . . . demands consideration of related, less-spectacular manifestations as well. It may even be suggested that the general object of study is not the labor dispute, the strike or the lockout, but the total range of behavior and attitudes that express opposition and divergent orientations between industrial owners and managers on the one hand and working people and their organizations on the other (Kornhauser *et al.*, 1954: 12–13).

The variety of industrial conflict has been indicated by Clark Kerr:

Its means of expression are as unlimited as the ingenuity of man. The strike is the most common and most visible expression. But conflict with the employer may also take the form of peaceful bargaining and grievance handling, of boycotts, of political action, of restriction of output, of sabotage, of absenteeism, or of personnel turnover. Several of these forms, such as sabotage, restriction of output, absenteeism, and turnover, may take place on an individual as well as on an organized basis and constitute alternatives to collective action. Even the strike is of many varieties. It may involve all the workers or only key men. It may take the form of refusal to work overtime or to perform a certain process. It may even involve such rigid adherence to the rules that output is stifled (1964: 171).

All these are actions which are taken by workpeople; managements have a similar armoury at their disposal (Kornhauser *et al.*, 1954: 14–15).

Organized and unorganized conflict

The distinction between organized and unorganized conflict is of great analytical importance (though occasionally difficult to draw in practice). While both types of activity represent workers' response to a work situation which causes dissatisfaction or deprivation, the nature and implications of this response differ markedly. Put simply, in unorganized conflict workers typically respond to the oppressive situation in the only way open to them *as individuals*: by withdrawal from the source of discontent, or, in the case of certain forms of individual sabotage or indiscipline, by reacting against the immediate manifestation of oppression. Such reaction rarely derives from any calculative strategy; indeed, unorganized expressions of conflict 'are often not regarded as conflict by the persons in the situation' (Scott *et al.*, 1963: 40).

Organized conflict, on the other hand, is far more likely to form part of a conscious strategy to change the situation which is identified as the source of discontent. The different levels of rationality displayed in these two types of response will be analysed further in a later chapter.

Forms of conflict as alternatives

Evidence from a number of studies suggests that in any industrial situation in which workers experience sufficiently acute deprivations, unrest will be expressed in some form. The circumstances of the case will however influence what form this expression of conflict takes. Thus in any situation, the different varieties of industrial conflict may represent alternatives.

For discontent to be expressed in a strike, a minimum of worker solidarity and organization is presupposed almost by definition.

> The very action of striking is a collective act and implies a certain amount of understanding and belief in the efficaciousness of mass action. While it is true that strikes are occasionally spontaneous outbursts due to accidental circumstances or long periods of repression, one may generalize to the extent of saying that workers with no feeling of solidarity or common interest would be unlikely to undertake a strike (Griffin, 1939: 98).

While car workers are sufficiently cohesive to display their unrest in strike action, 'with young unskilled women in the clothing industry, say, it may appear in a high rate of labour turnover' (Knowles, 1952: 210). (This does not mean, incidentally, that women are never prominent in industrial disputes; the London match girls' strike of 1888 is one of the most famous episodes of British labour history, and many other examples of female militancy are cited by Knowles. Indeed, women clothing workers took part in one of the most prominent stoppages of 1970. But women tend to be employed in industries and occupations where collective organization is least strong, and they strike far less frequently than men.)

There is statistical evidence that different types of conflict function as alternatives. Knowles concluded that 'figures covering the end-period of the Second World War suggest that strikes and absenteeism in coal-mining are to some extent "interchangeable"' (1952: 225). Subsequently a more detailed study in the same industry has offered corroboration (Scott *et al.*, 1963). Miners in higher-skilled occupations, who form more cohesive work groups and possess greater bargaining strength, are most likely *both* to pursue grievances through the formal negotiating procedure *and* to engage in strikes, go-slows, and overtime bans. Lower-skilled groups, who figure least prominently in such collective activities, have the highest level of involvement in the measurable forms of unorganized conflict. Very similar findings emerge from a study in American manufacturing industry: 'apathetic' work groups which lack sufficient cohesion to engage in collective conflict 'were not trouble-free, but only super-ficially so. . . . There was evidence of worker discontent, but often it was not found in terms of specific demands or grievances' (Sayles, 1958: 8).

One implication of such findings is that attempts to suppress specific manifestations of conflict, *without removing the underlying causes of unrest*, may merely divert the conflict into other forms. There is the case of the major motor company which, two decades ago, dismissed a number of leading shop stewards as 'trouble-makers'. The resulting demoralization at shop-floor level led to a temporary fall in strike figures; but absenteeism, accidents, and turnover all rose sharply (Turner *et al.*, 1967: 190–1). (It may be significant that labour turnover in the strike-prone car industry appears much lower than in manufacturing industry generally.) In coal-mining, the period of contraction since the mid-1950s has been associated both with a decline in strike action and with a rise in absenteeism (Handy, 1968). While these examples show the expression of conflict changing from organized to unorganized form, the reverse may also occur. At one Midland factory, after severe local unemployment had reduced the normally high rate of turnover, an unprecedented series of strikes took place (Hyman, 1970). It is plausible to assume that disgruntled employees who would normally have found more congenial jobs elsewhere were instead induced to take collective action to improve conditions.

Just as the expression of unrest may change between organized and unorganized form, so situations will influence what type of organized conflict is more regularly used. Flanders has noted 'the increasing use of "cut price" industrial action such as overtime bans, working to rule or going slow' (1970: 112); this may be seen as reflecting an economic situation in which workers have been stimulated to growing self-assertiveness, but because of mortgage and HP commitments are perhaps less willing than previously to lose earnings through strike action. (This point should not be overstressed: on occasion workers *are* ready to make major sacrifices in a dispute, and in any case few strikers initially anticipate a protracted struggle. Today, moreover, the presence in many households of more than one wage-earner ensures some income even during a strike.) If social and economic conditions can influence the choice of 'cut-price sanctions', so, more dramatically, can managerial policy. When firms in the American rubber industry (with union collaboration) introduced severe disciplinary penalties for unofficial strikers, workers turned from stoppages to go-slows, with considerable success: 'management has found slow-downs more difficult to combat. . . . Moreover, they do not carry the opprobrium of walkouts in the eyes of the public' (Kuhn, 1961: 176–7). Other American employers have had the same experience: a typical comment is 'Give me a good clean wildcat any day' (Slichter *et al.*, 1960: 671). The predominant view of those British managers who have had experience of both is also that other sanctions are more effective than strikes. It may be predicted that if anti-strike legislation in Britain does reduce the number of stoppages, this is likely to accelerate the growth of alternative forms of collective action. Those responsible for the Industrial Relations Act paid little heed to this possibility; presumably they were unwilling to admit that the very structure of work in industry generates conflict, and that the strike is only its most manifest form of expression.

Explanations of strike-proneness

There are two main ways in which sociologists can try to account for strikes. The first is to examine variations in strike-proneness: to consider why the incidence of industrial conflict differs between work groups, between firms, between industries, or between regions and even nations. Industrial sociologists have devoted considerable ingenuity to efforts to explain these variations, and the 'man in the street' tends to hold some sort of theory about this also. The second approach involves a different level of analysis: examining the causes of strikes in general, and exploring the rationale behind them. Questions of this order will be considered later in this book; in the present section, some theories of the first type are examined.

Agitators

A widespread assumption about strikes, even if rarely coherently formulated, is that disputes are fomented by agitators. As was suggested earlier, such an interpretation seems to underlie proposals to control industrial conflict through penalties against strike 'leaders'. Widely held among politicians and owners of newspapers, this view is also cherished by many industrial managers, who 'seek to persuade their employees and the public at large that industry is a harmony of co-operation which only fools or knaves choose to disrupt' (Fox, 1966: 5).

Such beliefs, as will be shown in Chapter 6, possess important ideological utility. Yet they reveal a fundamental ignorance of the manner in which industrial disputes typically occur. The shop steward is the usual target for the 'agitator' label; but as was seen previously, the steward's role is more often associated with attempts to prevent strikes than to foment them. The popular theory also fails to explain why it is that agitators are apparently so much more influential in some industrial situations than in others. As Turner has argued,

> where industrial situations are likely to lead to conflict, they will generally find leaders to organize it anyway: and such leaders are naturally likely to be people of aggressive temperament, and so also to acquire strong views. The ability of such individuals to *create* conflict in the absence of circumstances that would induce it anyway seems to me to be highly marginal (1963: 12).

The point has been tersely stated by Knowles: 'one cannot agitate successfully without widespread grievances' (1952: xii).

This does not mean that in certain situations, militant representatives do not perform a significant role in articulating conflict. For conflict to take a collective character it is usually necessary for someone, initially at least, to take the lead in giving an organized form to workers' discrete discontents. And on occasion, shop stewards' strategical skill may be crucial to the effectiveness of a strike. Yet if this is 'agitation', it need not reflect any sinister underlying motivation. Shop stewards tend to be elected, or at least to retain their positions, only if they serve the wishes of their own members. To attribute industrial disputes to agitators is therefore, at best, to point to the instrument of conflict rather than its cause. More often it is to imply that strikes are of such questionable rationality that evil machinations must lie at their root. This thesis is thus profoundly *un*sociological, seeking to explain social processes exclusively in terms of the interventions of 'influential' individuals. It is the mirror image of that approach to history which relates events of major social significance solely to the actions of 'great men'. The sociologist, by contrast, is aware of the contraints which the social situation itself normally imposes on the influence of any individual, and it is this which she or he seeks to analyse.

Communications

The 'human relations' school is the title commonly applied to a loosely knit group of American industrial sociologists and social psychologists, who developed their main theories in the 1930s and 1940s and were particularly influenced by the ideas of Elton Mayo. The name indicates their central argument: that the key to worker 'morale', high productivity, and industrial peace lies in the quality of 'human relations' in industry. Exponents of this approach insisted that employers could best attain their objectives by encouraging cohesive social relationships within the labour force, by providing workers with 'supportive leadership', and by ensuring the existence of effective channels of communication between management and employees.

This approach has long attracted hostile criticism. Its advocates have been charged with managerial bias, a manipulative approach to workers, the treatment of the factory as a closed community, the denial of the rationality of industrial conflict, the neglect of the role of trade unions. Many of the writings in the human relations tradition have merited such criticism; and attempts to validate experimentally the early human relations assumptions and prescriptions have tended to demonstrate their inadequacy. Yet while the more naïve views of the human relations school are academically discredited they remain widely influential, particularly within management education.

An early application of this approach to a strike situation is the attempt by Scott and Homans to explain the persistent outbreaks of unofficial stoppages in wartime Detroit (1947). They argue that whatever the immediate issue involved in disputes, 'in the long run a number of the strikes seemed to stem from faulty communication'. With the labour force swollen by an influx of new employees, workers were unable to penetrate company or union bureaucracies with their grievances, and struck instead. To illustrate how this problem could be overcome the authors cite the case of 'K', a manager who 'had been interested in psychology at college'. Hearing that men in his department were planning to strike after the lunch break, K visited the canteen and 'began talking to various men about the importance of staying on the job'. They were persuaded, and afterwards 'he went around and talked with the men to tell them how much he appreciated their staying on. There was no more trouble that night or later.' Scott and Homans conclude that 'our industrial society is held together by thousands of men like K'.

A similar analysis can be found in Whyte's (1951) account of industrial relations in a steel container factory. A new works manager displayed such autocratic behaviour towards union representatives that relations became hopelessly embittered. Tension soon exploded in a strike which dragged on over half a year; but even this traumatic experience did not improve relationships. Eventually middle management revolted, and told their superior that his own actions were partly responsible for the conflict which existed. The works manager saw the error of his ways, responded in a conciliatory manner to the union's next approach, and an era of harmonious industrial relations was gradually constructed.

Social phenomena are, in the last analysis, products of the actions and interactions of individuals; industrial relations are also interpersonal relations; and undeniably the attitudes and actions of specific individuals can in certain circumstances have far-reaching repercussions. But individual influence over social events is usually more limited. Bad human relations are more often a symptom of industrial conflict than its cause. As Kerr and Siegel have argued, examination of communications and interpersonal relations cannot explain why whole industries are more strike-prone than others.

> It may be true that face-to-face relations are worse between longshoremen and coal miners and their employers than between grocery clerks and theirs. . . . But why are face-to-face relations so unsatisfactory between coal miners and their employers? Is it because they always know less about semantics than construction workers and their employers, and is it only faulty communication systems which stand between them and ultimate harmony . . . ? It seems more likely that some situations are structured against good face-to-face relations and that this structure is the more basic cause (1954: 199).

This leads to the basic inadequacy of most writing in the human relations tradition: its assumption that industrial peace is the norm and conflict pathological. From this perspective, disputes must be attributable to ignorance or misapprehension; with knowledge of 'the facts' workers would have no desire to strike. Yet while some strikes may result from misunderstandings, it would be naïve to assume that disputes typically arise in this way. On the contrary, Kerr has suggested that 'misunderstanding and the misuse of words have probably made a substantial contribution to industrial peace' (1964: 174). There are many facts (for example, information concerning job changes or planned redundancies, profit ratios or directorial salaries) the communication of which to workers might tend to *stimulate* conflict. As Allen has argued, 'for those who believe that there is a correlation between communications and industrial unrest perhaps it is as well that communications are faulty' (1966: 109).

Community integration

Kerr and Siegel, whose criticism of the human relations approach has been quoted, have found from an analysis of the strike records of eleven countries that certain industries appear consistently strike-prone. In particular, miners, dockers, and seamen show the highest propensity to strike, with textile and lumber workers close behind.

The authors list a number of economic and technological

influences, but argue that these are 'insufficient to explain the bulk of the facts'. The factor they choose to stress is 'the location of the worker in society'.

> The miners, the sailors, the longshoremen, the loggers, and, to a much lesser extent, the textile workers form isolated masses, almost a 'race apart'. They live in their own separate communities. . . . These communities have their own codes, myths, heroes, and social standards. There are few neutrals in them to mediate the conflicts and dilute the mass. All people have their grievances, but what is important is that all the members of each of these groups have the same grievances (1954: 191–2).

Such workers, they argue, readily develop a consciousness of collective grievance, form a strong emotional attachment to their unions, and are insulated from societal norms deprecating overt industrial conflict.

By contrast, Kerr and Siegel see workers with a lower propensity to strike as more closely integrated into the wider society. 'They are more likely', they argue, 'to live in multi-industry communities, to associate with people with quite different working experiences than their own, and to belong to associations with heterogeneous memberships. In these communities their individual grievances are less likely to coalesce into a mass grievance which is expressed at the job level' (pp. 193–4).

This is a persuasive explanation of the exceptional strike records of workers in a small number of industries. As a more general theory of industrial conflict it is less satisfactory. For there are industries – such as steel manufacture – which are highly strike-prone in some countries but not in others; while there are also significant variations in strike activity within industries in a single country (Eldridge, 1968: 38–9). Since the majority of workers in any industrialized nation fall within Kerr and Siegel's single undifferentiated category of 'community integration', their theory – as they themselves recognize – is necessarily unable to explain contrasts in the experience of conflict of different sections of these 'integrated' workers. (Their argument could, however, be extended to suggest that certain types of worker, while residentially integrated within an urban community, may because of a strong craft tradition or unusual working hours form a cohesive occupational community; they may therefore possess unusual solidarity and show a particular readiness to engage in collective conflict.)

Technology

Many sociologists have focused on technology as a key determinant of the texture of relationships in industry. Among the early applications of this perspective are a number of analyses of work in the motor industry, which argue that the monotony and dehumanization of assembly-line technology are an inevitable source of deprivation and conflict (Chinoy, 1955; Walker and Guest, 1957).

This approach is generalized by Woodward, who has analysed the implications for management of different degrees of technical complexity: unit and small batch manufacturing, mass production, and process technology. She suggests that

> the attitudes and behaviour of management and supervisory staff and the tone of industrial relations . . . seemed to be closely related to . . . technology. In firms at the extremes of the scale, relationships were on the whole better than in the middle ranges. Pressure on people at all levels of the industrial hierarchy seemed to build up as technology advanced, became heaviest in assembly-line production and then relaxed, so reducing personal conflicts. Some factors – the relaxation of pressure, the smaller working groups . . ., and the reduced need for labour economy – were conducive to industrial peace in process production (1958: 18).

The link between technology and industrial conflict has been examined directly by Kuhn in his analysis of 'fractional bargaining' – the unauthorized pursuance of demands backed by unofficial sanctions – in American industry. His main conclusion is that 'the incidence of fractional bargaining is greatly influenced by the technology of production', and he explores in detail the manner in which this influence appears to operate. To Kuhn, four aspects of technology seem crucial: regular changes in work methods, standards or materials; the opportunity for considerable interaction between workers; the grouping of the labour force into a small number of roughly equal departments; and the sequential processing of materials into a single end product.

> The first and second of the above characteristics stimulate willingness of members of the work group to engage in fractional bargaining. The third tends to weaken the political authority of the local union over the work groups, and the fourth enables the work group to disrupt the plant's total production at a cost to itself which is small in relation to the cost it inflicts upon management. The less pronounced these characteristics are in a production technology, the less important should fractional bargaining be (1961: 148).

A very similar analysis is made by another American, Sayles, in his attempt to explain variations within establishments in the behaviour of different work groups. His conclusion may be briefly stated: 'it appears as though all of our relevant variables are related to the technological system designed by the company to organize the work process' (1958: 93).

It is indisputable that the technology of a firm or industry can have an important conditioning effect on worker-management and union-management relations. But a theory which sees technology as *all*-important is demonstrably inadequate. (This has been recognized, for example, in more recent work by Woodward.) Why is the steel industry strike-prone in some countries when – as was noted earlier – in others, under the same technological conditions, it is relatively peaceful? Or why does the strike record of the British motor industry contrast so markedly with the comparative harmony in Germany or Japan, when the technology of car assembly is internationally uniform? Single-factor explanatory theories, it is clear, do scant justice to the complexity of social reality.

One influential attempt to consider both technology and other aspects of the work environment is developed by Trist and his associates in their study of the north-west Durham coalfield. They argue that work relations should be viewed as structured within a 'socio-technical system'.

> Any production system requires both a technological organization

– equipment and process layout – and a work organization relating to each other those who carry out the necessary tasks. . . . Although technology places limits on the kind of work organization possible, it does not uniquely determine its form. . . . A work organization has social and psychological properties of its own that are independent of technology (1963: 6).

The development of mining in the twentieth century is used to illustrate this thesis. The traditional face-worker was a 'complete miner', performing a whole cycle of operations on his own or as part of a small group. But as mining became mechanized the three main tasks – mechanically cutting into the face at the bottom of the seam, removing the coal from above this cut on to conveyors, and moving forward the machinery ready for the next cycle – as well as various ancillary operations, were each allocated to a separate task group. Each group worked on only one shift of a three-shift cycle, and was paid for the successful completion of its own task on the basis of a complex bonus system. According to the authors, this narrow specialization diminished job satisfaction; conflicts developed between groups, each of which had an incentive only to perform the precise operations for which it received payment rather than to facilitate the whole production cycle; and the result was low productivity and a high degree of unorganized conflict (as well as organized conflict over payment disputes).

The researchers insist that this situation was not the inevitable result of technical progress: it was simply that when mechanization was introduced, a rigid division of labour was considered the most 'scientific' means of organizing work. The study describes experiments with a different form of work organization: work teams were highly flexible, individuals were encouraged to acquire several skills, and all workers on each face shared in a common bonus payment. The reported result was reduced conflict and increased output.

Another study in which the interaction of technology and social organization is emphasized relates to the steel industry (Scott *et al.*, 1956). Here, a notable peculiarity is the occupational career structure of production workers: recruitment to each grade above the lowest is by promotion, strictly according to seniority, from the grade below.

This system 'not only ties an employee to the industry and indeed to a single firm, but also, by establishing a pattern of aspiration and promotion for his working life, gives him a feeling that he has a real stake in it' (pp. 252–3). This system, incidentally, also gives managements and union a powerful sanction over potential dissidents. By contrast, this system does not apply to maintenance craftsmen who are thus mobile between firms and even to other industries. Scott and his associates indicate how these distinctive occupational structures were reflected in differences of attitude between production and maintenance workers. It may be added that this also helps explain why strikes in British steel are the virtual monopoly of maintenance workers.

The industrial relations system

While the socio-technical approach is considerably more sophisticated than simple technological determinism, its analysis stops at the factory gates; it ignores all influences on the nature of industrial relationships which derive from the wider society. A theoretical framework designed to overcome this limitation is Dunlop's concept of the 'industrial relations system' (1958). According to Dunlop, 'an "industrial-relations system" is to be viewed as an analytical subsystem of an industrial society' (p. 5).

An industrial-relations system is comprised of three groups of actors – workers and their organizations, managers and their organizations, and governmental agencies concerned with the work place and work community. These groups interact with a specified environment comprised of three interrelated contexts: the technology, the market or budgetary constraints and the power relations in the larger community and the derived status of the actors. An industrial-relations system creates an ideology or a commonly shared body of ideas and beliefs regarding the interaction and roles of the actors which helps to bind the system together (p. 383).

Dunlop applies this framework to the parallels and contrasts in international experience in industrial relations in two industries, coal-mining and construction. He also uses it to analyse industrial relations in Yugoslavia and in developing countries.

Explicitly or otherwise, this theoretical perspective has tended to underlie a number of post-war studies of industrial conflict. The account given by Knowles, for example, of the strike-proneness of various British industries would fit comfortably within Dunlop's conceptual framework. And since the publication of his volume in 1958, the notion of an industrial relations *system* has become widely adopted within the academic study of the subject – even if some of its implications are not always fully appreciated.

The limits of structural explanation

All the sociological theories considered so far (with the exception of the human relations school) have focused on *structural* determinants of industrial relations. The assumptions inherent in this type of sociological perspective have been clearly summarized by Fox.

> We may think of the social organization of the enterprise as a structure of inter-related roles which to varying extents determine the behaviour of their occupants. We must note also that the organization exists within an environment, and is related to it by a network of contacts between roles within the organization and roles outside it. . . . But much of the industrial behaviour in which we are interested is not role behaviour in the narrow sense of being officially required. A man's behaviour – or more likely a group's behaviour – in relation to the job contains much more that is not officially prescribed. Work-groups may make their own rules, go on strike, behave unco-operatively. Similarly managers may manipulate returns, conduct feuds, form cliques. But it is of the essence of the sociologist's approach that these kinds of behaviour are not viewed as random or idiosyncratic. His contention is that just as role behaviour, narrowly construed, is shaped by the nature and definition of the role that the occupant is called upon to fill, so these other kinds of behaviour take systematic, patterned forms which can be related directly to given roles and other 'structural' aspects of the situation in that they tend to evoke it in regular and

uniform ways. The point needing stress is that this is just as much 'structured' behaviour as that prescribed by role in the officially defined sense. It is called forth by the nature of the total situation (1966: 16–17).

The sociologist's point of departure, certainly, is that people's social actions are not merely 'random or idiosyncratic', but can normally be related to the pressures inherent in the situations in which they find themselves. Sociological analysis is indeed possible only because we tend to act in similar ways when confronted by the same type of social situation.

Yet this basic truth is often overstated. Many social theorists view human behaviour as mechanically determined by the social structure. This common fallacy is known as '*positivism*'. Such terms as 'role' or 'social institution' or even 'society' are used by sociologists to refer to the stable patterns of relationships which they discover; but positivism involves treating such concepts as real entities with an independent existence over and above the activities and relationships of human individuals. People are treated, in effect, as wholly passive: the helpless playthings of 'social forces'. Something akin to this type of approach is evident in the passage just quoted: it is assumed that a fixed pattern of behaviour is 'called forth' by a specific social situation.

Structure and consciousness

Such assumptions must be rejected. 'Society' (or 'social institutions' or 'roles') is not a mystic entity which obliges us to behave in a predetermined manner; it is the shorthand expression we use to refer to the stable and predictable regularities – the 'structure' – in our activities and relationships. Humans not puppets; they consciously interpret the situations in which they find themselves, and in the light of these interpretations they select their responses in accordance with the goals which they wish to achieve. Only by exploring the subjective dimension – human consciousness and the interrelation of people's definitions and responses – is it possible to understand the regularities and patterns which exist in industrial relations or in any other area of social life.

Few sociologists – though there are some – are so crass as to ignore entirely the consciousness of those whose actions they study. But its treatment is often unsatisfactory. This is true, for example, of Talcott Parsons, the high priest of American sociological orthodoxy. It is fundamental to Parsons' perspective that a society is an integrated system, that stability and equilibrium are the norm, that the social fabric is cemented by 'shared values'. Yet nowhere in Parsons' work is there a satisfactory investigation of the origins and the dynamics of these values. Accordingly, 'Academic Sociology is characterized both by the importance it attributes to values *and* by its failure to develop ... a distinctive sociology of moral values' (Gouldner, 1970: 140–1).

The uncritical assumption that beliefs and values increase the integration and stability of a 'social system' has been carried over into industrial relations theory by Dunlop, who acknowledges the influence of Parsons on his own thinking. The consequences are baneful. One element in Dunlop's definition of the 'industrial relations system' is 'ideology': 'a set of ideas and beliefs commonly held by the actors that helps to bind or to integrate the system together as an entity' (1958: 16). Yet rather than explaining *how* the actors' ideologies interact with the other components of the 'system' to produce order and stability, he merely asserts that this *is* their effect. Thus he writes that 'the idea of an industrial-relations system implies a unity, an interdependence, and an internal balance which is likely to be restored if the system is displaced' (p. 27). And of the actors' ideas and beliefs he states that 'an industrial-relations system *requires* that these ideologies be sufficiently compatible and consistent so as to permit a common set of ideas which recognize an acceptable role for each actor' (p. 17; emphasis added). This is sheer mysticism. If it is part of the definition of an industrial relations system that it contains built-in tendencies towards equilibrium, and that radical conflict is excluded from the actors' ideologies, then it cannot be assumed that industrial relations in the real world constitute a system at all. The extent to which the beliefs and values of different participants may converge or diverge has to be treated as problematic.

To put the point another way, social structure and social consciousness are dialectically related, each acting upon and influencing the other, and in some situations leading to increased stability, in others to heightened conflict. This has been recognized by Eldridge, who has insisted that the analysis of industrial conflict must take account of 'the interaction of cultural, economic and organizational factors', and has applied this prescription to an essay on industrial relations in the British steel industry (1968). He notes the familiar contrast between the militant history of the industry in South Wales, and the amicable relations which have long characterized north-east England – despite the structural similarity of the two contexts. The explanation he offers centres around the 'principle of cumulation': the thesis that in certain situations a succession of minor occurrences – 'historical accidents' – can prove mutually reinforcing and so set relationships in a persistent mould. Eldridge cites the account which Phelps Brown has given of the development of industrial co-operation in the north-east:

> One man's initiative would be reciprocated by someone on the other side; no economic storm came to break up the arrangement they made between them: a tradition was established, and drew enough strength from its own success. Human relations build up like that, but in either direction. Started in the wrong direction, not by malevolence but perhaps by some twist of circumstance, they can generate ever new conflicts out of the bitter memories of past ones. Each friendly act is suspect as a trap, each unfriendly one is vital to self-defence; and all because that is how it was yesterday (1960: 157).

The implications are clear: that ideologies are not mechanically determined by structural forces; and that whether the understandings which arise are shared or conflicting may be a matter of contingency.

The mediation of meaning

As the quotation from Phelps Brown illustrates, social action is not merely 'called forth' by the structure of the objective situation but depends also on how that situation is perceived and defined. Action stems also, of course, from the goals and motives which the participants bring to the situation. To neglect the possibilities of variation in perceptions and definitions, goals and motives, is to trammel sociological analysis.

The attempt to provide explanations from the point of view of the 'system' entails the neglect of the point of view of the actors involved. . . . The orientation which workers have to employment and the manner, thus, in which they define their work situation can be regarded as *mediating* between features of the work situation objectively considered and the nature of workers' response (Goldthorpe *et al.*, 1968: 183, 182).

This argument has obvious relevance for the study of industrial disputes; for workers' ideas and beliefs are directly related to their willingness to engage in specific forms of conflict activity. The complex subject of strikers' goals and motives will be considered in detail in Chapter 5; the present chapter concludes with some remarks concerning the varieties of meanings of industrial conflict for workers involved.

A form of unorganized conflict which can be perceived in radically different ways is absenteeism. In mining there is considerable evidence that voluntary absence represents a major managerial problem; studies of mining communities suggest that workers assert as a right their freedom to 'have one off', and many even argue that they have a duty to stay away from the pit if they feel at all unfit in order to avoid endangering their workmates. A totally different situation has been described in a study of a British steel factory: employees shared management's definition of voluntary absenteeism as morally improper. Men would thus feel obliged to attend the factory despite severe work-related stresses, and the result was often that they would – quite literally – worry themselves sick (Hill and Trist, 1955). In a significant sense it might be argued that absenteeism is not the same action in the two situations, because it is defined so totally differently by the actors themselves.

Such differences in definitions may be even more marked in the case of organized conflict. McCarthy has described what he terms an 'endemic strike situation': a plant with eighty-three recorded stoppages in the space of a year.

Virtually all piece rate and lieu rate demands, together with an elaborate and costly system of waiting time, had been negotiated by shop stewards under the more or less constant threat of walkouts. Sudden stoppages took place over almost every conceivable issue, e.g. if the gangways were obstructed, or if lavatory facilities were felt to be below standard on a particular day. Many of these strikes were spontaneous demonstrations on the part of the workers themselves, although the larger and more important ones were usually led by stewards, who had strategically calculated when they would be most effective. Yet there was also something different about the use of the strike sanction in this firm. Elsewhere, in the plants we studied, the strike was very much a weapon of last resort, employed on the rare occasions when frustration, or a sense of immediate injustice, appeared to demand a sudden demonstration, or when it was thought to be strategically necessary to apply maximum pressure as fast as possible. Here, on the contrary, disputes tended to reach the point at which the strike threat was made or carried out much sooner, and much more readily. In effect the strike had become a part of the normal custom and practice of industrial relations in the firm, an endemic feature of factory life accepted by *both* sides as being largely inevitable (1966: 23).

This situation could be typified as one in which immediate collective action is the culturally expected response of workers to any grievance. Less extreme examples of such expectations are common in industrial relations: management have learned to take workers' complaints or demands seriously only if the latter are willing to strike over them; the workers know what is expected of them. Here the respective perceptual frameworks of management and workers interact in such a way that regular stoppages are virtually guaranteed. Doubtless the origins of such cultural patterns may be sought in the 'principle of cumulation'.

Contrast such situations with factories where strike action is unprecedented. The 'regular' striker (one who may expect to be involved in a stoppage once or twice every few years) might regard a stoppage as a natural and even routine event; but the worker who takes a decision which overturns a tradition of industrial peace must perceive a strike quite differently. During the Pilkington dispute, for example, 'there was a feeling of elation, a feeling of liberation about the place, even though everyone did seem to be confused about what was going on. The way some of the men were talking it was as though they had done something big for the first time in their lives' (Lane and Roberts, 1971: 104–5). Sexual imagery being as common in industry as elsewhere, a labour force which strikes for the first time is often described as losing its virginity. The workers may previously have regarded striking as morally improper; having taken the plunge they may be expected to experience a sense of achievement, but possibly also feelings of doubt, apprehension and even guilt; and having done it once – especially if the experience is rewarding – they will probably be far readier to do it again.

As with absenteeism, the *meanings* attributed to a strike will vary so much between situations where stoppages are routine and those where they are unprecedented that it is unhelpful to define it as the same action in both cases. Where the significance of their action is so differently regarded by the strikers themselves, the precipitating causes are likely to be similarly distinctive.

The need for a dialectical sociology

In this section an attempt has been made to show that it is essential to consider how 'structural' influences on industrial conflict – technological, economic and political forces – are mediated by those processes which shape workers' (and managers') definitions of the situation.

In recent years, the neglect of the subjective viewpoint – which is so characteristic of sociological orthodoxy – has led to something of a reaction. An increasingly influential school argues that

> In industrial sociology what may be termed an action frame of reference could, with advantage, be more widely adopted; that is to say, a frame of reference within which actors' own definitions of the situations in which they are engaged are taken as an initial basis for the explanation of their social behaviour and relationships (Goldthorpe *et al.*, 1968: 184).

The current emphasis on the 'action frame of reference' is not, however, without its dangers: for some sociologists, in their reaction against positivism, have neglected the structural influences of which the actors themselves may be unconscious. In effect, the views and definitions of the actors are treated as a sufficient explanation of the social situation being investigated.

This approach is itself misguided. Our consciousness does have a certain independence from such structural factors as the level of technology, the system of economic relations, and the institutions of political and industrial control; and it can influence the development of these components of the social structure. Yet consciousness is not wholly autonomous. Definitions of reality are themselves socially generated and sustained, and people's ability to achieve their goals is constrained by the objective characteristics of their situation.

Put technically, it might be said that there exists a 'structured dialectic of social structure and social consciousness' (Coulson and Riddell, 1970: 93). There is, in other words, a complex two-way process in which our goals, ideas and beliefs influence and are influenced by the social structure. To do justice to its complexity, industrial sociologists must be attuned to this dynamic interaction between structure and consciousness. A static or a one-way analysis necessarily distorts social reality, and is therefore an inadequate basis for understanding industrial behaviour or predicting its development. The greatest potential for further progress in the sociology of industrial conflict (and the same is indeed true of sociology in general) must lie in the elaboration of a dialectical approach.

4. The Institutionalization of Industrial Conflict

Discussion so far has focused primarily on relations between employers and workers, while little reference has been made to those between employers and trade unions. This has been deliberate; for while strikes and unions may, in the popular imagination, be inseparable, in practice it has been seen that the typical stoppage in contemporary Britain is largely dissociated from the formal trade union organization.

Yet – as with Sherlock Holmes and the dog that did not bark – the very absence of a large number of official strikes might itself be regarded as a fact of great significance. For though the degree of past conflict can easily be exaggerated, at one time trade unions were certainly more directly involved in strike activity than is now the case. To explain this change it is necessary to consider the theory of the institutionalization of industrial conflict.

The 'functions' of social conflict

The 'commonsense' view of conflict is of a process which is disruptive and destructive; and a similar assumption predominates among sociologists also. Sociological orthodoxy has something of a fixation about 'order', and tends to treat any threat to the stability of the *status quo* as a 'problem' to be deplored and if possible eliminated. Another sociological tradition, very much in the minority, has tended to define the *status quo* as the 'problem' and to welcome conflict as a possible precursor of an alternative form of social order. There is however a third, and increasingly influential approach which insists that, paradoxically, the expression of conflict can act as a means of *reinforcing* the *status quo*.

The best-known exponent of the latter theory is Lewis Coser. In his book *The Functions of Social Conflict* he insists that

> conflict, rather than being disruptive and dissociating, may indeed be a means of balancing and hence maintaining a society as a going concern. . . . A flexible society benefits from conflict because such behaviour, by helping to create and modify norms, assures its continuance under changed conditions (1956: 137, 154).

The proposition indicated in the title of Coser's study, that conflict is 'functional' for society, raises complex issues concerning the questionable assumptions of functional theory in general. These are unfortunately too far removed from the subject of the present work to justify discussion here.

Coser's relevance for an analysis of strikes lies in his use of industrial relations experience as evidence for the proposition that conflict, when articulated in an organized manner, becomes self-regulating. Organizations of employers and workers, he insists, through engaging in a struggle in which neither side obtains final victory over the other, eventually elaborate 'rules of the game' which both sides become anxious to protect. Despite the deprivations inherent in the structure of industry, conflict thus becomes institutionalized, and 'peace can be concluded and maintained effectively' (pp. 129–33). It is necessary to examine in some detail the validity of this argument.

The management of discontent

Trade unions arose as the collective response of working people exposed to the economic deprivations of an inhospitable society; and they found themselves repeatedly engaged in bitter conflict with the controlling elements in that society. Yet today, it is possible to describe trade unionism as 'an essential part of the mechanism of social control' within this same society (Fox and Flanders, 1969: 156). One formulation of this paradox has been provided by Dubin:

> That there are conflicts of interests in industry today seems scarcely questionable. That we have institutionalized the mode of this

conflict through collective bargaining is also clear. We have thus built, in the institutional practice of collective bargaining, a social device for bringing conflict to a successful resolution (1954: 47).

The ambivalence inherent in the trade union function has been succinctly stated by Wright Mills in his description of the union leader as a ' manager of discontent. . . . He organizes discontent and then he sits on it' (1948: 9).

Originating in the United States, where official unionism is far more intimately involved in plant-level industrial relations than in Britain, this interpretation of trade unionism as a source of social stability has become central to most academic theories. The arguments on which this thesis is based can be subsumed under three main headings: that trade unions, by their concrete achievements, have eradicated the causes of intense social conflicts; that industrial conflict is expressed in innocuous forms now that the legitimacy of trade unionism has been generally accepted; and that the 'institutional needs' of unions themselves lead naturally to moderate and conservative policies.

It could be argued that this theory overemphasizes the extent to which the expression of industrial conflict can become socially controlled. The 'management of discontent', as Wright Mills himself conceived it, is a highly precarious enterprise: a union which damps down workers' discontents too far destroys its own reason for existence. Many of the demands pursued by unions even within 'mature' collective bargaining can be at least potentially disruptive. And while institutionalization may provide an orderly formal system of industrial relations, with trade union officials behaving as very models of 'responsibility', this may fail to extend to the activities of rank-and-file workers and informal industrial relations on the shop floor (Hyman, 1971b). As will be seen below, there remain powerful social causes of conflict, and there are thus important limits to institutionalization. Nevertheless, it is precisely because the theories outlined below do possess a significant core of validity that they are so widely accepted.

Trade union achievements

Trade unions are widely credited with achieving a major improvement in the situation of the wage-earner since the 'bad old days' of the nineteenth century or even the 1930s; and this improvement is at times cited as evidence that society itself has been transformed. Indeed, some go so far as to argue that the alterations in social conditions have been so radical that unions are no longer necessary – a contention particularly popular in employer circles.

Attention is most often directed to such concrete changes as increases in earnings and reductions in hours of work. In fact, throughout this century the share of wages and salaries in the national income has barely deviated from the figure of 60 per cent. Trade unions have not succeeded in winning for their members any part of the percentage of production accruing to profits; they have merely held on to the same relative share within a growing economy. There are many economists who argue that the trend of wages would have been basically the same even if no unions existed. This is something which cannot be proved one way or the other; but at least most union members *believe* that their organizations are responsible for increasing earnings, and would be most unwilling to rely solely on the generosity of their employers or the working out of impersonal economic laws.

Many writers on industrial relations would insist that, whether or not trade unions should be credited with raising wages, this whole controversy diverts attention from an even more significant achievement: 'the protection and advancement of workers' rights and freedoms on the job' (Harbison, 1964: 275).

The public's preoccupation with the union's economic role in labour markets has meant that an even more important role has been neglected and insufficiently understood. That is the role of union organization within the workplace itself in regulating *managerial* relations, i.e. the exercise of management authority in deploying, organizing and disciplining the labour force after it has been hired (Fox, 1966: 7).

A similar argument has been urged by Allan Flanders: 'this surely is the most enduring social achievement of trade unionism; its creation of a social order in industry embodied in a code of industrial rights' (1970: 42).

It is hardly surprising that many writers have interpreted the gains which unions have achieved as at least blunting the edge of workers' discontents and thus contributing towards social stability. This view has been forcefully summarized by Harbison:

> Collective bargaining, where it operates with reasonable success, fulfils three major functions: first, it provides a partial means for resolving the conflicting economic interests of management and labor; second, it greatly enhances the rights, dignity, and worth of workers as industrial citizens; and, third, as a consequence of the first two functions, it provides one of the most important bulwarks for the preservation of the private-enterprise system (1954: 274).

Legitimacy and stability

The relatively pacific role of modern unions is also often attributed to the legitimacy which they have achieved within contemporary society. In their formative years, unions were viewed by employers (and also governments) as dangerous and subversive organizations. The brutal resistance encountered by even the most modest union activities was the main cause of most of the spectacular conflicts of the period. Nineteenth-century British employers made frequent use of the 'document' – a declaration by each employee that he was not a union member; this was the cause of major disputes in building, engineering, and several other industries. In America as recently as the 1930s, leading companies spent thousands of dollars on espionage, acquired private arsenals of guns and tear gas, and hired thugs and assassins, as part of a war against union organization. In both countries, local and national government at times aided employers in such resistance. But now that managements and the state have for the most part come to terms with unionism, the argument runs, harmonious industrial relations have become possible.

Such an assumption underlay the main foundation of American

labour legislation, the Wagner Act of 1935; its preamble insisted that 'the denial by employers of the right of employees to organize and the refusal by employers to accept the procedure of collective bargaining lead to strikes and other forms of industrial strife and unrest'. The other half of this argument – that unions, if their right to exist is accepted, will act 'moderately' and 'responsibly' – has long been pressed by union officials themselves. William Allen, secretary of the Engineers, told a Royal Commission a century ago that 'we believe that strikes are a complete waste of money. . . . We endeavour at all times to prevent strikes. It is the very last thing that we would think of encouraging.' The pioneer theorists of industrial relations, the Webbs, insisted that conflict was reduced when unionism and collective bargaining were accepted (1897: 220–1).

Such arguments – from union leaders and their sympathizers – might at one time have been viewed as special pleading; but in recent years they have become part of academic orthodoxy. Two examples will suffice: Dahrendorf and Lipset. In the words of the former, 'industrial conflict has become less violent because its existence has been accepted and its manifestations have been socially regulated. . . . By collective bargaining the frozen fronts of industrial conflict are thawed' (1959: 257, 260). Lipset has taken the thesis a stage further with his assertion that

> when the conflict of interest groups is legitimate, these 'conflict' organizations contribute to the integration and stability of the society. Trade unions should not be viewed primarily in their economic-cleavage function. They also serve to integrate their members in the larger body politic and give them a basis for loyalty to the system (1959: 113).

Such a process can of course be deliberately fostered. Sophisticated labour relations textbooks urge companies to display 'a positive acceptance of the union', to strive 'to integrate it into the administrative structure of the enterprise instead of treating it as a thing apart'; the collaborative relationship which results, it is suggested, 'can contribute to efficient management'. Wright Mills described the evolution of such relationships in the US, less than a decade after the bitter and often bloody struggles to achieve union recognition. What was occurring, he argued, was the amalgamation of 'the union bureaucracy with the corporation's' (1948: 223). In Britain, the more enlightened managements have long been attempting to achieve a similar process of incorporation.

Governments, too, have sought to capture the unions by kindness – particularly in time of war or economic difficulty. By co-opting union leaders on to numerous (though typically ineffectual) consultative committees, and by offering knighthoods and similar rewards for good conduct, the attempt is made to ensure a 'responsible' trade union movement. The pressures involved have been clearly expressed by the Labour Correspondent of *The Times*.

> The unions had become in a very real sense a part of the 'establishment'. Their association with the Government and employers on scores of committees of all kinds and their accepted right to be consulted on any subject affecting their members directly or indirectly made them an important influence in the nation's councils and also, many people felt, imposed a responsibility on them. They had become a part of the body of the State in many of its intricate ramifications, instead of, as they once were, something outside the State and in some senses a rival power. . . . Belonging, as they now did, implied loyalty (Wigham, 1961: 11–12).

Union leaders have in general willingly endorsed this bargain, exercising restraint both in the scale of their demands on employers and in their use of official strike action.

These developments underlie the theory of 'mature' industrial relations. It is held that as unions gain acceptance, so industrial conflict is rendered increasingly institutionalized, professionalized, and antiseptic. Situations rarely impel union leaders to wield the strike weapon; and when such situations do arise, the conflict itself takes a notably peaceful form. In America, where large-scale stoppages often do accompany the negotiation, every few years, of company-wide agreements, these have become ritualistic engagements: with unions co-operating in an orderly shutdown of production, and companies often providing shelter and refreshments for pickets. And even the British General Strike of 1926 –

symbolically the apogee of union militancy – is today, at times, somewhat erroneously remembered primarily as the occasion for football matches between police and strikers.

The 'institutional needs' of unions

Why is it that trade unions apparently accept so willingly the incorporating embrace? This can to a large extent be explained by considering the concept of 'goal displacement' (Hyman, 1971a: 195–205). Organizations are created, more or less deliberately, in order to achieve some specific purpose; but these original goals tend, over time, to become supplemented and extended; procedures devised for the efficient attainment of these goals become sanctified as ends in themselves; and those in charge of the organization become committed to 'institutional' goals which are considered necessary for its security and stability but which may conflict with its overt purposes. This same process appears inherent in trade unionism: 'unions as social organizations have developed a certain "functional autonomy", that is, their growth and integrity have become ends in themselves' (Tannenbaum and Kahn, 1958: 3). The German-born sociologist Michels was one of the first to discern this process in the organizations of the labour movement, arguing that it conferred on them 'a profoundly conservative character':

> The . . . doctrines are, whenever requisite, attenuated and deformed in accordance with the external needs of the organization. Organization becomes the vital essence. . . . More and more invincible becomes its aversion to all aggressive action. . . . Thus, from a means, organization becomes an end (1915: 369–73).

Such institutional pressures create within unionism a perpetual ambivalence. An established union may have arisen as 'an expression and vehicle of the historical movement of the submerged laboring masses for social recognition and democratic self-determination', but it also performs the more prosaic and often contradictory role of 'a businesslike service organization' (Herberg, 1943). This dichotomy is expressed in the contrast between the 'agitational motive' and the 'organizational motive' (Ross, 1954). While unions have often first recruited mass membership among unorganized workers through agitation and militant action, mass enthusiasm has usually proved relatively transient. So in the long run, membership stability has tended to depend on union ability 'to convert temporary movement into permanent organization' (Flanders, 1970: 43). This in turn has provided a strong incentive to joint involvement with managements in job regulation; which has usually meant union acceptance of some form of 'peace obligation' in return for management concessions towards 'union security'. This is why far-sighted employers are often happy to agree that all employees must be union members (in common language, to operate a 'closed shop'): they see this as a contribution towards a situation in which

> the leaders of labor will deliver a responsible, which is to say, a well-disciplined, union of contented workers in return for junior partnership in the productive process, security for the union, and higher wages for the workers (Wright Mills, 1948: 119).

It is important to note, however, that the structure of industrial relations has made this situation far less easily attainable in most British industries than in the United States. And even in America, recent experience has shown that conflict cannot be suppressed simply by incorporating the union hierarchy: workers still find means of expressing their grievances.

The leaders and officials of the union will naturally assign a special salience to furthering what they consider to be its 'institutional needs'. This helps explain the conflict of roles which was described in Chapter 2: the 'responsibility' of the representative as against the volatility of the rank and file. Concern for union security is likely to make the official particularly committed to the bargaining relationship with the employer, and thus particularly reluctant to take militant action where this appears to jeopardize relations. For the same reasons, union leaders have a strong inducement to seek and preserve the social legitimacy of unionism, and to accommodate their relations with governments and with employers nationally to this end. It is scarcely surprising, then, that the pressures towards caution and conservatism are normally so powerful.

The withering away of the strike?

The theories and interpretations discussed in the previous section have become commonplace, among academic analysts of industrial relations at least: and their implications for any analysis of strikes are obvious. 'The actual use of the strike as a conventional implement is dwindling', was the conclusion of one study of statistical trends in fifteen countries.

> Man-days of idleness in the late 1950s are fewer than in the late 1940s or the late 1930s, despite the increases in population and union membership. . . . The decline is most dramatic when described in comparative terms. One significant measure of industrial conflict is the number of strikers in relation to the number of union members. This proportion has fallen off sharply. . . . Secondly, those strikes that do occur have been growing much shorter (Ross and Hartman, 1960: 4).

'The strike has been going out of fashion,' the authors argued; indeed they labelled their analysis 'the withering away of the strike'. While reluctant to predict that these trends would inevitably continue, one of their final remarks was that 'we do not see any substantial evidence of any impending revival of strike activity in the Northern European countries' (p. 176).

Only one important criticism can be made of this analysis: it is wrong. It is true that, internationally, striker-days in the post-war period have been substantially below their pre-war level. But as the discussion of British strike trends showed, this merely reflects the relative infrequency today of large-scale and protracted stoppages; it in no way indicates that striking as such 'has been going out of fashion'. Rather, post-war experience in Britain has demonstrated that in terms of their absolute number strikes are 'flourishing rather than withering' (Eldridge, 1968: 40). It is also misleading to imply, as Ross and Hartman do, that the massive trial of strength was once the normal form of strike action and that the nature of the strike has therefore been transformed. While such major battles once provided the overwhelming bulk of striker-days, there is no evidence that they were ever more than a minority of strikes as such.

Even at the time of writing, then, Ross and Hartman may be said to have misinterpreted in important respects the post-war trends in international strike activity. Experience since they wrote has destroyed any plausibility which their thesis may have possessed at the time. This can be seen from recent statistics of disputes in the fifteen countries examined by Ross and Hartman (see Table 4.1).

On the thesis of the withering away of the strike (which, it must be noted, the authors did not consider applicable to every country) the figures for both strikes and striker-days should show a consistent decline. In fact, over the two halves of the 1960s, this occurred in only one of the fifteen countries: Norway. By contrast, strike activity in several major countries increased considerably during the decade. But it is the evidence of the early 1970s that is decisive; both indices rose *in every single country* on Ross and Hartman's list; while mass unemployment in the past decade has caused no general decline. Indeed in half of the fourteen countries for which both indices are available, strikes and striker-days were *both* higher in 1975–85 than two decades earlier despite the unfavourable economic climate. Internationally, it is clear, the strike is obstinately refusing to wither.

The mainsprings of conflict

If industrial conflict has shown such resistance to permanent domestication, the presumption must be that there exist powerful underlying causes. To diagnose these causes necessitates an interpretation of the basic structural realities of our society. Such an analysis is inevitably controversial; but it is essential if any explanation is to be given of the continuing prevalence of the strike and related activities in modern society.

Unquestionably the most important point to be emphasized is that class divisions are fundamental to our social structure. The concept of class, it is true, is as unfashionable in contemporary sociology as it is in everyday discourse. Most sociologists talk not about class but about 'social stratification'; they examine such factors as income levels and ownership of television sets, and report that the present-day class

Table 4.1
Average annual strikes and striker-days in fifteen countries

	Strikes						Striker-days ('000)					
	1955–9	1960–4	1965–9	1970–4	1975–9	1980–5	1955–9	1960–4	1965–9	1970–4	1975–9	1980–5
Australia	1,159	1,144	1,537	2,557	2,179	2,167	713	707	1,058	3,280	3,012	2,282
Canada	223	309	563	730	1,024	823	2,003	1,198	4,867	6,438	8,211	5,859
Denmark	33	40	29	96	222	273	226	485	71	846	168	579
Finland	60	57	90	946*	1,857	1,569	1,602	322	180	1,270*	854	816
France	2,040	2,003	1,885†	3,651	3,567	2,485	2,340	2,810	2,483†	3,436	3,681	1,430
India	1,409	1,611	2,406	2,971	2,551	2,339	6,504	5,714	15,682	21,984	26,432	44,199
Italy	1,896	3,522	3,080	4,692	2,819	1,819	5,548	13,280	15,420	19,614	21,368	12,014
Japan	785	1,215	1,467	3,164	2,099	858	5,151	4,479	3,343	5,871	3,015	536
Netherlands	60	69	25	33	30	19	81	117	22	217	115	89
Norway	20	10	6	12	19	18	241	147	11	79	49	98
South Africa	89	68	78	194	205‡		12	23	11	74	36†	
Sweden	14	18	18	74	100	131	51	17	94	215	109	877
United Kingdom	2,530	2,512	2,380	2,885	2,345	1,286	4,602	3,160	3,929	14,077	11,663	9,806
United States	3,844	3,466	4,742	5,458	5,048	104§	24,340	18,600	36,540	43,412	35,319	13,309§
West Germany			Not available				871	482	148	1,251	1,079	982

* Part of the increase in Finnish figures reflects a change in official compilation methods.
† French statistics are not available for 1968, the year of the near-revolutionary strike wave. Were these available and included, strikes and striker-days in 1965–9 would almost certainly be well above the figures for the two earlier periods.
‡ South African statistics are not available after 1977.
§ Since 1980, US statistics have excluded strikes involving less than 1,000 workers.
Source: International Labour Office, *Yearbook of Labour Statistics.*

structure consists of nothing more than a series of minor variations in styles of life and standards of living. The picture drawn by the press and politicians follows a similar outline: today, it is argued, almost everybody is 'middle class', and class-consciousness is therefore out-of-date and somewhat disreputable.

This is a serious fallacy. Levels of income and styles of consumption are only one, fairly superficial indication of class. And even in this respect, the argument that old social divisions have been eliminated is in fact misplaced. As was seen earlier, the share of wages and salaries in the national income has altered very little throughout this century. Income tax returns show some reduction in the extreme inequality of incomes since the 'bad old days'; but this reduction has been only limited, and is in any case exaggerated by the statistics since there are many devices – legitimate and illegitimate – whereby the very rich minimize the amount of their income recorded for tax purposes. Moreover, what equalization there has been seems to have occurred mainly in the 1940s; since then the trend has if anything been reversed. (The statistics show that the 'wage explosion' of 1969–70 raised the share of wages and salaries in the national income by some 3 per cent. This disproves the common argument that large wage claims are self-defeating; but this gain scarcely amounts to a substantial redistribution of income, and may be only temporary.) The widespread belief that there has been a drastic equalization of incomes in recent years is very convenient for the rich; but the main change since the nineteenth century is simply that the absolute income of all groups has risen with the increase in total national income.

Inequalities of income mirror, and are largely derived from, massive inequalities of wealth. An analysis by the *Economist* (15 January 1966) showed that 7 per cent of taxpayers owned 84 per cent of all private wealth in Britain, while 2 per cent owned 55 per cent of the total. At the other end of the scale, 88 per cent of taxpayers shared less than 4 per cent of personal wealth, with an average property of only just over £100. The idea that Britain is now a classless society is therefore a myth. As the *Economist* noted, wealth generates more wealth: 'the rich do not only have more money; they also make it multiply faster'. The greater a person's wealth, the more profitably he can invest it. In the longer term, not only do the children of the rich inherit their parents' wealth; they also enjoy overwhelming advantages within the educational system, which further increase their prospects in terms of occupational advancement, high salaries and fringe benefits, and social influence and prestige (Westergaard, 1965). Thus is inequality perpetuated from generation to generation.

This is, however, only half the story, for one of the accompaniments of wealth is power. 'The uninterrupted, albeit modified, dominance, of the property-owning classes, in a society which has long been the most highly "proletarianized" in the world, is surely one of the most striking phenomena of modern times' (Worsley, 1964: 22–3). The disproportionate power of the rich in social and political life generally is well documented, though space prevents a detailed discussion of the evidence here (Worsley, 1964; Westergaard, 1965; Miliband, 1969). It is however essential to emphasize the specific *industrial* consequences of inequality.

What is at issue, of course, is the ownership not just of wealth but of the whole productive system. Industry in our society is capitalist industry (another term which is rarely used in 'respectable' discussion); this means that industry is for the most part privately owned, and its basic dynamic is the provision of profits for its owners. Recent surveys have revealed that only 4 per cent of the adult population hold shares in industrial or commercial companies, while 81 per cent of privately owned shares are in the possession of 1 per cent of the adult population. Yet gross profits account for roughly 20 per cent of the national income. (In most years, over a third of profits is paid out directly as dividends; roughly a quarter is paid in tax; while the remainder is reinvested. But since net investment adds to company assets, this enhances share values and so provides shareholders with a capital gain.) This is another aspect of the radical division within society: while the wealthy minority do not have to work (since the bulk of their income derives from property), the mass of the population can live only by putting their labour at the disposal of those who own and control the means of production. Those who depend on their wages or salaries in order to live are 'the people who, generally, "get the least of what there is to get", and who have to work hardest for it. And it is also from their ranks that are, so to speak, recruited the unemployed, the aged poor, the chronically destitute and the sub-proletariat of capitalist society' (Miliband, 1969: 16).

It is true that some theorists have argued that modern industry is no longer capitalist, since it is run not by shareholders but by salaried managers. This is a doubly fallacious argument. The company directors and top managers who make the key decisions in industry are themselves usually men of considerable wealth, and almost without exception their social origins and social values are those of the rich minority (Westergaard, 1965: Blackburn, 1967; Nichols, 1969). And in any case, the pursuit of profit derives not simply from the personal acquisitiveness of those who run industry but from the very dynamic of a capitalist economy. If sufficient dividends are not paid to keep shareholders happy then share values will fall, it will become difficult to raise further funds on the stock market, and the danger of take-over will loom. If companies do not expand and innovate as rapidly as industry generally, their competitive position will be undermined. Thus the 'logic of the market' obliges managers to pursue profits high enough both to placate shareholders and to finance new investment (Blackburn, 1965). This 'logic of the market' can of course be highly illogical from any humane viewpoint. It can dictate lavish expenditure on luxury office accommodation while thousands of families are homeless – and while building workers suffer large-scale unemployment. It can dictate the depletion of natural resources and the pollution of the environment to produce commodities which are elaborately designed to work inefficiently ('built-in obsolescence'), and which consumers would have little inclination to purchase in the absence of massive advertising campaigns. It can dictate the extreme intensification of work pressure for some employees, while others are in consequence made redundant.

To say that the logic of the market dictates such processes is, in a sense, to evade assigning responsibility for the consequences of social actions. More accurately, it should be said that we tolerate a system of economic anarchy. In a capitalist society it is true almost by definition that there is an absence of deliberate overall control directing industrial production towards the rational and efficient satisfaction of human needs. In consequence, decisions which seem perfectly logical at the level of the individual capitalist enterprise can have cumulative effects which are obviously irrational at the level of society as a whole.

The subordination of industry to the dictates of profitability occurs in its most extreme form when the productive system is privately owned by a wealthy minority. But by itself, even 'public ownership' need not alter the situation in any fundamental way. In Britain, nationalized industries are explicitly committed to adopt the criterion of profitability, and are thus firmly integrated within the basic structure of a capitalist economy. And even where state ownership is virtually total, it is not inevitable that capitalist priorities will give way to more humane considerations. Those who refer to Russia and other East European countries as 'state capitalist' societies imply that while the legal ownership of industry may have been transformed, the system of management and the economic rationale adopted do not differ over-much from those in Britain or the United States. It could be argued that a privileged and self-perpetuating élite makes the crucial economic decisions, and along basically capitalist lines, even in the so-called 'communist' countries. The irrational and often brutal consequences of a class-divided society cannot be expected to be overcome unless working people as a whole are able to take the key decisions in the organization and direction of production.

Income distribution

Workers in a capitalist society are *employees*. The value of the products of industry, after all other costs of production are allowed for, is divided between wage- and salary-earners and the owners of capital. What is income for the employee is a cost for the employer, which the latter will naturally seek to minimize. Thus how the proceeds of industry are divided between employers and workers will depend primarily on the power relationship between the two sides.

This is a persistent source of conflict, and for two main reasons. First, the balance is constantly disturbed by changes in the cost of living, costs of materials and other factors of production, and the value of output. 'The conflict over distribution exists over every additional increment of revenue. If productivity increases there is no law or custom which will guarantee that its proceeds will be shared out in a predetermined manner' (Allen, 1966: 113).

There is also a more basic reason why conflict over income distribution is endemic. A famous American labour leader, asked what it was that trade unionists wanted, answered tersely: 'more'.

There exists a naïve theory that within an 'affluent society', with the absolute economic deprivation of the past no longer the lot of most working people (though by no means eliminated), pressure for increased income should diminish. But what is important is not absolute but relative deprivation: the gap between people's actual income and that to which they feel they can reasonably aspire (Runciman, 1966). It is hardly surprising that workers still want 'more' when they are daily urged by TV commercials and advertisement hoardings to strive for a style of life which is beyond their means; and when they see that this life-style is already enjoyed by some sections of society (particularly by those who pontificate about 'greedy' trade unionists). Tawney's memorable words are as true as ever:

> The idea, which is popular with rich men, that industrial disputes would disappear if only the output of wealth were doubled, and everyone were twice as well off, not only is refuted by all practical experience, but is in its very nature founded upon an illusion. For the question is one, not of amounts but of proportions; and men will fight to be paid £30 a week, instead of £20, as readily as they will fight to be paid £5 instead of £4, as long as there is no reason why they should be paid £20 instead of £30, and as long as other men who do not work are paid anything at all. . . . If the community can afford to pay anything at all to those who do not work, it can afford to pay more to those who do (1921: 42).

Job security

Not only does conflict centre around the price of labour; it stems from the very *fact* that labour is in our society treated as a commodity to be bought and sold. The remainder of this section considers a number of the implications of this fact for relations in industry.

The status of labour as a commodity has obvious repercussions on the worker's security of employment. It is in the employer's interest to retain a worker in employment only when it is profitable to him to do so, and when it is more profitable to use his labour than to manufacture his products in any other way. This means that the worker's job is always at the mercy of economic and technological vagaries. The point is clearly stated in a standard textbook on industrial sociology:

> Since the worker's job depends on the needs of production and on the demands of the market, his job is always in jeopardy. This is particularly true in times of depression, but even in times of general prosperity, there may be severe local depression caused by technical conditions, shortages of raw materials, or the situation in a particular industry. . . . Perhaps the major threat to the worker's security stems from technological change. . . . The greatest threat to the worker undoubtedly lies in the ever-present possibilities of unemployment; not only single workmen but whole towns may be displaced by some technological change. The machine is thus a constant threat to the workingman's most basic need – to be the holder of a job (Schneider, 1969: 221–3).

Strictly speaking, of course, it is not 'the machine' which threatens the worker's security; it is machinery owned and controlled *by someone else*. Technological change as such could in principle be wholly welcome to the worker and to society, allowing more to be produced with less drudgery. It is not inanimate machines that throw people out of work, but the decisions which are taken as to how these machines shall be used. It is because the worker lacks any direct control over these decisions that his desire to establish a right to his job is always a potential source of conflict.

Power and control

This lack of control is one example of a more general powerlessness which follows from the status of labour as a commodity. This peculiar relationship has been analysed by Blackburn in a passage which it is useful to quote at length.

> In capitalist society the productivity of labour derives from its collective and co-operative nature, yet it is remunerated on an individual basis. The employer is well placed to reap the difference between the individual price of labour and its social productiveness. What the employer buys is the worker's *ability* to

work rather than that work itself. By selling his labour power the worker is effectively making it over to the employer for a stipulated period during which its organization and application will not be his own responsibility. There is something distinctly curious about this attempt to buy and sell labour just as if it were any other commodity.

The first thing to note is that the labour contract is not an exchange of equivalents: it is structurally asymmetrical. It is not just that the labourer has to sell his work in order to live whereas the capitalist is not similarly constrained to buy labour. By the terms of the contract, the worker receives a definite – and usually public – rate for the job whereas the employer receives an incalculable potentiality whose ultimate development it is for him to determine. The worker's wage is thus negotiated and bargained for in a manner quite distinct from the manner in which dividends and capital gains arise in the production process. From the employer's side the labour contract is open-ended. In principle the nature of the exact tasks the worker has undertaken to perform becomes the province of management. The workshop or office operates on a command structure in which the powers of decision rest with the owners' chosen representative, the manager (1967: 38–9).

Thus the employment relationship subordinates the worker to a structure of managerial control, designed to maximize the effort and application which he devotes in exchange for his wages.

That the exercise of this control generates conflict can be seen from the example of the Halewood strike. To reduce labour costs, four men were ordered to perform a dangerous and demanding task when in their view the normal five men were required. Management asserted its authority, and the result was a strike of 10,000 men. Such instances are legion. At one extreme, the employer may decide on a massive redundancy. More routinely, a company may attempt to change work methods and speed up production. Or managers may try to cut down on rest periods and tea breaks. (To most outsiders, tea breaks are a cause of hilarity. To the worker, they may be an essential respite from the physical and emotional pressures of the job, and the only opportunity for social relationships during working hours.) Hence the exercise of managerial control is a persistent basis for conflict.

The natural tendency for a power relationship to generate conflict is subject, however, to an important constraint: the degree to which subordinates accept the right of those in control to issue orders. Where such a right is recognized it is usual to speak of 'authority' rather than simply of 'power'. 'Authority that is viewed as legitimate is not felt as coercion or manipulation, either by the man who exercises it or by the man who accepts it' (Simon, 1957: 108). To present the contrast in a stark manner, it could be said that authority normally attracts ungrudging obedience, whereas a simple power relationship is characterized by involuntary or calculative compliance.

The dominant values in societies generally tend to underwrite the legitimacy of those in positions of control. As Gouldner has argued, there is a tendency for might to *make* right: 'like any other behavior, the judgement that something is legitimate can be coerced and rewarded situationally' – it can be imprudent to question the right of those in control to be there. Moreover, it is often more comfortable for those who are subject to apparently inescapable control to define their compliance as morally proper. 'Thus are power and morality brought into equilibrium' (1970: 293). So it is not surprising that the 'right of management to manage' is rarely directly questioned by working people. And for this reason, the exercise of managerial control leads only sporadically to overt conflict.

Yet it is only within limits that managerial control is buttressed by the dominant social values. Indeed, managerial legitimacy is vulnerable in four distinct ways. First, the values of society are themselves less than consistent. While the virtue of 'respect for authority' is rarely disputed, our culture also values highly such abstract ideas as 'freedom' and 'democracy'. In consequence, there is often considerable reluctance to speak of industry in terms of control at all – certainly when those who are *controlled* are considered. 'Common parlance has it that those on top of the industrial hierarchy are "bosses" or "managers", thus accenting their command functions; but those filling subordinate positions are spoken of as "workers", focussing on their technological responsibilities' (Gouldner, 1955: 164). Since it is uncomfortable within a liberal-democratic ethos to define workers as 'obeyers' or 'the managed', the moral basis of managerial authority is reduced.

Secondly, and partly in consequence, social values offer little guidance as to the degree of managerial authority and hence worker obedience which is appropriate. Workers do not normally define themselves, nor are they defined by managements, as 'wage slaves'; hence it is not assumed that they surrender their autonomy *absolutely* during working hours as part of the employment contract. But in this case,

> *which* commands has the worker promised to obey? Are these commands limited to the *production* of goods and services only? Under the terms of the contract, may an employer legitimately issue a command unnecessary for production? *Who* decides this anyhow, worker or employer? (Gouldner, 1955: 162–3).

It is probable that workers will be inclined to define their own obligations more narrowly than management would wish. If employers then seek to impose their own wider conception of authority, this will probably be perceived by workers as a naked exercise of power – and as such resisted.

Thirdly, 'there can be strong or weak authority. Accordingly it may be useful to consider degrees of commitment *to* management rule as being on a common scale with degrees of commitment *against* it' (Fox, 1971: 44). Workers may only partially accept the dominant social values; and to the extent that these values themselves are ambivalent, they may embrace those elements that are least favourable to managerial control. So while workers may not reject their employer's authority, the veneer of legitimacy which it holds in their eyes may be thin indeed. Simply because the existing structure of industrial control exists they may acquiesce in the demands made of them, without explicitly challenging management's right to issue orders, yet without any strong belief in its legitimacy.

Finally, the actual exercise of managerial control can generate resistance even from workers who do not ordinarily question its legitimacy. Any assertion of managerial prerogative may potentially violate some aspect of workers' expectations (even if only some vaguely formulated sense of 'fairness'), forcing them to question critically what before was taken for granted. The Pilkington dispute, sparked off by a minor friction, is said to have had such consequences.

> A worker sells more than his labour when he undertakes to work for an employer – as well as undertaking to perform certain tasks he also undertakes to abide by a set of rules, he submits to a system of authority. From this it follows that whether the worker likes it or not, whether he is primarily interested in money or not, he nevertheless sacrifices certain areas of freedom, a sacrifice furthermore that is not likely to be lost on him. It is quite unrealistic to suppose that because a worker works only for money he accordingly shuts off his mind to his daily experiences at the factory. If he treats his *labour* as a commodity it does not follow that he expects himself, a person, to be treated as a commodity. Neither does it follow that he will be prepared to put up with anything if the money is right. . . .
>
> The modern attitude to authority was well expressed by those workers who, in the act of striking, experienced feelings of elation and liberation. These feelings are, we suspect, extremely common amongst those who spark off a wildcat strike. They are feelings characteristic of those who have momentarily dissolved the shackles of authority (Lane and Roberts, 1971: 227–9).

'Momentarily' must be recognized as a key word in this passage: such conflicts, in which traditional attitudes to authority are dramatically overturned, must inevitably be followed (unless the whole structure of society is in the process transformed) by a return to the old relationships. But even so, workers' acceptance of the propriety and inevitability of these relationships may never be quite the same again.

'Industrial democracy'

This analysis might appear to contradict the thesis, outlined earlier, that trade unions, through collective bargaining, have replaced traditional managerial control by 'joint regulation'. Certainly the continuing realities of control in industry are inconsistent with some of the more idealized conceptions of the impact of unionism which make use of such exaggerated descriptions as 'industrial democracy' or 'a secondary system of industrial citizenship'. It would be fatuous to deny, however, that in some industries at least the rise of trade unionism has affected the impact of managerial prerogative on the worker. Little more than a generation ago, many employers possessed almost unrestricted power to hire and fire, and their powers over employees within the workplace were correspondingly autocratic. Managerial autonomy is today subject to important constraints: many decisions which were once unchallengeable are no longer tolerated; others can be taken only after consultation with workers' representatives. This is an achievement which is understandably valued by trade unionists with experience of the previous state of affairs.

Yet the transformation in relationships must not be exaggerated. It is important to scrutinize carefully the nature of the 'joint regulation' which is often argued to have displaced managerial autonomy. One way in which unions can be said to have curbed employers' prerogatives is by controlling their *arbitrary* exercise: the penalizing of a worker, for example, is likely to be permitted only if management can offer what appear to be good reasons. Arbitrary rule has had to give way to consistency of treatment, an achievement which it would be foolish to underrate. From the managers' own viewpoint, their authority is indeed considerably circumscribed; and workers have at least a better idea where they stands when management is obliged to follow some form of 'rule of law'. (Though in the last resort, of course, collective bargaining does not eliminate management's right to act unilaterally if the two sides disagree.) Nevertheless, the fundamental implications of managerial control need be little less oppressive if the basic policy decisions – what sort of reasons are to count as 'good reasons', what sort of rules are to constitute the 'rule of law' – continue to be determined by the criterion of the economic interests of the employer.

So the crucial question which must be asked concerning 'joint regulation' is this: how far has collective bargaining shifted the type of consideration which determines managerial policy over such key issues as the worker's security of employment, or the availability of occupations compatible with human dignity? The answer must be: very little. It is true that those who emphasize the significance of 'joint regulation' might insist that 'it is the *method* that is valued here, not necessarily the *results*' (Fox, 1966: 7). But from the employer's viewpoint it could well be that the method is acceptable precisely because the results do not strike at any of the really crucial 'rights of management'; indeed, the most perceptive managements might suspect that involvement in 'joint regulation' tends to inhibit union representatives from pressing demands which go 'too far' for fear that the continuance of the bargaining relationship might be endangered if the 'rights of capital' were too directly challenged. There is a wealth of meaning in Flanders' declaration that 'the paradox, whose truth managements have found it so difficult to accept, is that they can only regain control by sharing it' (1970: 172). The sceptic might suggest that while collective bargaining has eliminated some of the more glaringly brutal accoutrements of managerial control, it has consolidated the basic structure. The legitimation which trade unionism accords to management – for in collective bargaining, the obverse of employer recognition of the union is union recognition of the employer – is particularly welcome, simply because workers' organizations might otherwise act as vehicles of oppositional ideology.

The idea that collective bargaining replaces managerial control by industrial democracy must therefore be rejected. Management still commands; workers are still obliged to obey. Trade unionism permits debate around the terms of workers' obedience; it does not challenge the fact of their subordination. 'Joint regulation' is *not* joint management (Flanders, 1970: 233–6). And even as a process of joint rule-making, the implications of collective bargaining should not be exaggerated. Flanders has argued (1970: 240) that unions give workers a basis for 'participating as directly as possible in the making and administration of these rules in order to have a voice in shaping their own destiny and the decisions on which it most depends'. But this presupposes that workers generally are positively involved in the control of their own union. Yet in most cases, official union machinery is marked by the almost total absence of membership participation; and it can be argued that the 'organizational motive' which shapes union collective bargaining policies in fact encourages such apathy (Hyman, 1971a: 206–24). It would be over-simple to suggest that unions are therefore undemocratic; but clearly they do not function as agencies for the active involvement of workers generally in the control of their industrial destinies.

Moreover, many of the most important restrictions on managerial autonomy derive not from the formal institutions of trade unionism but from the spontaneous organization of workers on the shop floor. Such informal organization has always set some limits to the powers of management. A study half a century ago offered a perceptive and highly detailed survey of such autonomous enforcement by work groups of their own rules (Goodrich, 1920). While inter-war depression weakened workers' position in this respect, the relatively full employment of the years 1940–70 enhanced the effectiveness of shop-floor organization. Some of the implications of this informal union activity at the point of production have been described in Chapter 2. Another dimension is the ability of workers to sustain 'custom and practice' in the face of management attempts to overturn established working conditions.

This direct and collective assertion by workers of their own power and individuality – their refusal to accept the managerial definition of their role as mere instruments of production – is at times supported by the official union machinery. But far more often it is completely detached from the formal institutions of collective bargaining; and often it is disowned by union officials. Arguably, these shop-floor controls have a better claim than orthodox collective bargaining to be considered a form of 'industrial democracy'. This would still be an exaggeration: the employer continues to make the fundamental policy decisions, while the control which workers have carved out impinges only on the implementation of this policy. Indeed, management is normally able to tolerate this situation precisely because the workers themselves – or at least their shop-floor representatives – realize that their restrictions on management must not go 'too far'.

Nevertheless, the confrontation within the workplace of two bases of control provides a constant source of instability and conflict. Management, particularly when under competitive pressure, is always liable to attempt to push back the frontier of control. A recently popular mechanism directed to this end is the 'productivity bargain', in which workers are offered a financial inducement to surrender their unilateral controls over managerial initiative (Flanders, 1964; Topham, 1967; Cliff, 1970). A central concern of the Donovan Commission was also to advise managements how to regain those areas of authority which had been eroded.

In the present situation, managerial resistance to the existing powers of workers at the point of production is probably the more potent cause of conflict. But the process can also occur in reverse, with workers attempting to extend the frontier of control.

> A determination not to have the conditions of their work entirely dictated to them . . . constantly expresses itself in the struggles of workers on the shop floor, whether they refuse the foreman the right to swear at them, resist speed-up, or deny that management has the right to decide how long a girl may spend in the lavatory (Cliff, 1970: 201).

As Goodrich has argued, 'the demand not to be controlled disagreeably . . . runs through all trade union activity' (1920: 37). But struggles over this demand can potentially lead to a more conscious questioning of the system whereby management is able to command and workers are obliged to obey. From disputes which are trivial in themselves, a conscious aspiration for real industrial democracy may at times be generated.

Workers are human

This leads to the final source of conflict within our system of industry: its impact on workers as total human beings. We possess an almost unlimited variety of actual and potential interests, aptitudes, and abilities. Yet the way in which production is socially organized may either develop and extend our creative potential, or else may stunt and constrain it.

It is widely recognized that industrial work, as it exists today, is of the second order. This has been eloquently expressed by Gouldner.

> In large reaches of our society, but particularly in its industrial sector, it is not the man that is wanted. It is, rather, the function he performs and it is the skill with which he performs it for which he is paid. If a man's skill is not needed, the man is not needed. If a man's function can be performed more economically by a machine, the man is replaced. This has at least two obvious implications. First, that opportunities for social participation in the

industrial sector are contingent upon a man's imputed usefulness, so that in order to gain admission to it – and the rewards it brings – people must submit to an education and to a socialization that early validates and cultivates only selected parts of themselves, that is, those that are expected to have subsequent utility. Secondly, once admitted to participation in the industrial sector, men are appraised and rewarded in terms of their utility and are advanced or removed in accordance with their utility as compared with that of other men.

One consequence is that a section of the working population is unable to obtain work at all – is unemployed. But a second consequence is that a major portion of each individual's talents cannot be utilized: in Gouldner's words, each worker possesses an 'unemployed self'.

The individual learns what the system requires; he learns which parts of himself are unwanted and unworthy; he comes to organize his self and personality in conformity with the operating standards of utility, and thereby minimizes his costs of participating in such a system. In short, vast parts of any personality must be suppressed or repressed in the course of playing a role in industrial society (1969: 348–9).

An organization of work which forces people to suppress much of their individuality is one aspect of what is known as alienation – an important but much abused concept. Workers do not control the process of production; the process of production appears to control *them*. The fact that work is carried out under a form of compulsion gives it an 'alien' character. In contemporary industrial societies, we do not collectively decide what it is socially desirable to produce. Instead, 'wants' are artificially stimulated (through advertising and other forms of 'marketing') to suit what it is *profitable* for employers to produce. Nor do we collectively decide how the work process can be organized in a manner compatible with human dignity; instead, workers must accommodate themselves to the narrow and often degrading requirements of profitability. As Marx expressed it, for the alienated worker the production process exists *outside him*, independently, as something alien to him, and . . . becomes a power on its own confronting him. . . . His labour is therefore not voluntary, but coerced; it is *forced labour*. It is therefore not the satisfaction of a need; it is merely a *means* to satisfy needs external to it (1961: 70–2).

The pioneer French sociologist Emile Durkheim, in his classic analysis of the division of labour, recognized the manner in which modern industry could have alienating consequences.

It has often been accused of degrading the individual by making him a machine. And truly, if he does not know whither the operations he performs are tending, if he relates them to no end, he can only continue to work through routine. Every day he repeats the same movements with monotonous regularity, but without being interested in them, and without understanding them. . . . He is no longer anything but an inert piece of machinery, only an external force set going which always moves in the same direction and in the same way. Surely, no matter how one may represent the moral ideal, one cannot remain indifferent to such debasement of human nature.

He went on to insist, however, that 'the division of labour does not produce these consequences because of a necessity of its own nature, but only in exceptional and abnormal circumstances' (1933: 371–2). This is a crucial argument. 'In large measure, the deadliness of much of modern work derives from the manner in which it is organized socially' (Gouldner, 1970: 280). It is not modern technology which makes work stultifying and degrading; technology is potentially liberating, providing the possibility of removing the drudgery from human labour. Whether the consequences of technology are in fact liberating or enslaving depends on *how* it is decided to use the machines, and on *who* makes these decisions. To attribute unpleasant social consequences to inanimate machinery is to evade examining those *human* actions which – deliberately or by default – are in fact responsible.

The assumption that technical 'progress' necessarily involves the dehumanization of work can, however, become a grotesque form of self-fulfilling prophecy. A recent study has argued that

> with the machines that now exist, and still more with those under development, a rapid shift is taking place from the human being to the machine. In these systems no longer is the producer a man serviced by machines but a machine serviced by men. For the possibilities of this new situation to be realized a change is required in the work culture from a man-centred to a machine-centred attitude – a *machine culture* (Trist *et al.*, 1963: 259).

That intelligent authors – who, no doubt, are pleasant enough individuals, kind to children and dumb animals – should coolly argue for the explicit subordination of human beings to inanimate machines is evidence of the degree to which dehumanization is already implicit in the organization of work in our society.

One indication that the existing situation is indeed, in Durkheim's words, 'exceptional and abnormal' is the degree of conflict which it generates. Within every worker there exists a human being trying to get out.

> Here, then, in the exclusions of self fostered by an industrial system oriented towards utility, is a fundamental source of the sense of a life wasted which is so pervasive, even if muffled, in an industrial society. For the excluded self, while muffled, is not voiceless and makes its protest heard (Gouldner, 1969: 349).

The assumption within our culture that work cannot be expected to possess intrinsic meaning and creativity can lead workers to express 'satisfaction' with their jobs, if these merely appear to suffice as a means of 'earning a living' – the implication being, of course, that one cannot expect to 'live' during working hours. Yet such 'satisfaction' has shallow roots.

> Men questioned about their responses to work may respond on either of two levels: in terms of how far they have adjusted to work as it is, and in terms of how far they have any picture of work as it might be. . . . Workers may present one picture of themselves when they are speaking from a position of resignation to certain

total or partial deprivations (which they have been conditioned to see as largely inevitable), and a very different picture when they allow themselves to dwell on the nature of those deprivations (Fox, 1971: 22).

The adaptability of humanity is immense; but the very fact that workers are human cannot but lead to at least sporadic revolt. Let the last word on this question rest with William Straker, a miners' official speaking in 1919.

In the past workmen have thought that if they could secure higher wages and better conditions they would be content. Employers have thought that if they granted these things the workers ought to be contented. Wages and conditions have improved; but the discontent and the unrest have not disappeared. Many good people have come to the conclusion that working people are so unreasonable that it is useless trying to satisfy them. The fact is that unrest is deeper than pounds, shillings, and pence, necessary as they are. The root of the matter is the straining of the spirit of man to be free (Topham, 1967: 133).

The causes of industrial peace

If such sources of conflict are fundamental to the way industry is organized in present-day society, it might be asked why this conflict is so *rarely* expressed. As Cole has put it, 'as soon as we begin to examine the economic system from a human point of view . . ., the difficulty is to understand not why unrest and strikes exist, but why they are not more prevalent' (1920: 6). One reply would be that while the typical worker strikes for less than a day a year, this is only the tip of the iceberg of organized conflict; while as the preoccupations of industrial sociologists indicate, such usually unorganized conflict as sabotage, indiscipline, 'restriction of output', absenteeism, labour turnover, and sheer bloody-mindedness constitute a chronic managerial problem. Nevertheless, the fact that industry functions at all is evidence that a certain degree of industrial harmony is the norm.

One reason is that, despite the argument of the previous section, there exists an area of common interest between those who control industry and those who work in it. If a firm goes bankrupt, employers and employees both suffer losses. This is not to say that workers do not still suffer deprivations if, in order to stave off bankruptcy, they accept speed-up, redundancies, and the erosion of whatever control they may have over the physical process of production. Nor does it mean that, at a different level of analysis, the perpetuation of the whole system of ownership and control of industry based on stocks and shares, dividends, take-overs, and – inevitably – bankruptcies and redundancies, does not represent a fundamental and unbridgeable opposition of interest between employers and working people. But in everyday life it is the narrow yet immediate area of common interest which is most easily perceived; and extremely influential forces encourage members of society to continue to interpret the situation in this way.

Sheer force of habit also makes at least a minimum of day-to-day co-operation between employers and workers seem the norm. So for workers to break out of their everyday routine and engage in some form of overt conflict, a specific incident or grievance must usually generate the necessary momentum.

Another cause of industrial peace has already been mentioned: the social values which attribute legitimacy to managerial control.

Collective action has traditionally been regarded as a violation of [managerial] rights because it challenges the prerogative of employers to control their own businesses. . . . Strikes take place within a hostile environment even though they are a common every-day phenomenon. They are conventionally described as industrially subversive, irresponsible, unfair, against the interests of the community, contrary to the workers' own best interests, wasteful of resources, crudely aggressive, inconsistent with democracy and, in any event, unnecessary. The morality which assesses strikes in these terms acts on employees so that they approach strike action with serious inhibitions (Allen, 1966: 27).

One reason for the prevalence of unorganized conflict in some industrial situations may be precisely that it is not defined as a challenge to managerial authority.

Finally, those processes of institutionalization discussed at the beginning of this chapter add important reinforcement to these other causes of industrial peace.

The limits of institutionalization

Modern industrial societies thus contain countervailing tendencies to those factors generating conflict. As was seen earlier, current academic orthodoxy in industrial relations is inclined to accept the theoretical argument that social conflict, if openly expressed and organized, is naturally self-correcting. Such an assumption, while rightly rejecting the naïve view of conflict as exclusively destructive, is itself one-sided; for not all conflicts are capable of containment and absorption by the social structures which give rise to them.

Those who predict the 'withering away of the strike' commit the fallacy of assuming that short-term trends will continue indefinitely.

As always in social affairs, however, development is by no means unilinear. . . . The fact that industrial conflict has become less violent and intense in the last century does not justify the inference that it will continue to do so. . . . It is certainly conceivable that the future has more intense and violent conflicts in store. To some extent there are already indications of such a development (Dahrendorf, 1959: 278–9).

Dahrendorf's arguments have been validated by subsequent events. He noted that the institutionalization of conflict through trade unionism led in turn to dissension within unions, and to unauthorized action in the form of unofficial strikes. 'It is hard', he added, 'to see how trade unions propose to check this development.' As was seen earlier, the scale of unauthorized conflict has increased, and official union efforts at its suppression have failed. The more sophisticated union response is to attempt to control such conflict by leading it – hence the revival of the official strike. But this response may itself, by giving legitimacy to the activities and aspirations of union rank and file, serve to encourage further conflict. Thus the present situation has been described as one of 'cumulative disorder'. The relatively full employment of the post-war era has given workers the power to challenge managerial control over a wide range of issues; the main inhibition on their use of this power has been their own limited aspirations and their doubts as to the legitimacy of militant action. Such constraints appear to be disintegrating, the actions and demands of one group of workers setting an example to others (Fox and Flanders, 1969).

Given the analysis presented earlier in this chapter, such a conclusion is in no way surprising. The conflicts and contradictions inherent in the capitalist system of industrial society, and in the worker's role within it, must be expected to find expression – often in unpredictable fashion. It could be suggested that the abandonment in Britain today of the traditional government policy of 'voluntarism' (that is, virtual legislative non-intervention in industrial relations), in favour of repressive legislation, is clear evidence of how precarious industrial stability is officially regarded. Yet few who are aware of the fundamental roots of industrial conflict will imagine that a policy of repression will restore stability. On the contrary, the growing size and bureaucratization of industrial organizations, the application of advanced technology with minimal regard to the needs and interests of employees, the increasing interference by governments in collective bargaining – all these developments seem likely to accentuate discontent. Unless and until the basic structure of industry and society is radically recast – with workers controlling the process of production, in the interests of human welfare, rather than being controlled by it, in the interests of profit – the institutionalization of industrial conflict will of necessity remain partial and precarious.

5. The Rationale of Industrial Conflict

Meanings and motives in human action

In Chapter 3 the structural analysis common to most studies of industrial relations was contrasted with interpretations of conflict which explore the meanings and motives of those directly involved. This duality of approaches is one which pervades sociology generally, and reflects an ambivalence which permeates social reality.

The subject matter of the human studies (sociology, economics, pyschology, history) is distinguished from that of the natural sciences primarily by the fact that human activity is purposive. Inanimate matter does not understand its own behaviour or that of the objects around it. But human beings possess goals, define situations, assign meanings to the actions of others, develop expectations, frame intentions, and act in accordance with their interpretations of the choices open to them. 'Actions are not just physical movements; they are informed by purposes, guided by thought and based on interpretations of reality. They, in their turn, reveal these purposes, thoughts and interpretations' (Rickman, 1967: 59).

The sociologist can therefore make sense of the social world only by taking account of the meanings which it holds for social actors and the motives which underlie their actions. This is not to say that the sociologist should be concerned only with their subjective viewpoint. Our actions do not always have the intended results, and often the unintended consequences of human activity are patterned by unrecognized structural determinants. Meanings and motives are themselves typically socially generated and sustained, in ways of which the actors themselves may be unaware. But a sociology which focuses – as much sociology has done – exclusively on the unrecognized determinants and unintended consequences of action is a one-sided and inadequate sociology. The proper concern of the

110

sociologist should be the complex interaction of subjective meanings and objective reality.

The nature of rationality

The purpose of this chapter is accordingly to examine strikes from the striker's viewpoint, as a form of rational social action. But two preliminary comments must be made.

First, exclusive attention to the striker's viewpoint does not imply acceptance of the naïve assumption that a strike is nothing but an aggressive act on the part of workers. 'A motivational analysis of industrial conflict is concerned with the behavior of all persons and groups significantly involved in the relationships between labor and management' (Kornhauser, 1954: 75). In common parlance, it takes at least two to start a fight. The act of striking is merely one point in a chain of events: it may be interpreted, for example, as a natural response to the obstinacy or provocation of the employer, which may in turn be explained by reference to a wider network of inter-relationships. It would be impossible to understand any specific dispute, then, without exploring the meanings which it holds for all types of participant. But for the purposes of this chapter, the workers' viewpoint *is* central: for it is they who must define the employer's action as obstinate or provocative, and must perceive a stoppage as an appropriate and efficacious response.

Second, to speak of strikes as a form of rational social action presupposes some understanding of the nature of rationality. On close examination, the concept is extremely difficult to define satisfactorily. One sociologist has suggested the following: 'action is rational in so far as it pursues ends possible within the conditions of the situation, and by the means which, among those available to the actor, are intrinsically best adapted to the end for reasons understandable and verifiable by positive empirical science' (Parsons, 1937: 58). Yet in everyday life, human action is simply not rational if so rigid a definition is applied. The standards of the real world are not the ideal standards of 'positive empirical science': assumptions regarding empirical reality are for the most part beliefs taken for granted; few actions are based on detailed consideration of the possibilities inherent in the situation; most means to ends are merely known to work tolerably well, like cookery-book recipes, rather than being carefully scrutinized as the best available (Schutz, 1964).

Thus if the concept of rationality is to be of any utility for the analysis of social action, the above formulation requires several qualifications. First, a rigid dichotomy between means and ends is unhelpful, for in real life ends and means (or terminal and instrumental values) interpenetrate. Most academic books, for example, are written with several aims: increasing knowledge, propagating a viewpoint, furthering the author's reputation, and earning some money. But such objectives cannot in practice be ordered into a tidy hierarchy; moreover, writing a book is usually also a source of intrinsic satisfaction – an 'end in itself'. A similarly complex interrelationship of means and ends is normal in work situations. A second qualification is that in the real world a complete knowledge of the facts of any situation is in principle impossible. And thirdly, for an actor to make a systematic appraisal of all alternative courses of action is likewise impossible. Accordingly, rationality in social action cannot be evaluated against any absolute standard. It is not a question of all or nothing but rather of more or less. Moreover, in assessing the rationality of an action (or perhaps more appropriately, a series of actions), there are numerous dimensions which need to be considered: one recent author has listed eleven (Cohen, 1968: 89–90). But simplifying considerably, it is possible to suggest three main points to be considered. First, how far does an action or series of actions represent a considered choice of alternatives, in the light of its significance for the actor's overall interests? (The latter clause is important: someone buying a house might be expected to study the market more carefully than one buying a box of matches.) Second, how accurate and complete (given the same qualification) is the actor's knowledge and understanding of the situation? Third, how far do means and ends form a coherent system?

In practice there will be difficulties in applying these criteria to actual conflict situations. In some cases, for example, people may offer a plausible explanation of their actions, yet an observer may be sceptical. Are the reasons given merely rationalizations? Are they perhaps unconscious of the real sources of their discontents, and displacing their sense of hostility on to some substitute object serving as a scapegoat? Or if the action makes sense in terms of their own stated objectives, might their interests be better served by different goals? Questions of this kind will in fact arise in the ensuing discussion. It must be stated here that on occasion an observer will be able to present convincing evidence that people fail to appreciate the real sources of their grievances, or are insufficiently aware of their own best interests, or are not fully conscious of their own motivations. Usually, as suggested above, this will involve a question of degree rather than of all or nothing. Often, however, actor and observer will merely be offering alternative interpretations of reality each of which possesses credibility; and different observers may come to different conclusions. For example, such differences of interpretation underlie the argument whether wage disputes 'really' are economic in motivation or reflect more fundamental deprivations.

Are strikes irrational?

Before considering further the rationale of industrial conflict there is a red herring to dispose of: the objection that it is pointless to analyse strikes as rational social action because they are in fact irrational. This common argument can take at least four forms: the denial of any conflict of interest in industry; the assertion that all conflicts of interest could best be resolved by peaceful means; the suggestion that the costs of a stoppage to the strikers themselves normally outweigh the gains; and the insistence that the spontaneous origins of most disputes demonstrate the absence of rational consideration.

Conflict of interests in industry

The suggestion that there is no conflict of interests within modern industry cannot be taken seriously. The previous chapter described in detail the sources of irreconcilable conflict within our society between employers and workers: the distribution of income; security of employment; power and control over decisions during work; and the subtle and pervasive conflicts generated by workers' obligation to treat as a commodity their ability to labour. Since the denial of any conflict of interests is so obviously false, the only interesting question which arises is why this opinion is so often expressed. This will be examined in the next chapter.

The possibilities of peaceful settlement

Slightly less naïve is the thesis which accepts the existence of a conflict of interests but insists that this conflict is resoluble by peaceful means alone. Since most claims and grievances are settled by negotiation, without recourse to overt sanctions, it is argued that all issues could be so disposed of were the parties to industrial relations sufficiently rational.

One variant of this doctrine proposes as the rational course that any questions not settled by negotiation between the two sides should be referred automatically for the decision of a third party. Whatever plausibility this idea may possess derives however from a misconception of the nature of industrial arbitration. For this is in practice less a judicial than a political process. The choice of arbitrator, and the principles to be applied, can be as potent a basis for dispute as the issues referred. There exists no 'neutral' body of industrial jurisprudence to guide the arbitrator: however high-flown the reasoning which accompanies the award, this can never deviate too far from an estimate of the likely outcome if the disputants had fought the matter out for themselves. Other things equal, it would be irrational for either party to agree to arbitration if past experience showed that a more favourable settlement could be expected from a strike or lock-out. It is interesting that an inter-war study found identical proportions of strikes and lock-outs on the one hand, and arbitration awards on the other, resulting in favour of the employers, in favour of the unions, and in compromise (Flanders, 1968: 95). A comparison of two recent national disputes referred to third-party settlement after lengthy strike action is also relevant: the local authority manual workers, who caused considerable disruption with their stoppage at the end of 1970, received a far larger award than the postal workers, whose strike in early 1971 was comparatively ineffectual. This is strong evidence that the power relationship of the parties – shaped ultimately by an assessment of the damage that each can inflict in open conflict – provides the background to any resort to arbitration.

To this argument it might be retorted that if the parties were rational, each could assess its own power and that of its adversary, could predict the probable outcome of a stoppage, and would therefore be willing to negotiate terms of this order without incurring the costs of a strike (Hicks, 1932: 144–6). Such a response involves a misapprehension both of the nature of power and of the nature of collective bargaining. Power is not quantifiable, nor is it even a visible attribute of a group or individual. The relative power of the parties to a dispute is a function of their control over resources and over the actions of others; but such control becomes manifest only when it is put to the test. 'Since power can often be appraised only in its actual exercise, accommodation may frequently be reached only after the contenders have measured their respective strength in conflict' (Coser, 1956: 135). There is a further point which Hicks recognized: 'weapons grow rusty, and a Union which never strikes may lose the ability to organize a formidable strike, so that its threats become less effective' (1932: 146). Bargaining strength depends to a large extent on the assessment each side makes that workers are prepared to back their discontent with action; but as was seen earlier, this willingness is itself affected by workers' previous strike involvement.

The indeterminacy of power is accentuated by the fact that within the collective bargaining process there always exists 'an ignorance which it may be to the interest of the parties to perpetuate' (Knowles, 1952: 251). If the union allows the employer to learn the minimum it is willing to accept, the employer will naturally refuse to offer more. Collective bargaining has often been likened to a poker game: an appropriate analogy, except that the complexities of the situation are far greater. It is an essential characteristic that each side strives to manipulate the other's assessment of the question at issue and its own determination (Walton and McKersie, 1965). It is not merely a question of the respective power of the two sides, but of the likelihood that the opponent will mobilize this power over the particular question at issue. If either side so misjudges the other's position that a strike occurs, this may represent a natural outcome of the structure of collective bargaining and need not reflect on the rationality of either party.

Finally, the overemphasis of the possibility of peaceful resolution of disputes often involves a simplistic view of the nature of industrial disputes. Commonly it is assumed that these always fit the model of wage negotiations, with the issues readily defined and quantified, and the eventual settlement precise and unambiguous. But conflicts which centre on the obligations which the employee undertakes in return for wages are quite different in character. As was seen in the previous chapter, these can never be wholly formalized in the employment contract. The limits of managerial control and worker obedience are therefore continuously defined and redefined in a shop-floor struggle which may at any time erupt into overt conflict. The suggestion that disputes can be eliminated by a 'co-operative' and 'problem-solving' approach is thus based on a totally inadequate conception of industrial reality.

The balance of costs and outcomes

Commentators are often bewildered by the fact that the costs incurred in a stoppage may seem out of all proportion to the point at issue. 'Editorial columns are studded with mathematical demonstrations that the workers would have been much better off if they had accepted the employer's final offer and stayed at work' (Ross, 1948: 47). If, say, 2 per cent separates the final positions of the two sides, it is argued that the wages lost in a fortnight's strike would take two years to recover even if the strikers' demands were won in full. That workers do strike in such situations is taken as sufficient evidence of irrationality.

One reply could be that long and costly strikes rarely occur when employers have full order books: as was seen earlier, such disputes typically occur in periods of economic recession. Hence wages lost in a stoppage might have been lost anyway.

It is in any case fallacious to assess the stakes in an industrial conflict solely in terms of the immediate issue in dispute. A military analogy is possible: as Marshall argued, there is

> no advantage in comparing the expense of any particular strike with the total direct gain to wages . . . because a strike is a mere incident in a campaign, and the policy of keeping up an army and entering a campaign has to be judged as a whole. The gain of any particular battle is not to be measured by the booty got in it (1899: 379).

If either side is to argue credibly that it has a sticking-point, then it must be prepared if need be to stick to it, even though the margin between this and peaceful settlement may be minimal. The repeated concession of a slender margin may represent, over time, the surrender of substantial ground. In political terms, the fact that one side proves its refusal to compromise beyond a specific point may exert a profound influence over subsequent negotiations. 'A sixty-day strike over 2 cents an hour may be irrational in the economic lexicon, but viewed as political behavior it may have all the logic of survival' (Ross, 1948: 74).

There is a somewhat different argument which may be mentioned in this context:

> the strike cannot be treated as the economist might like to treat it, as a rational phenomenon, in which each side nicely calculates the expected benefit of another day's strike and weighs this against an equally nicely calculated loss. It is, in part, a catharsis, a release of tensions, but it is also a drama, something which brings excitement and a sense of purpose into otherwise humdrum lives (Boulding, 1963: 217).

Leaving aside the rather patronizing nature of these remarks, two comments are called for. First of all, many modern strikes are singularly undramatic affairs; and even where strikes do generate excitement, this does not mean that they cannot also function as part of a calculative bargaining strategy. And secondly, economic rationality is not the only form of rationality. Economists tend to assume that nothing has a value unless it has a market price: an exceedingly narrow-minded conceit. If workers use a strike as a form of release from a work situation which they find uncongenial and oppressive, this is perfectly rational behaviour.

The problem of spontaneity

The interpretation of industrial conflict as catharsis or drama leads to a final version of the denial of the rationality of strikes: the argument that the very spontaneity which commonly characterizes their outbreak is evidence that they are emotional outbursts unrelated to any considered strategy.

It is true, as Knowles has noted, that strikes are rarely 'carefully planned and premeditated; still less often are they dictated by considerations of strategy. Most often they are more or less spontaneous outbursts against "injustice"' (1952: 6). But to act spontaneously is not necessarily to act irrationally. If an action is decided on 'the spur of the moment', this indicates deficient rationality only if haste causes faulty judgement: if the typical actor, after full consideration, would have decided otherwise. And indeed, some situations *demand* immediate action; deliberation is itself then scarcely rational.

Thus many strikes are probably spontaneous because the context makes this necessary: the Halewood workers felt they must respond at once to the dismissal of a shop-floor representative. And even where 'spontaneous' action involves less perishable issues, the strikers may have laboured under a sense of grievance for a considerable time, and also have been fully aware that a stoppage offered a possible solution to the problem. In the case of the 'downers' described by Clack, 'the issues involved were not frivolous; nor was the action the outcome of irrationality or hot temper' (1967: 61). A decision to strike, in such situations, may already hang in the balance, and need only a minor incident to become effective.

Degrees of rationality

This is not however to argue that all strikes are wholly rational; 'pure' rationality is as impossible in industrial conflict as in social life generally. As Coser has recognized, 'the distinction between realistic and nonrealistic conflict involves a conceptual abstraction from concrete reality in which . . . an admixture of both "pure" types will be found' (1956: 53). Strikes, like any other social action, can display greater or lesser degrees of rationality.

It is necessary to add, however, that human actors – and in particular such people as strikers – are often credited with less rationality than is justified. 'People cannot allow deviation to threaten their picture of what their society is about' (Cohen, 1971: 19). To admit the rationality of strikes is to accept that strikers have a case:

that genuine deprivations underlie industrial conflict. Those who deprecate industrial conflict – employers and, in some cases, sections of workers also – have a powerful incentive to deny that it is rational or meaningful. Such obscurantism must of course be transcended by those whose aim is to *understand* reality. The argument of a recent study of industrial sabotage is particularly apposite:

> We cannot as sociologists impute 'irrationality' or 'meaningless-ness' without detailed consideration of the context in which the act occurs, without obtaining evidence from the individual's workmates and friends, and finally without taking into account the reasons which have led him to offer an 'irrational' solution when he was pressed to state his intention. We will often not have to go through all these stages. In many cases the meanings which inform sabotage are explicitly intentional (Taylor and Walton, 1971: 225).

In the context of strikes, a parallel argument is certainly as valid.

The formulation of grievances

At the beginning of this chapter it was emphasized that it is normally presupposed by strike action that the strikers themselves 'define the employer's action as obstinate or provocative, and . . . perceive a stoppage as an appropriate and efficacious response'. In this section, the first of these processes will be considered: the worker's definition of a situation as one of conflict.

Gouldner's attempt to outline a 'general theory of group tensions' is a helpful introduction to this topic. He points out that 'men under stress verbalize their grievances', and refers to such verbalizations as 'symptomatic complaints': 'a symptomatic complaint constitutes a statement of frustrated expectation' (1955: 125). The complaints expressed by people in a conflict situation are therefore evidence of the expectations which have been violated, and the elements in the situation (including the actions of others) which have served to frustrate these expectations.

The reasons given for striking

Strikes offer particular opportunities for analysis in these terms, since the strike situation itself obliges those involved to specify their grievances; negotiations for a settlement are otherwise impossible. The reasons given for striking are in turn classified and published as part of official dispute statistics. While all such classifications are somewhat arbitrary and strike issues are often far more complex than the official categories can represent, the figures are nevertheless of considerable interest.

Until recently the Department of Employment listed nine 'causes of strikes': claims for wage increases; other wage disputes; hours of labour; demarcation disputes; employment and dismissal questions (including redundancy); other personnel questions; other working arrangements, rules and discipline; trade union status; and sympathetic action. Only four of these categories of strike issues figure at all prominently: the two classes of wage disputes, employment and dismissal questions, and 'other working arrangements'. The remaining five categories have together accounted for only 10 to 15 per cent of stoppages in recent years, and often less than 10 per cent of striker-days.

Knowles has grouped these categories under three headings: 'basic' causes (wages and hours), 'solidarity' (union status and sympathetic action), and 'frictional' causes (all the other categories). Analysing the trends between 1911 and 1947, he argued that 'strikes on basic questions have declined in relative importance, and strikes on frictional issues have correspondingly increased. . . . It is significant that wage-increase strikes in particular have shown a very marked decline' (1952: 235). McCarthy, continuing the analysis up to 1957, has added that 'it is clear . . . that this trend has continued' (1959: 24). An ambitious attempt to explain this trend is offered by Turner:

In twenty years of high employment from 1940 the proportion of strikes about 'wage-questions *other than* demands for increases', and (particularly) about 'working arrangements, rules and discipline' rose remarkably: from one-third of all stoppages to three-quarters. Now a close look at disputes so classified suggests that their increase mainly involves three types of demand. First, for what some have called an 'Effort Bargain' – that is, for the amount of work to be done for a given wage to be as explicitly negotiable as is the wage itself. Secondly, for changes in working arrangements, methods, and the use of labour to be also subject to agreement – or to agreed rules. And thirdly, they concern the treatment of individuals or groups by managers and supervisors. One *could* say that these disputes all involve attempts to submit managerial discretion and authority to agreed – or failing that, customary – rules: alternatively, that they reflect an implicit pressure for more democracy and individual rights in industry (1963: 18).

This analysis has been cited by Cliff as evidence that 'the urge for workers' control is becoming more stridently expressed in strikes' (1970: 201).

While there is much evidence of growing pressure of this kind, this is not the main explanation of post-war trends in strike issues. As was seen in Chapter 2, from the war until the early 1960s the mining industry provided the majority of recorded strikes; and its own pattern of strike issues dominated the statistics. The structure of national wage bargaining, together with the collaborative attitude of the Mineworkers' Union towards the Coal Board (in this period there were no official stoppages whatsoever) virtually excluded the possibility of strikes for straightforward wage increases. But the system at the coal-face of 'management through the wages system', with piece-rate bargaining over 'not only main tasks but sub-tasks and ancillary activities' was a central focus of conflict, while any work conditions or arrangements which adversely affected earnings could easily provoke a stoppage (Trist *et al.*, 1963: 64–5). Hence for many years, some 90 per cent of mining strikes fell into the categories 'other wage disputes' and 'other working arrangements'.

The pattern in other industries has always been quite different. Throughout the 1960s roughly half of all non-mining strikes involved wages, and a substantial majority of these were officially classed as claims for straightforward increases; only 30 per cent of these stoppages fell into the categories which dominated the mining statistics. In the last few years straightforward wage claims have become even more important, at the same time as the number of strikes in mining has fallen sharply. This is reflected in the 1970 statistics: wage disputes accounted for 62 per cent of all recorded stoppages; only 8 per cent of strikes were attributed to 'other wage disputes'; while 15 per cent concerned 'other working arrangements'.

The rationale of wage demands

It should be no cause for surprise that the grievances expressed by workers in strike situations centre primarily around wages. 'In a market economy, very many of the things that workers, and others, seek can be secured only through cash transactions' (Gouldner, 1955: 32). As one factory worker has put it, 'work, at factory level, has no inherent value. The worker's one interest is his pay-packet. The accent on money is understandable – after all, we are shorter of it than most' (Johnson, 1968: 12). Or as another sociologist has argued, more grandly,

> the primary goals of the worker relate to economic advancement and economic security for himself and his family. His taking a job is a means to this end. . . . In industrial conflict, to give paramount importance to satisfaction with wages is not necessarily an acceptance of simple economic determinism. In our society . . . we have reduced all forms of motivation to a pecuniary accounting. In a free market money has been known to buy anything from men's brains to women's virtue. Since income remains the all-important means for satisfying human wants and needs, wages will continue to be a major consideration in industrial conflict (Katz, 1954: 95).

As was argued in the previous chapter, there is no reason to assume that any given level of income should satisfy workers – particularly in a society where so much ingenuity is devoted to *stimulating* our desires for material acquisition and gratification, and where such acquisition is to a large extent culturally prescribed.

Wages are therefore desired for their own sake – or more accurately, in most cases, for the goods and services they can buy. But in addition, income often represents an index of status (Whyte, 1955). Within our culture, to inquire as to a person's worth is usually to invite an answer in cash terms. Conflict is thus inherent in any situation in which people's income fails to match their self-evaluation. As a study in the mining industry has indicated,

> a man's status as a strong and skilled worker, and as a man worth his pay, is conveyed by what shows on the pay-note. Any factor helping to cut down the amount of his wage is an attack on the whole status of the . . . worker. All this adds intensity to his attitude towards wages questions (Dennis *et al.*, 1957: 65).

This double significance of wages increases their contentious character. Workers may feel aggrieved if their income fails to keep pace with rising prices or their own aspirations for a higher standard of living. They may feel entitled to more money if productivity and profitability increase. But wages can also constitute a source of discontent when they compare their situation with that of other employees. If wages represent a badge of status, the principle of 'fair comparisons' is assumed to require equivalent remuneration for workers in analogous occupations; where the pay of any group appears out of line, the situation will be perceived as 'unfair'. And in deciding what level of wage increase is 'fair' and thus acceptable, workers' expectations will be shaped – if only because of the paucity of other criteria – by their knowledge of what has been agreed elsewhere.

It follows that the wage *structure* – the interrelationship of pay levels of different grades of employees – can constitute an elaborate and precarious system, with changes in the pay of one group creating a sense of grievance among others. The car industry study by Turner and his associates revealed that 'very many of the strikes officially classified as due to demands for wage-increases in fact spring from differences in rates or earnings between related jobs in the same plant or firm' (1967: 63). Often, conflict may arise because the standards which workers apply when comparing their earnings with other groups have become more ambitious. Ford workers have demanded 'parity' with the higher-paid car workers of the Midlands. Women have demanded, and have won some legislative support for, equal pay with men for equal work (though this will be little help to them if they remain excluded from most higher-paid occupations). Such groups as dustmen decide that their value to the community has previously been under-rewarded. Men and women with such aspirations will feel aggrieved unless and until they succeed in improving their relative position; but this will necessarily involve a deterioration in the relative position of someone else. Thus an attempt to reduce differentials in favour of the lower-paid may well be interpreted by those with higher earnings as an assault on their established rights. Recent public discussion of the principles which might form the basis of a 'just' structure of incomes is likely to persuade some groups that their pay is too low; but few are likely to accept that their wages are too high. This could well result in an increasing number of mutually incompatible expectations and aspirations, and hence more workers dissatisfied with their relative earnings. Government intervention to enforce any specific pattern of pay settlements may serve to compound their sense of grievance.

Manifest and latent issues

Even where the overt focus of a dispute is something other than wages, it may be possible to argue that an economic grievance underlies it.

> In discussion with officials of the National Coal Board an attempt was made to discover the attitude of the administration to the large number of disputes in the Yorkshire coalfield. One principle dominated the replies: *'Every strike is a wages strike'*. Men may go on strike because of bad roof conditions, because of water, because of difficulties caused by mechanical breakdowns; but in all these cases it is the effect on the pay-note that is really at stake (Dennis *et al.*, 1957: 64).

Identical attitudes are reported in another mining study: 'when wage demands are presented, management rarely suspects that the source of trouble may lie elsewhere; but when other demands are made, management is often convinced that wage demands really lie at the root of the matter' (Wellisz, 1953: 350–1). Similar assumptions are held by managers in most other industries. No doubt certain expressed grievances, ostensibly concerning some other aspect of work conditions, are more or less ingeniously disguised wage claims. But it would require an extreme cynicism – as well as an extreme commitment to the model of 'economic man' – to argue that no disputes over non-wage questions are to be taken at their face value.

If all stoppages are sometimes seen as at root economic, the precisely opposite interpretation is itself not uncommon.

> In fact, the majority of wage claims are revolts against . . . oppression – revolts against the systematic mutilation of the worker's personality, against the stunting of his professional and human faculties, against the subordination of the nature and content of his working life to technological developments which rob him of his powers of initiative, control and even foresight. Wage claims are much more frequently motivated by *rebellion against working conditions* than by a revolt against the economic *burden of exploitation* borne by labour. They express a demand for *as much money as possible to pay for the life wasted, the time lost, the freedom alienated* in working under these conditions (Gorz, 1965: 319).

From very different theoretical assumptions, the human relations school (or at least its early exponents) also argued that wage disputes reflected not simply economic deprivations but also workers' frustrated desires for social satisfactions at work. Some social psychologists have presented a similar analysis:

> It is precisely because he is not permitted truly to actualize his potential that [the worker] makes a decision to 'simplify' his personality, making money and other material factors most important. It is as if the employee says to himself, 'I want to be a healthy creative human being; I cannot be and still produce what I am required to produce. Therefore, I will say "To hell with my total personality", and place the major emphasis on money' (Argyris, 1967: 215).

Attempts to interpret strike issues in any of the above fashions reflect a belief that the observer must make a distinction between manifest and latent conflict in industrial relations, for the motives that are channelled into industrial strife and the values that are being disputed, are not to be estimated in terms of their outward manifestations alone. It is widely acknowledged that the precipitating causes of strikes may be quite different from their underlying causes. . . . General social conditions are inevitably reflected in the behaviour of employers and employed towards each other (Lockwood, 1955: 337–8).

Such an approach is often criticized. As McCarthy has put it, 'one assigns causes to strikes according to one's personal bias or predilections. A Marxist will draw up one list, and an industrial psychologist another' (1959: 17). 'Some people', adds Turner, 'think that the stated grievances of strikers are merely phenomenal or accidental, and that conflict is inherent in our socio-economic arrangements, or in common psychological postures or cultural situations, or in deficiencies of managements' sociological and "communicative" technique' (1963: 8).

To dismiss the reasons which strikers themselves give for their actions is obviously to refuse to treat their behaviour as rational – or else to accuse them of deception. Yet it is possible to go beyond their own reasons – to distinguish manifest from latent issues – without questioning either their rationality or their sincerity. *What is involved here is a difference in levels of explanation and analysis.* That workers formulate specific grievances in the course of a dispute is a crucial fact about the situation; to attempt to account for their action without reference to their own expressed demands would be absurd. Yet the sociologist must also investigate further than the strikers' own formulation of the issues. In Gouldner's terms, analysis 'requires study both of the expectations which have been frustrated, and the conditions frustrating them' (1955: 127). Strikers are rarely trained sociologists, and may not have examined deeply the social sources of their own expectations or of the conditions frustrating these. The sociologist *is* interested in such questions, and may well need to refer to features 'inherent in our socio-economic arrangements' in a search for an explanation. In addition, we may have to consider various aspects of the 'structure' of particular work situations (its technology, for example) in search of factors likely to prove particularly frustrating to the typical worker's expectations. At all times, however, the most sensitive sociological perspective is one which succeeds in synthesizing the different levels of analysis by illuminating the processes which lead from the latent or underlying sources of conflict, via the workers' expectations and perceptions, to the immediate or manifest issues of dispute.

Non-economic sources of wage demands

A classic example of this perspective is provided by Gouldner's *Wildcat Strike*. At the factory studied, managerial control which had traditionally displayed considerable leniency gave way rapidly to far stricter supervision; shortly afterwards an unofficial strike (the first stoppage in the plant's history) took place in pursuit of a wage claim. Gouldner's argument is that the first development constituted the underlying cause of the second.

Gouldner's reasoning may be summarized as follows. Stricter supervision violated workers' expectations regarding the behaviour of management. However, the expectation that management should act leniently was 'of tenuous legitimacy in an *industrial* situation' – it was difficult to deny that management had the formal right to exercise rigid supervision if the company thought this appropriate. The men's grievance could not therefore be raised as such through the formal negotiating procedure, and so remained unresolved and 'latent'. The subsequent wage negotiations between union and management served to reactivate these latent hostilities. In this case the workers perceived no obstacle to the aggressive pursuit of their claim: 'a wage demand is always legitimate'. The workers' attitudes were for the most part ambivalent: in part their hostility over the supervision grievance was displaced on to the wage issue, which was seen as a way of hitting back at the company where it would hurt most; but also, higher wages were viewed as compensation for the deprivations suffered as a result of management's stricter policy.

Other authors have reached similar conclusions. In the strike described by Warner and Low, 'most of the formal demands of the strikers concerned wages and the recognition of the union, but interviews with workers during and before the strike clearly showed that many of the basic grounds for dissension had little to do with the amount of wages received' (1947: 131). In a situation of discontent, wages can take on an important symbolic character. Thus Kornhauser has argued that

> a stated goal of higher wages may veil unverbalized strivings for self-respect and dignity or vague hostilities toward the boss, the machine, and the entire industrial discipline. The unstated motivations may be inferred at times from the fact that the discontent continues after the wage increase is granted (1954: 64–5).

One reason why certain strivings are unverbalized and certain motivations unstated may be that these are unsuited to the language and the structure of collective bargaining. 'Demands framed in terms of hours and wages conveniently define what is at stake. Precise, quantitative demands give a concreteness and urgency to the opposition of groups that vaguely felt, but unfocussed, dissatisfactions about the quality of life would never do' (Lockwood, 1955: 338). A wage claim is readily comprehensible to negotiators on both sides, and usually offers an ample 'bargaining range' within which compromise is possible. In addition, 'wage demands provide an excellent rallying cry, and they are accepted by management as falling within the permissible range of labour aspirations' (Wellisz, 1953: 350). Non-wage issues are often far less precisely formulable and may involve questions of principle on which compromise is difficult if not impossible. Not surprisingly, research suggests that of all issues arising in shop-floor industrial relations, wage disputes are disproportionately liable to be referred for negotiations involving full-time union officials. The structure of the bargaining institutions themselves appears to encourage this bias (Hyman, 1972).

Gouldner's emphasis on legitimacy relates closely to this point. Since managerial control is legitimized in our culture, it is not surprising that acceptance of a wide area of managerial prerogative is one of the foundations of collective bargaining. Workers, too, cannot formulate explicitly those grievances which stem from the exercise of managerial control without questioning their very subjection to this control. The basic necessity that every strike must be settled means, moreover, that workers are obliged to specify their grievances in a form which permits resolution *in negotiation with employers*. Where workers' deprivations derive from their very status as employees, the requirements of the strike situation prevent this grievance from receiving articulation. Collective bargaining is the art of the possible – within a narrowly defined framework of possibility. Hence it can be argued that

> workers insist on being paid as much as possible not because they put wages (money and what it can buy) above everything else but because, Trade Union action being what it is at present, workers can fight the employer only for the price of their labour, not for control of the conditions and content of their work (Gorz, 1965: 319; emphasis omitted).

In consequence, as Lane and Roberts argue, during unofficial strikes 'it is not unusual for the demands to be formulated *after* the strike has started. It often appears that the only way that strikers can make themselves understood is by putting a price on their return to work even though the original reason for coming out may have possessed only the most tenuous relationship to money' (1971:17).

The argument that grievances of a non-economic nature typically underlie wage demands is not one which can be definitely proved or disproved. It reflects a belief that workers' deprivations are never experienced as exclusively economic; and this in turn presupposes that there are certain aspirations and motivations so essentially human that no worker can permanently forgo all satisfaction in the job and control over the work process, however high the earnings, without some conflict being generated. Such assumptions provide not so much a description of work and society as a framework for interpretation. They cannot therefore be simply true or false, though they can accord more or less comfortably with the reality of the situation. It is relevant that sociological investigators of strike situations are unanimous in discerning non-economic motivations as influential. It is also relevant that those who adopt this approach are able to explain convincingly why so many strikes do have wage demands as their immediate focus: this is only to be expected because wage demands, unlike aspirations for workers' control, are culturally defined as legitimate.

Multiple motivation of strikes

An assumption that the causes of a specific dispute must be *either* economic *or* non-economic is in any case a false dichotomy. The grievances expressed by strikers themselves are rarely simple. As Knowles has argued, 'few strikes have a single immediate cause, and it is therefore difficult to be certain of the main question at issue. . . . Many strikes take place on a multiplicity of immediate issues, the relative importance of which may change during the strike itself' (1952: 228).

Knowles himself suggests that latent hostilities generated by the worker's situation may be 'rationalized – in the form of a particular grievance – as the immediate cause of the strike' (p. 214). To speak of rationalization is however an unwarranted devaluation of workers' own account of their grievances. In most industrial situations, conflict in some form is never far from the surface. 'The industrial worker, for the most part, works harder than he likes at tasks which are frequently arduous, usually monotonous, and sometimes dangerous. On the job he is nearly always subject to the direction of higher authority. His income is seldom sufficient to cover what he thinks his needs demand. The natural state of the industrial worker, therefore, is one of discontent' (Harbison, 1954: 278). If the consciousness of deprivation is continuous, little additional sense of grievance or provocation may be needed to trigger off a militant response. As was discovered by a government investigation during the First World War, 'often the immediate cause of an outbreak merely marks the culminating point of a series of troubles, most of which in themselves are of trifling importance, but the cumulative effect of which in view of the unfriendly relations between both parties, constitutes a serious menace to industrial peace' (Commission of Inquiry into Industrial Unrest, 1917, cited in Knowles, 1952: 229). Which grievance the strikers in such a context choose to present as the reason for their action may be to some extent arbitrary – and may well be determined, as suggested above, by a sense of the type of demand appropriate for collective negotiation between union and employer. Or an attempt may be made to present the issue in a manner which the 'general public' can understand; and a wage claim is readily comprehensible.

But it must be emphasized that the demand put forward can *both* constitute a genuine aspiration of the strikers, *and* fail to represent the sum total of their grievances. And in such a context, it is predictable that different strikers will give different reasons for their actions; in particular, strikers who feel a strong need to justify their action (both to themselves and to others) may well articulate a whole catalogue of their discontents. Complex grievances reflect complex situations: thus the Halewood dispute which opened this book was provoked by the dismissal of a steward; but the strikers saw the issue as closely linked with a perceived attack on conditions of work and shop-floor union organization. The strike thus qualifies for inclusion under three of the official categories of 'causes of stoppages', even without examination of possible 'underlying causes'.

Another form of complexity which is widespread in situations of industrial conflict derives from what has been termed the 'effort bargain'. While the employment contract of necessity leaves open the precise obligations on the employee, most workers seem to have a rough conception of the degree of effort which represents a 'fair' exchange for their wages. Changes in technology, and the employer's pursuit of profits, persistently threaten to disrupt this effort bargain by intensifying the demands upon the worker (Behrend, 1957; Baldamus, 1961). The form which the effort bargain takes is determined by the pay system within each workplace: those paid by results will negotiate job times or piece rates; those paid by time rates will argue over the workload (Turner *et al.*, 1967: 64). Conflict involving an effort bargain may be resolved *either* by reducing the workload, *or* by increasing wages, *or* by a combination of the two. Those who consider workers to be 'instrumentally oriented' might interpret a strike in such circumstances as a calculative pursuit of pecuniary reward; those who take a contrary view might see it as a protest against the deprivations engendered by an increased pressure of work. Most such disputes in fact involve elements of both motivations; an instrumental orientation in workers is basically a question of degree.

This same point may be extended in considering the trend of strikes within contemporary 'affluent society'. There is no need to treat the various possible explanations of strike causes as exclusive alternatives. The growing readiness of workers to perceive and express grievances may be seen as a reflection *both* of a natural heightening of economic aspirations, *and* of the tentative articulation of discontent at oppressive managerial control and dehumanizing conditions of work in a situation where the absolute burden of economic exploitation need no longer constitute an overwhelming preoccupation.

Responses to grievances

Strikes are 'both a reaction against frustrating situations and an instrument of positive action' (Wellisz, 1953: 365). Having considered the ways in which workers perceive their situation as one of frustrated expectations, it is now necessary to examine how the strike is chosen as an appropriate response.

The meanings of strike action

As was argued in an earlier chapter, the meanings which a stoppage holds for workers will vary according to the cultural context and their previous experience of strike action. Workers with a similar sense of grievance may therefore evaluate the appropriateness of a strike in quite different fashions.

This variety of meaning is particularly evident in respect of attitudes to the legitimacy of strike action. As Allen argued in a passage quoted earlier, workers tend to be affected by social values which deprecate industrial disputes, and therefore 'approach strike action with serious inhibitions'. Press reaction often plays on these sentiments to considerable effect – as with the power workers' work-to-rule at the end of 1970. Many factors will however affect the degree to which such inhibitions are felt. The values of a particular occupational sub-culture may generate sufficient consciousness of class conflict and the need for worker solidarity for the dominant social values to be wholly neutralized. This insight forms part of the theory of Kerr and Siegel, discussed earlier, that occupations which form part of a tight-knit community isolated from society at large will show the greatest propensity to strike.

At the other extreme are occupations particularly strongly committed to the dominant social values, such as professional and many other types of white-collar employees. Traditionally these have often regarded a stoppage as 'unprofessional' and hence illegitimate whatever the provocation. In part this may reflect social origins: members of the higher white-collar occupations tend to come from that minority section of society which is usually identified with 'public opinion' and hence is particularly strongly attached to the ruling values of society. In addition, as Turner has noted, most professions have been able to exert powerful control over the employment conditions of their members without needing to resort to anything as vulgar as a strike. Conversely, the reluctance to strike in many less exalted white-collar occupations is often associated with the general weakness of trade union values – and may well have similar causes: for example, workers' identification with the values of higher managerial strata into which they aspire to achieve promotion.

It should be noted, however, that such inhibitions appear to be weakening. As Allen has put it, strike action 'is a spreading phenomenon which is overcoming all manner of social barriers' (1966: 112). One explanation might point to changes in the employment situation of previously non-striking groups: a factor also associated with extensions of trade unionism (Lockwood, 1958; Bain, 1970). A related hypothesis might be that employers have traditionally been sufficiently considerate (or sufficiently perceptive of their own long-term interests) to ensure that white-collar employees did not lose out through their high-minded abstention from collective action; but that in a period of rapid price inflation combined with competitive pressure on employers, such employees perceive themselves as falling behind in the 'free-for-all' and feel obliged to abandon their former self-denying ordinance. It is not unduly cynical to suggest that if workers' consciousness of grievance is sufficiently strong, and if a strike appears to offer the only remedy, scruples as to the legitimacy of such action cannot persist indefinitely. Recent strikes by such groups as airline pilots, bank employees and schoolteachers would appear to support this contention.

Workers' attitudes to the legitimacy of strike action may also be affected by the nature of the dispute. A recent survey of workers' attitudes to unconstitutional stoppages found that only one in four thought these justified in *any* situation; but nearly three in four thought them legitimate if management had broken an agreement, was resorting to unreasonable delays in dealing with grievances, or had dismissed a workmate unfairly (Government Social Survey, 1968: 143). This helps, incidentally, to explain some of the findings of 'opinion polls', which are considered in more detail in the next chapter. A recent NOP survey asked respondents: 'Some people say laws are needed to control the power of big unions so they cannot shut down an entire basic industry like steel or cars. Do you think such laws are needed or not?' Confronted by so loaded a question, presenting strikes simply as economically disruptive events caused by big and powerful unions, it is not surprising that a majority even of trade union members voiced approval for anti-strike legislation. But when such trade unionists consider strikes, not in the abstract but with an appreciation of the grievances which lead men and women to stop work, their attitudes may be very different.

Perceptions of strike efficacy

For workers to respond to a grievance by strike action it is necessary not only that they should overcome any doubts as to the legitimacy of a stoppage, but also that they should perceive this as an effective solution to their predicament. At this point of analysis, the 'action approach' and the search for 'structural determinants' clearly overlap considerably: for many of those situational factors which are associated with a high strike propensity in fact increase the prospects of successful action – and are so perceived by workers themselves.

Such factors may be said to have a conditioning effect on workers' readiness to strike.

The fundamental causes of labor disputes can be divided into two classes: (1) permissive conditions, or the absence of obstacles to the ability to strike, and (2) sources of active unrest among the workers. Among the first the presence of labor organization is a strong encouragement to use the strike as a weapon; otherwise conflict is more likely to appear in individual or spontaneous group form. Furthermore, an organization in an isolated setting has even more striking power than one subjected to cross-pressures in a pluralistic community. In addition, the financial strength of workers' organizations is a major permissive factor; strikes occur with much greater frequency during periods of prosperity. Finally, strikes are more frequent when the government allows this type of expression, and less frequent when the government represses them (Smelser, 1963: 52).

The findings of such researchers as Kuhn and Sayles are relevant here: groups with a key position in the production process may be readier than others to threaten strike action since they know that this will achieve an immediate impact. (Paradoxically, they may not actually strike particularly often, if managements are sufficiently impressed by the threat alone; British printing workers – or, applying the concept of strike action somewhat more loosely, British doctors – are a case in point.) Conversely, workers in some other occupations and industries may refrain from striking from an accurate appreciation of their own lack of strategic strength.

Less concrete elements in a situation may also affect workers' assessment of the prospects of a successful stoppage. Past experience is an obvious guide: previous success may increase the readiness to strike – particularly if this is taken as evidence that a stoppage is 'the only language this company understands'. In this respect, the human relations school provided a valid insight: management's response when workers express grievances in the absence of strike action will shape the latter's assessment of the need for militancy. Past defeats, on the other hand, may discourage future stoppages (though this effect may be outweighed by a heightened sense of grievance).

Consciousness of the efficacy of strike action can also be affected by the experience of other groups of workers. Such a 'demonstration effect' may be particularly apparent in periods of rapid increase in strike incidence. In the period of 'labour unrest' before the outbreak of the First World War, for example, many stoppages occurred among groups of lower-skilled workers lacking any previous tradition of collective action or organization. 'Simply because the breakthrough *had* been achieved among sections who had previously appeared equally hopeless, such workers now saw no reason why they too should not be successful (nor often did their employers)' (Hyman, 1971a: 194–5). A very similar explanation has been suggested for the British 'strike explosion' of recent years.

The rationale of 'irrational outbursts'

In a previous section attention was given to the argument that the very spontaneity of most strikes is evidence of irrationality. It was argued that in some cases the situation may demand immediate action; while in others the strikers may be pressing a long-standing grievance, their exasperation having accumulated to the point of eruption. Yet it is scarcely deniable that some stoppages occur after minimal attempts to remedy the grievance in question; the timing of the strike may be singularly inopportune from any strategical viewpoint; the strikers may appear unable to state clearly the reasons for their action. Are such disputes demonstrably irrational?

One answer is to view such a stoppage as intermediate between mass absenteeism and more orthodox strike action. And this indicates a significant complexity in the nature of the strike itself. Strikes normally serve three separate functions: they are a means of withdrawal from the work situation; a display of aggression; and a calculative attempt to obtain alterations in the work situation or the employment relationship. On occasion, particularly where stoppages are regarded as routine, they may be purely calculative acts with minimal emotional overtones. But in other situations, the calculative component may be minimal; demands may be formulated during the course of the strike simply because, conventionally, strikes have to focus around some demand: they can only be settled if there is something to negotiate about.

It is important, where strikes appear to lack substantial calculative content, that they should be evaluated on their own terms. To stop work is a significant act, whether or not a specific demand is attached to the stoppage: and when work is uncongenial (as it is, to greater or lesser degree, for virtually all industrial workers) this is in itself surely an eminently rational thing to do. In the early nineteenth century, the term 'holiday' was often used to denote a strike; later the term 'playing' was common. Hence the withdrawal from work inherent in a strike was once explicitly valued for its own sake. In the same way, the opportunity to release the tensions accumulated in an oppressive work situation gives many apparently irrational walk-outs a convincing rationale.

Levels of rationality

So far this chapter has been concerned to argue that strikes in general can properly be interpreted as a form of rational social action. This is not to deny that the degree of rationality displayed in specific disputes can vary. In terms of the definition proposed at the beginning of the chapter, engaging in a stoppage at a particular point of time may be singularly ill-considered, in that the prospects of success are negligible; or a specific demand or grievance may be based on misinformation; or strikers' purposes may be confused and contradictory. It is appropriate for the sociologist to explore these dimensions of the rationality of particular disputes, and to attempt to explain any shortcomings in strikers' information or strategical wisdom or clarity of purpose. (The investigator should beware, however, of basing this assessment on a misunderstanding of the strikers' own motives and intentions.)

If degrees of rationality can vary, so too can *levels* of rationality. While a person's information concerning his situation can be more or less accurate, it can also be more or less profound. The assessment of the probable consequences of an action can show better or worse judgement; the range of alternative actions considered can be wide or narrow. A strategy may be better or worse suited to achieving the redress of a particular grievance; it may also be more or less oriented to eradicating the source of the grievance. Thus a man may act rationally in killing flies which invade his kitchen; but if they breed in a dung-heap outside his back door, it may show a higher level of rationality to remove the dung-heap. A similar appraisal may be made of different forms of industrial conflict.

The definition of the situation

In evaluating workers' formulation of grievances, it is possible to examine how penetrating is their analysis of the situation which frustrates their expectations. At one level, workers may object to the speeding-up of their jobs. At another level, managers may argue that their company will go bankrupt if productivity is not increased: they may accept that workers' expectations are indeed frustrated, yet insist that these expectations are in the situation not realizable and hence not rational. This was the situation in the plant described by Gouldner: management felt obliged to tighten discipline because of acute market pressures and in order to achieve maximum output from expensive new machinery; the firm could not survive while maintaining traditional managerial leniency. At yet another level, however, it might be argued that an economic system in which competitive pressures compel an intolerable deterioration in work conditions is itself a remediable source of deprivation. It may be suggested that to the extent that workers striking against speed-up have pursued these different levels of analysis of their situation, so their action is based on a higher or lower level of rationality.

This example should indicate that an appraisal of levels of rationality in strike situations may vary with the viewpoint of the observer. Those who hold, for example, that wage increases are the main cause of price inflation will argue that demands for higher pay are self-defeating: while strikes may succeed in raising money the increases will be eroded by higher prices. Others might reply that there is no law preventing increases in wages at the expense of profits; if employers choose to respond to wage increases by raising prices, they might well have done so anyway. (And as was shown in the previous chapter, there is some evidence that the recent British 'wage explosion' has caused a slight increase in the share of the national income obtained by wage- and salary-earners.)

Analysis in terms of levels of rationality is particularly relevant in the case of conflicts between different groups of workers. Demarcation disputes (which, incidentally, have caused only 2 per cent of stoppages in recent years), over such issues as who should fit a particular nut to a bolt, are frequently attacked for their triviality. This criticism misses the point. Given the insecurity of employment with which ordinary workers are faced, it is perfectly natural for them to attempt to establish some form of property rights in their job by drawing a demarcation line around it. To the outsider such a line may seem arbitrary, and conflict over minor infringements absurd; but the workers can reasonably respond that their 'right to the job' will be soon eroded if they do not resist all encroachments, however trivial in themselves. At a different level, however, it could be suggested that attempts to gain job security by erecting barriers to competition from other workers are unlikely to prove successful in the long run. They can be expected to provoke resentment among workers who are excluded, and the employer may exploit any such divisions. It might show a higher level of rationality were workers to devote their collective energies to resistance to the employment status which condemns them to permanent insecurity.

In the context of wage disputes, similarly, the determination of workers to defend 'traditional differentials' is understandable; particularly since, as has been seen, pay is widely treated as a badge of status. Yet relative superiority within the ranks of employees might be regarded as a poor alternative to a dignified status for all workers. More prosaically, if workers' economic aspirations are shaped by an exclusive concern with relativities, then the share of production accruing to profits remains unchallenged; workers ignore the fact that their earnings fall considerably short of the value of their labour.

A more radical assessment of the level of rationality involved in orthodox wage bargaining has been made by Gorz.

> Pure wage claims deflect and conceal much deeper claims – worse than that, they are a dead-end which the workers' movement has reached. For wage disputes by themselves tend to serve the employer's own wishes: to be left with the power to organize the productive process at will, the power to regulate, qualitatively and quantitatively, the content and relations of labour; in compensation for which – and for the additional mutilations they can now impose – the employers are ready to grant wage increases. Wage claims as such accept the fundamental criterion of a profit-motivated economy, that you can do anything and everything with human beings as long as you pay (1965: 319–20; emphasis omitted).

From this perspective, to fight for higher wages while accepting the commodity status of labour is like killing bluebottles while ignoring the dung-heap outside the kitchen door.

The selection of responses

In similar fashion, the observer's own definition of industrial reality will colour any assessment of the levels of rationality displayed in workers' responses to their grievances.

Several writers have attempted to classify reactions to situations which conflict with individuals' aspirations or expectations. One of the best-known typologies is Merton's definition of four 'deviant modes of adaptation': 'innovation' (breaking the rules when one's aspirations cannot be satisfied legitimately); 'ritualism' (following the rules and lowering one's aspirations to match the outcome); 'retreatism' (dropping out of conventional social life altogether); and 'rebellion' (aspiring and attempting to change those aspects of social structure which cause the frustration of one's expectations) (1968: 193–211). While Merton is concerned with responses to frustrated aspirations at the level of society generally, his analysis is readily applicable to the work situation (Fox, 1971: 82–100).

A different set of categories is put forward by Taylor and Walton in their study of industrial sabotage. They suggest that three types of motives may underlie attempts to destroy or mutilate objects in the work environment: '(i) to reduce tension or frustration, or (ii) to facilitate the work process, or (iii) to assert some form of direct control' (1971: 226). The first type of action is spontaneous, the choice of the object of sabotage is fairly arbitrary, and there is no aim to make work easier, alter power relationships, or present a direct challenge to authority. The second type is planned and is directed against a specific target, is designed to make the job easier and may accordingly challenge some aspects of managerial control, but is not designed to restructure power relationships. The third type presents the most explicit challenge to managerial authority, and does aim to restructure power relationships (pp. 227–35).

It is reasonable to interpret all three types of sabotage as rational social action, in that even the first type brings some relief to an oppressive situation – even if only fleetingly. However, it could be argued that an action designed to achieve continuing relief within physically or emotionally debilitating work displays a higher level of rationality than an act which brings only a temporary respite. By the same token, an attempt to tackle the root cause of dehumanizing conditions of work may be said to be of a higher order still.

This argument may be generalized to all types of worker response to industrial deprivations. Purely individual forms of conflict activity would normally appear to reflect a relatively low level of rationality; for the typical worker can marshal sufficient power to effect a significant alteration in the work situation only by acting collectively. Thus such unorganized conflict as absenteeism or turnover brings only temporary withdrawal from an uncongenial job, or else transference to another usually only marginally preferable; while the ability of employees individually to breach or evade managerial rules is in most contexts rigidly circumscribed.

Some forms of collective action also provide little more than a limited distraction from the oppressiveness of the job itself. 'Fooling around' is a universal form of relief in industrial situations, which can easily shade into the first variant of sabotage described above. Its limited objectives are clear from this description by Roy: 'patterns of fun and fooling had developed within a matrix of frustration. Tensions born of long hours of relatively meaningless work were released in the mock aggressions of horseplay' (1960: 167). It would be foolish to deny the value of such adaptations in assisting people to retain their sanity in the face of appalling drudgery; but they are *only* adaptations, unrelated to any strategy to alter the situation.

Most forms of organized conflict are however evidence of a higher level of rationality, insofar as they represent an explicit attempt to exert control over the employment relationship itself. Yet often, as suggested above, such disputes may be the mutually frustrating efforts of specific worker groups to gain a relative advantage over others. Even where this is not the case, industrial action is conventionally directed at securing improvements within the confines of the existing employment relationship; and as was argued in the previous section, the structure of collective bargaining itself tends to channel workers' grievances into relatively innocuous forms.

So it is possible to imagine a higher level of rationality: in the categories of Taylor and Walton, the attempt to assert control; or in Merton's terms, rebellion. Touraine has suggested a distinction which seems particularly applicable to these two levels of orientation in strikes: on the one hand 'solidarity – upholding the interests of a group or a category in an organizational system'; and on the other 'labour action – oriented directly towards the development of creativity in work and of control by workers over their working conditions' (1965: 22). The selection of this second level of response presupposes a similarly high level of rationality in the definition of the situation: an attempt to restructure power relationships is to be expected only if these relationships are perceived as the underlying cause of workers' deprivations.

In what ways can workers come to relate the basic structural realities of industry in our society to the deprivations which they themselves endure? Some writers consider that involvement in industrial conflict can itself generate a heightened consciousness. Eldridge suggests that

> unofficial strikes . . . may be seen as a particular expression of dissatisfaction with the existing rules of the industrial game. . . . The work group becomes more than usually aware of the essentially coercive nature of the rules and rebels from a sense of oppressiveness. The unofficial strike then becomes a gesture of defiance against their industrial lot (1968: 90).

Others have argued that as the structure of control in the wider society is seen to set narrow limits to what can be achieved by strike action at the level of the individual firm or industry, so the focus of industrial conflict may be raised. This view was put forward by Lenin in 1899, in one of his earliest articles on strikes.

> A strike teaches workers to understand what the strength of the employers and what the strength of the workers consists in; it teaches them not to think of their own employer alone and not of their own immediate workmates alone but of all the employers, the whole class of capitalists and the whole class of workers. . . . A strike, moreover, opens the eyes of the workers to the nature, not only of the capitalists, but of the government and the laws as well (quoted in Hyman, 1971b: 41).

Such an analysis is open to question. It is true that revolutionary situations have often been accompanied by widespread strikes, but there is little evidence that strikes themselves have initiated the process. Anderson's argument is relevant here:

> The trade union's . . . maximum weapon against the system is a simple *absence* – the strike, which is a *withdrawal* of labour. The efficacy of this form of action is by nature very limited. It can win wage increases, some improvements in working conditions, in rare cases some constitutional rights. But it can never overthrow a social regime. As a political weapon, strikes are nearly always profoundly ineffectual. . . . The strike is fundamentally an economic weapon, which easily boomerangs if used on terrain for which it is not designed (1967: 265–6).

For strikes to function as an explicit challenge to the structure of control within industry and society, they would have to cease functioning as instruments of collective bargaining. If workers should become increasingly conscious of the deprivation engendered by their status as wage-earners within a capitalist society – and it would be a rash prophet who would argue just how workers' consciousness may or may not develop – then conceivably the trend of strikes could be in this direction. But such a development would meet the resistance, not only of the dominant social values and of those in positions of social dominance, but also of the institutions of collective bargaining – on both sides of industry.

It is therefore difficult to imagine that strikes could ever spontaneously develop into the mechanism of an open assault on managerial authority, let alone broader political authority. If workers' struggles should acquire a higher rationale than they at present possess, they would almost certainly need to transcend purely industrial forms of organization. Trade unions, by their nature, are unsuited to any extensive involvement in activities of an explicitly political kind; insofar as such involvement has occurred, this has been essentially 'as a by-product and auxiliary' to their primary concern with collective bargaining (Flanders, 1968: 75). Though questions of power and control are at least implicit in many of the day-to-day struggles which take place in industry, trade unions have traditionally resisted the suggestion that control of industry – and ultimately of society itself – is directly related to the problems and deprivations which confront trade unionists in their employment. So if industrial conflict were to extend into an explicit challenge to existing structures of control, this challenge would require the organization and articulation of an openly political movement.

6. Strikes and Society

Strikes as a 'social problem'

Conventional attitudes to strikes

The approach of this book has intentionally diverged from the orthodox assumption that industrial conflict is by definition a 'social problem', and that its analysis and interpretation must be geared to the elimination, or at least the diminution, of its 'disruptive' effects. Instead, Eldridge's dictum has been accepted: 'in sociology, the sources of conflict and co-operation, order and instability must have an equally valid claim to problem status' (1968: 22).

By contrast, conventional attitudes to strikes are at best ambivalent and in most cases unreservedly hostile. In Frayn's words: 'public opinion, so far as I can tell, unquestionably concedes the right of men in a free society to withdraw their labour. It just draws the line at strikes' (1967: 160). As has been noted earlier, the dominant social values tend to define open industrial conflict as illegitimate; and these values, impinging on workers' own definitions, often act as an inhibiting factor in disputes.

'Public opinion' as a social delusion

Conventional hostility to strikes is based on three main assumptions. First, that industrial conflict is outdated, unnecessary, or irrational. Second, that strikes result directly in severe economic disruption. Third, that they are evidence of excessive trade union power.

None of these arguments is based on significant empirical foundations. It should be unnecessary to rehearse the analysis of the previous chapters: conflict is endemic in the organization of industry in our society, and the consequent deprivations experienced by workers provide a rational justification for striking. The economic costs of stoppages were also considered previously. Few who have examined this question in any detail would seriously dispute Turner's conclusion:

> The supposedly peculiar costs of the British pattern of industrial conflict have not been satisfactorily demonstrated by those who allege them, but have been stated in terms which (by comparison with such general evidence on the economic effects of strikes as is available) are certainly much exaggerated. One can perhaps add that what seems currently a widespread public assumption that Britain is notably strike-prone appears to have little justification (1969: 44).

The third proposition reflects what Toynbee has termed the 'Myth of the Two Giants'.

> This is the widely-shared assumption that we live in a community which is largely, though perhaps regrettably, controlled by two huge but similar social forces. These powers are sometimes referred to by those supremely abstract terms, 'Labour' and 'Capital': more often, perhaps, because the earlier terms still have a Marxist ring, by the words 'Unions' and 'Management' (1967: 95).

At times this view is held in an even more extreme form: that we inhabit a 'labouristic' society, in which unions alone are the dominant social force against which even employers are impotent. As was noted earlier, this accords uncomfortably with the fact that British strikes are overwhelmingly unofficial and that unions thus lack the power even 'to control their own members'. And as Lane and Roberts point out,

> to suggest that trade unions have become more powerful than employers would be laughable if it were not taken so seriously. The day to take such suggestions seriously will be the day when a shop steward has the power to sack his managing director. What is so often forgotten is that trade unions are primarily *defensive*

organizations: where employers are in a position to set economic change in motion, the trade unions can normally only *react* to change. . . . One of the acid tests of power is the distribution of economic resources, and on this count alone it is clear that the trade union movement is no more powerful now than it was in 1900. Since 1900 there has, contrary to popular belief, been no significant redistribution of the national income (1971: 234).

It is worth repeating the basic contention of Chapter 4: unions have achieved (or have at least been associated with) important improvements in the conditions of work and the status of the worker; nevertheless, the basic structure of power in industry and society has yielded little to the rise of trade unionism. Our industrial system remains a capitalist one.

Popular attitudes to strikes are thus 'based on a false view of economic and political realities' (Lane and Roberts, 1971: 234). For the sociologist, the fact that industrial conflict is so extensively defined as a 'social problem' – and with so little apparent reason – is itself a highly significant problem. Its explanation may well provide important information not only about strikes but also about society itself.

One reaction to the deluded character of popular attitudes would be to dismiss these as irrational. Clegg, for example, having noted that 'our attitude to strikes is remarkable rather for its vehemence than for its close reasoning', has concluded that any explanation of the hue and cry about strikes 'cannot be provided by the student of strikes, but only by the social psychologist' (1956: 43). Yet if the argument of the last chapter is to be taken seriously, it is important that the sociologist should take pains to discern some rationale in popular attitudes rather than merely despairing at their illogicality.

The social visibility of strikes

One attempted explanation has pointed to the *social visibility* of strikes.

Probably the basic explanation for this exaggerated view lies in the *overtness* of the strike. Glaring and palpable, it thrusts itself rudely above the surface of society. Although not the most significant source of economic loss, it is certainly the most conspicuous. The number of workers participating in strikes is roughly of the same order of magnitude as the number suffering industrial accidents. The accidents occur quietly, however, generally one by one, whereas strikes are showy mass phenomena. They are not the only form of economic conflict but merely the most conspicuous (Kornhauser *et al.*, 1954: 8).

This argument is not wholly convincing. It is true that major strikes are mass phenomena; and on occasion they are accompanied by mass picketing, demonstrations, the circulation of statements and appeals, and so on. But very few strikes are nowadays 'showy' in this sense. Most disputes, indeed, involve mass action only in the decision to stop work, the holding of occasional strike meetings, and the eventual decision to return. For most of the time the strikers are dispersed – perhaps digging the garden, decorating the house, or helping with the family shopping. Striker bears no stigmata to identify them as such: they are intrinsically far less socially conspicuous than a worker who is maimed in an industrial accident. And if accidents are usually suffered individually – though surely not 'quietly' – the daily procession of injured workers through the casualty wards of any large hospital is itself a noteworthy social phenomenon. There is nothing about the factory gate which makes it intrinsically more visible to the public at large than the hospital.

This indicates that social visibility is not merely an inherent quality of phenomena; it relates also to what people are looking for, and what is brought to their attention by the media of communication. This can be indicated by considering two possible newspaper headlines: 'clergyman divorced for adultery with barmaid' and 'company fined for permitting unguarded machine'. Since both refer to reports of judicial proceedings, the public visibility of the events denoted may be assumed to be roughly equal. The fact that a company puts the lives and limbs of its employees at risk is not of obviously less significance than the moral peccadilloes of curates or barmaids. Which event, however, is more likely to be prominently reported in most newspapers? The evidence is that public attention to particular areas of social activity, and public definitions of certain social phenomena as problems, do not occur spontaneously; they result from identifiable social institutions and social processes. 'Public opinion', it could be said, is socially produced.

The social production of opinion

Strikes are one example of what sociologists commonly term 'deviant' behaviour – which means, roughly, behaviour which is commonly regarded as out of the ordinary and is labelled as a 'social problem'. Sociologists are increasingly recognizing, however, that 'social problems are not the result of an intrinsic malfunctioning of a society but are the result of a process of definition in which a given condition is picked out and identified as a social problem. . . . The societal definition, and not the objective makeup of a given social condition, determines whether the condition exists as a social problem' (Blumer, 1971: 300–1). As Stanley Cohen has argued,

> a 'social problem' consists not only of a fixed and given condition but the perception and definition by certain people that this condition poses a threat which is against their interests and that something should be done about it. . . . So, whenever we see terms such as deviance and social problem, we must ask: 'Says who?' (1971: 14–17).

The structure of persuasive definitions

'Says who?' is the essential starting point for any analysis of allegedly 'public' attitudes. It is a famous sociological dictum that situations which people define as real are real in their consequences. While providing a highly significant insight, this is also at best a half-truth.

The dictum has been elaborated by Merton in his discussion of the 'self-fulfilling prophecy'. Rumours of insolvency, by causing a 'run on the bank' as worried depositors seek to withdraw funds, may themselves suffice to *cause* insolvency. Or the beliefs which one racial group holds about another may prove self-validating: if whites exclude blacks from their unions 'because negroes work for low wages', blacks will indeed be *forced* to take jobs in low-paid, non-union factories and occupations (Merton, 1968: 475–90).

Yet not all social definitions are self-validating. If workers in a factory define their employer as a man of exceptional generosity, this may prove insufficient to bring them an increase in wages. Or to take another example, a general expectation of a Labour victory in the 1970 election failed to keep Wilson in office.

Two factors seem to make definitions liable to prove self-validating. One relates to the context in which such definitions occur: a relatively unstructured situation is most favourable for the self-fulfilling prophecy. If international financiers and speculators lose confidence in sterling, there will be a run on the pound and possibly devaluation. But since (despite popular stereotypes of 'gnomes of Zurich') there is little planned co-ordination of the activities of financial speculators, the confidence which each has in the stability of sterling derives in large measure from his estimates of the confidence of others. Rumours of a possible devaluation would have to be taken seriously and acted on, for fear that others may act on them. A system of interaction which is unstructured – lacking overall co-ordination and control – is thus often one precondition of self-validating definitions. Another is that individuals have a strong motive for basing their actions on their guesses of what others will do. A belief that most of the electorate supports Wilson is not a particularly cogent reason for not voting for Heath. But if balloting were public, and victors customarily rewarded friends and penalized opponents, such a belief would be important and could prove self-validating.

The other factor relevant for analysis of self-fulfilling prophecies is the fact that some people's definitions of a situation are more persuasive than others'. If the Director of Public Prosecutions defines a magazine as obscene, its editors may find themselves in prison. If 10,000 shipyard workers define the closure of their yards as a social and economic obscenity, they may still find themselves on the dole. So it is not enough to talk of *the* definition of the situation; often the appropriate question is *whose* definition.

In certain circumstances, anyone may be able to provide a persuasive definition of the situation. Any member of a cinema audience who stands up and shouts 'Fire' may well be widely believed. Where interaction is unstructured, rumours can simply 'get started'. But such cases are exceptional: we live in a society in which definitions of reality are not usually traded from hand to hand but are distributed wholesale. 'In modern urban societies there is extreme social segregation between different groups which leads to information being obtained at second hand through the mass media rather than directly by face-to-face contact' (Young, 1971: 35.) This means that the various media (radio and TV, newspapers, magazines) as well as such organizations as governments, schools, and churches – and those who control them – possess considerable power as merchants of persuasive definitions. The relationship between such influence, and power in society generally, is examined in the next section.

The media and the production of opinion

The mass media do not purport, for the most part, to provide a detailed and systematic analysis of the social phenomena which they report. This, it would be argued, is not the function of a television newsreel or a mass-circulation newspaper. One consequence of this is that what is socially distributed as 'news' is typically characterized by superficiality, trivialization, and sensationalism.

> The type of information which the mass media portray is that which is 'newsworthy'. They select events which are *atypical*, present them in a *stereotypical* fashion and contrast them against a backcloth of normality which is *overtypical*. . . . Out of this, simple moral directives are produced demanding that something must be done about it (Young, 1971: 35).

An analysis of the media's coverage of the October 1968 demonstration against the Vietnam war reported that 'viewers and readers were not presented with various interpretations focusing on different aspects of the same event, but with basically the same interpretation which focused on the same limited aspect – the issue of violence'. This exemplifies the extent to which 'the media provide us with a picture of what is happening only in a very selective sense. They structure "the pictures of the world" that are available to us and, in turn, these pictures structure possible modes of action' (Halloran *et al.*, 1970: 300–1, 313). Thus highly complex social situations tend to be defined as black-and-white 'issues'.

A further product of the communications industry is the modern concept of 'public opinion'. It is questionable whether 'the public' is sufficiently coherent an entity to be credited with *an* opinion; but at least traditional usage, recognizing this problem, defined public opinion as the outcome of collective discussion and debate. Today it is assumed that public opinion exists ready-made on every conceivable subject, without the need for any collective interchange of viewpoints on the implications of the question. Public opinion may be instantly manufactured and distributed merely by drafting a questionnaire and counting heads.

The media have thus provided themselves with an apparently 'democratic' instrument for transforming any social phenomenon into an 'issue' in respect of which a 'policy' is required. Unencumbered by any qualifications or detail, the public is presented with a yes/no dichotomy on which it is expected to offer an instant opinion – even if previously unaware even that the 'issue' existed. One inevitable consequence is that the opinions extracted may be based on a total absence of information. An American example makes this clear:

> In February, 1947, Gallup asked: 'Do you think Congress should or should not forbid jurisdictional strikes?' Some 68 per cent said yes, 25 per cent said no, and only 7 per cent said they didn't know. When asked however to define 'jurisdictional strike', only 12 per cent were able to give an approximately correct definition (Bell, 1954: 248).

Respondents who lack detailed knowledge of the subject in question are particularly susceptible to the instant moralizations of the media. Thus there is strong evidence that those most ignorant of industrial relations are most enthusiastic for legal penalties against unofficial strikers (Blumler and Ewbank, 1970). It is reasonable to assume that limited knowledge affected public attitudes towards the British Industrial Relations Bill, published at the end of 1970. This was a 140-page document, so complex that few labour lawyers claimed to understand it entirely; the general public was thus particularly dependent on the media's presentation, in which exposition, interpretation, and evaluation coalesced.

Another consequence of limited knowledge is that the phraseology of a questionnaire can be crucial to the outcome. It seems likely that the very presentation of such a question as 'should unofficial strikes be made illegal?' invites an affirmative response. Asking the question itself helps define the situation as a 'problem' about which, accordingly, 'something must be done' – and for which only one such solution is offered. Moreover, survey questions can be far more blatantly loaded than this. Bell cites a survey of attitudes to the closed shop in which 89 per cent expressed their hostility to it; when the question was reformulated this proportion fell to 45 per cent. In Britain, surveys often invite a response hostile to the closed shop by asking 'Should a worker be able to decide whether to join a trade union or not?' rather than 'Should trade union members be able to decide whether to work with non-unionists or not?' Similarly, polls conducted by Gallup in 1971 referred to strikes explicitly as a 'problem', and described the Industrial Relations Bill in the Conservative government's own terms as 'plans to reform trade union law'. It is perhaps less surprising that 51 per cent of respondents expressed support for such 'reform' than that 25 per cent declared their opposition and the remainder were 'don't knows'.

Social values and the power structure

Reference has been made at a number of points in this book to the 'dominant social values'. The values people hold – their standards of what is desirable and undesirable, legitimate and illegitimate – have a profound influence on social behaviour. These values are themselves socially derived, being absorbed by the individual from childhood through the various processes which sociologists label socialization.

The socialization process is normally related to the power structure within a society. As was pointed out in an earlier chapter, those who are subject to a system of control are far more likely to comply willingly if they define this control as legitimate – as authority rather than coercive power. Those who exercise control over the most important decisions in a society – in Britain today a fairly small number of wealthy industrialists, financiers, and members of the political 'establishment' – tend naturally to regard their own supremacy as legitimate, and equally naturally wish other members of society to share this view. If their right to take decisions with far-reaching consequences for the lives of the mass of ordinary people were widely and systematically questioned, the whole structure of power in society would be undermined. Fortunately for the stability of the structure, power in society normally extends to the mechanisms and content of socialization. Owners of newspapers are – necessarily – wealthy men, and members of what Wright Mills has termed the 'power élite'. Those who control such 'public' media of communication as the BBC are also members of this privileged élite. Considerable control over the educational system – which has a profound influence on social values – is vested here also.

There are therefore grounds for arguing that 'every stable society imposes on the majority of its members the social and economic attitudes of its beneficiaries' (Toynbee, 1967: 95). This is, however, an oversimplification. Most working people are accustomed to distinguish between 'them' and 'us': they are conscious of being controlled from above, and in a vague sense resent and question the legitimacy of this control. This is part of a more extensive working-class 'sub-culture' which itself helps socialize each generation of workers with values in part conflicting with the 'official' norms of society.

Nevertheless, this conflict of values is insufficient to threaten the stability of the whole system of social control, for it falls far short of an extensive or penetrating critique of existing social institutions. Social stability is reinforced, moreover, by the virtually universal acceptance of a number of concepts and definitions with profoundly conservative implications. The framework of ideas and beliefs which every person uses to interpret and make sense of the world around them is commonly termed an ideology. The term can be employed without any ulterior implications; but normally it suggests a set of ideas which serves the interest of a particular social group. As Berger has put it, 'ideology both justifies what is done by the group whose vested interest is served and interprets social reality in such a way that the justification is made plausible' (1966: 130).

One important component of the dominant ideology is the concept of 'the country' or 'the national interest'. It is normally taken for granted that such phrases are highly meaningful, and it is therefore important that their precise meaning should be carefully investigated. This will indicate how such ideas serve the interest of those with power in our society.

'The country can't afford it.' 'It' can be anything from free milk for schoolchildren to decent pay for postmen. Now 'the country' is, strictly speaking, a geographical expression. Of course people who talk like this do not really mean 'a collection of islands in the North Sea can't afford it.' If pressed, they will probably admit that what they mean is that 'the people living in these islands can't afford it.' Put in that way the statement is much less effective because it is obvious that we are talking about how to share out available income among these people. The trick is to give the impression that there is something called 'the country' which is somehow different from the actual people who live in it (Hallas, 1971: 31).

'The national interest' is the type of abstract idea which orients people's thinking in a particular direction. In this case, people are led to view the interests of a particular social group as common to the whole society – even though a fundamental *conflict* of interests may exist. Such powerful abstractions are a modern parallel to the fetish-objects worshipped by 'primitive' peoples.

The 'strength of sterling' is a good example of a modern fetish. What actually does it mean? Ask an economist and you will be told that if sterling is strong people will prefer to hold it rather than, say, dollars. But what people and why? Clearly not the mass of working people in this country. In fact most shops and pubs will not accept dollars anyway, so that whether sterling is weak or strong most of us have to 'hold' and use it regardless. The economist will probably brush aside this objection as frivolous. The 'people' he has in mind, he will explain, are bankers, brokers, and international currency speculators. Now they are not a very big group. Why do their preferences matter so much? If our economist is very patient he will tell us that if these bankers and speculators think that sterling is not a 'sound currency' they will convert their holdings into dollars or Swiss francs and this will 'upset our balance of payments'. In short these people have great *power*. But it is not power over pieces of paper or entries into bank ledgers. It is power over other people, specifically over working people. The paper and the entries are only tokens of that power. Having got so far we are well on the way to asking why on earth the working people of this or any other country should tolerate a state of affairs in which a handful of speculators can exercise such power. It is not a convenient question for the rich, which is why the mass media conjure up fetishes like 'the strength of sterling' (Hallas, 1971: 32).

Power, ideology and industrial conflict

The processes through which situations are defined and opinions manufactured have the power to exert a profound influence on social attitudes to industrial conflict. If those in control of these processes perceive such conflict as impinging on their interests, it would be surprising if this power were not utilized.

Strikes as a challenge to managerial control

Evidence presented earlier demonstrated that the economic costs of strikes are conventionally exaggerated, in that their effect on the level of national production, while not precisely calculable, is very small. However, an indirect consequence of workers' ability to strike was also noted: what Donovan terms 'the effects on management of the fear of the possibility of strikes even if they do not take place' (1968: 111).

This is to indicate that strikes – or the threat of them – are often successful in obliging managements to take account of the expectations and aspirations of their employees. Strikes are, quite simply, a challenge to the autonomy of managerial control. They are the means by which labour refuses to behave merely as a commodity. As was suggested in an earlier chapter, the extent of this challenge should not be exaggerated: strikes of the sort discussed by Donovan relate to particular exercises of managerial control and are not directed against the structure of this control as such. Nevertheless, 'any strike amounts amongst other things to a crisis in an established system of authority' (Lane and Roberts, 1971: 16). It is not therefore surprising that those who exercise managerial authority typically resent this limitation on their autonomy, and are sometimes haunted by the fear that strikes may escalate into an explicit challenge to minority control of industry.

The media and strikes

Accordingly, those who perceive a threat to their control have good reason to attempt to impose their definitions of reality on society. And in this they achieve considerable success.

> Organized labor and management compete for public approval, political favor, and desired governmental actions as well as for direct industrial objectives. In this competition it can scarcely be questioned that the business viewpoint, the social interpretations and values congenial to management, are the ones predominantly circulated. Since the media of mass communication are preponderantly in the hands of businessmen and depend on the support of management interests (advertisers), this tends almost inevitably to be the case. Moreover, influence in support of management philosophy, aims, and outlook must be reckoned with in many other quarters – schools and colleges, churches, political parties, everywhere that the prestige and power of wealth are felt (Kornhauser *et al.*, 1954: 507).

Press treatment of industrial disputes is evidence of the validity of this assessment. Lane and Roberts, in their study of the Pilkington strike, report that 'despite the leanings of some reporters, despite the editorial policies of the different papers, all of the press without exception managed to convey the impression that the whole thing was really rather lamentable. . . . The industrial *status quo*, in other words, always came out on top. This of course should not surprise anyone, for the press is part of the *status quo*' (1971: 75–6).

There are of course variations in the way in which the media produce definitions of strikes. The pressure on reporters to match their copy to editorial policy can differ considerably between papers. The nature and extent of sub-editing also varies, as does the readiness to mix reportage with editorializing. More basically, there are important differences in the way that particular stoppages and particular aspects of disputes are selected for reporting at all. The Halewood dispute received quite extensive coverage in all the 'quality' press, and reports did on occasion attempt to give a 'striker's-eye view'. (Possibly the fact that the stoppage occurred without warning, and at a considerable distance from Fleet Street, increased the chances of reporters' copy appearing unadulterated on the page.) By contrast, the 'populars' virtually ignored the dispute – perhaps because it could not readily be presented in terms of the stereotype of 'wildcat' action by 'greedy' workers.

Attempts at objectivity in some papers' accounts of some strikes in any case hardly extend to editorial generalizations, or evaluations of particular disputes. It is not uncommon for leader-writers to assail strikers as unreasonable and unreasoning, while a report on the facing news page makes obvious that neither accusation is justified. Editorial clichés have a built-in bias against collective action by workers. These have been examined in detail by Toynbee; one example will suffice:

> *'Holding up the public to blackmail.'* This is what the postmen were doing, according to *The Times*, when they demanded an increase on a basic wage of £11 10s 0d a week. This is what the dockers were doing when they announced that they would prefer to have their weekends off, like everybody else. This, of course, is what the seamen were doing when they demanded overtime pay for anything over and above a forty-hour week. And on the day when *The Times* was rebuking the postmen for exhausting its patience an article appeared on the same page which made a spirited defence of land speculators. It seemed that these enterprising men were not 'holding up the public to blackmail' but simply taking legitimate risks and making legitimate profits. Profits, for example, of two hundred per cent, made at the expense of local authorities and would-be house-holders (1967: 98–9).

In their generalized characterizations of industrial conflict, the media as a whole trade extensively in concepts and definitions which are profoundly ideological.

The unitary ideology and its uses

The view that there is a unique 'national interest', that the interests of those who control society are also those of 'the country as a whole', has its parallel at the level of the individual factory. It is an ideology that exerts considerable influence on conventional attitudes to industrial disputes: for the denial that strikes are necessary or rational makes no kind of sense without an assumption that the interests of employers and workers are fundamentally the same.

Alan Fox has described the conventional picture of the industrial firm as a 'unitary ideology'.

> A unitary system has one source of authority and one focus of loyalty, which is why it suggests the team analogy. What pattern of behaviour do we expect from members of a successful and healthily-functioning team? We expect them to strive jointly towards a common objective, each pulling his weight to the best of his ability. Each accepts his place and his function gladly, following the leadership of the one so appointed. . . . Most students of industrial relations would agree that this represents a vision of what industry ought to be like which is widespread among employers, top managers and substantial sections of outside public opinion (1966: 3).

'It might be asked', Fox continues, 'why employers and managers commonly supposed to be hard-headed and practical should subscribe to a "unitary" view of industrial organization which is so at variance with demonstrable facts' (p. 5). The sources of managerial ideologies have been discussed in detail by Nichols (1969), who shows how an image of the company as an 'organic whole' both serves managerial interests and gives managers a comforting definition of their own role. It is pleasanter for managers to see themselves as merely co-ordinating company policy in the interests of all concerned, rather than as exercising coercive control. Fox has made this same point succinctly:

> For many managers, the full and complete acceptance of the idea

that substantial sections of those whom they govern are in certain fundamental respects alienated is corrosive of self-confidence. This can be a powerful motivation towards believing that a basic harmony of purpose exists, and that any apparent demonstration to the contrary is due to faults among the governed – to stupidity, or short-sightedness, or out-dated class rancour, or an inability to grasp the basic principles of economics, or the activities of agitators who create mischief out of nothing. Such beliefs offer a high emotional yield, for failure and frustration can be projected onto others. Besides serving as a mechanism of defensive reassurance, the ideology also serves as an instrument of persuasion. Managers seek to persuade employees and the public at large that industry is a harmony of co-operation which only fools or knaves choose to disrupt. To the extent that they convince their employees their job is made easier; to the extent that they convince the public they gain sympathy whenever their policies are challenged by their workers. Arising out of this second point is the third. The propagation of the idea that the interests of the rulers and the ruled are identical helps confer legitimacy upon the regime (p. 5).

Given the interconnections of control over industry and control over the social production of opinion, it should cause no surprise that this ideology is so widely disseminated and embraced. Its implications for the interpretation of strikes are obvious: since the *structure* of industry is seen as essentially harmonious, conflict must be the result of ignorance or subversion. 'Employers who believed in the structural origin of strikes would, in effect, be approving of their own elimination' (Allen, 1966: 116); the belief that disputes reflect merely the wantonness of workers is both simpler and more satisfying.

But despite its rich ideological yield, the unitary perspective of industry has certain disadvantages for managements. Employees may absorb many of its assumptions; but while they may be willing to accept that *other* workers' strikes are irrational, they cannot feel the same about their own disputes. Managers themselves can be lured by these same assumptions into irrelevant or even counter-productive policies: attempting, for example, to root out the 'trouble-makers' who are thought to be responsible for conflict, and in the process making far more trouble than previously existed. What employers therefore require is an ideology which provides a more sophisticated approach than the unitary view yet retains all its basic advantages. And it is here that academic analysts of industrial relations are so important.

The academic analysis of industrial conflict

Academics are generally assumed to bring to the study of social affairs a more detached appraisal and more penetrating theoretical insight than those immediately involved in these affairs. At least in the context of industrial relations and industrial sociology, this is rarely more than partly true.

Fox has argued, in his discussion of managerial ideology, that 'the whole view of industrial organization embodied in this unitary emphasis has long since been abandoned by most social scientists as incongruent with reality and useless for purposes of analysis' (1966: 4). It is indeed true that 'most social scientists' are less unselfconsciously naïve than a generation ago. The starting point of the early human relations writers – that industrial conflict is a pathological deviation from the natural harmony of industry, that management is a neutral agency taking rational decisions in the interests of all, while resistance on the part of workers represents the irrational influence of 'sentiments' – is rarely stated by modern academics in so unsophisticated a form.

Nevertheless, the structural-functionalist school which has long dominated sociological theory, with its assumption that order and stability are the norm, has exerted a profound and continuing influence on the study of social relations in industry. Most exponents of the increasingly popular pseudo-discipline of 'organization theory' tend to the view that the natural state of the industrial enterprise is an equilibrium in which all co-operate in the pursuit of managerial goals. An even trendier variant, 'systems theory', has banished the very idea of conflict from its analysis in favour of such exotically loaded concepts as 'sub-optimal system functioning'. And as was seen in Chapter 3, the more traditional Parsonian model of a stable and integrated 'social system' has been taken over – even if not always consciously – as part of the theoretical framework of most analysts of industrial relations.

It is doubtful if more than a minority of academics concerned with social relations in industry have explicitly formulated a theoretical model in which conflict is treated as normal. And within this minority, by far the most popular approach is what Fox has termed 'the pluralistic frame of reference'. This perspective recognizes the reality of divergent interests in industry, but assumes – implicitly or explicitly – that this divergence exists within a higher-order framework of common interests. Managements which openly recognize the right of workers to organize collectively and to challenge company policies will be able, Fox argues, to negotiate a workable compromise whenever disputes arise, and will thus consolidate their own control.

> The pluralistic frame of reference, which openly concedes the severe limitations on management power, constitutes thereby a source of potential strength rather than weakness. It is a necessary – though not sufficient – basis for recognizing that co-operation is unlikely to be achieved in modern industry through the attempted manipulation of 'team spirit', 'high morale' and 'loyalty', but needs to be engineered by structural adaptations in work organization, work rules and work practices, and that direct negotiation with work-groups is an essential part of this process (1966: 14).

This approach has obvious affinities with the theories of institutionalization discussed in Chapter 4: the assumption that conflict which is potentially disruptive can be rendered harmless if the legitimacy of its expression is accepted. Conversely, Fox suggests, a manager committed to the unitary view of industry may adopt policies which will accentuate the intensity of conflict.

The pluralistic theory of industry can thus be of direct practical utility to employers of labour; it is also of considerable ideological utility. It accepts – what is obvious to an observer with any open-mindedness – that conflicts of interest do exist, but it denies that these represent a fundamental social flaw. The analogy used by Fox to illustrate the pluralistic approach is particularly revealing: the industrial enterprise ought to be 'viewed as a coalition of interests, a miniature democratic state' (p. 2). The meaning of these political comparisons is clear: a coalition is a government comprising two or more distinct parties; a democratic state is, at the very least, one in which the rulers are periodically chosen by the ruled, who can elect the opposition into office. To specify this is to demonstrate the absurdity of the analogy: workers do not elect their managers, and cannot vote them out of office; and in the employer alone is vested the right to govern the firm. As Dubin has candidly admitted, democratic principles are excluded from industry: 'should such a process be adopted, it seems clear that the workers, constituting the largest single group within the enterprise, would ordinarily outvote all other groups' (1954: 38). So it is clear that the pluralistic theory is itself incongruent with reality; it is little but a sophisticated variant of the view that industry is unitary harmony. And it too provides a legitimizing aura of approval for a system of minority control of industry and society.

It is this theoretical perspective which has shaped the bulk of recent academic writing in industrial relations. Rarely do academics suggest that conflict might be fundamental to industry and society as at present organized. Rarely do they consider whether workers might gain more by transforming the whole framework of power and control than they can possibly achieve within this framework. Rarely do they indicate the correct analogy for the modern industrial enterprise: a miniature *un*democratic state.

A theoretical approach which refuses to question whether minority control is 'normal' or 'natural' is associated with an orientation of research which in general serves the interests of those who exercise this control. As Merton has noted:

> Of the limited body of social research in industry, the greater part has been oriented toward the needs of management. The problems selected as the focus of the inquiry – high labor turnover and restricted output, for example – have been largely thus defined by management, sponsorship has been typically by management, the limits and character of experimental changes in the work situation have been passed upon by management, and periodic reports have been made primarily to management (1968: 625).

Many – probably most – academic studies of strikes have viewed these explicitly as problems for management. Many of the others have done so implicitly, as a result of the level of analysis chosen. Research into determinants of strike incidence at the level of the individual firm or industry necessarily isolate such factors as personnel policy, payment systems, disputes procedures – which can be manipulated by management in the interest of greater predictability and control. The passage quoted from Fox makes this explicit: 'co-operation . . . needs to be engineered by structural adaptation in work organization, work rules and work practices'.

The convergence of academic and managerial interests is often even more overt. Virtually all leading British academics in the field of industrial relations have worked at some time for the (now defunct) Prices and Incomes Board, the Commission on Industrial Relations, or the Department of Employment – the policies of each of which tend towards the consolidation of managerial control over wages and the use of labour at the level of the individual firm and industry or the economy as a whole. Other academics in the social sciences work directly as management consultants. Thus has arisen what Wright Mills has termed 'illiberal practicality': the consecration of academic expertise to servicing with advice and information those in positions of power, thus reinforcing their control over those beneath them (1959: 95–9).

At a more mundane level, 'illiberal practicality' is evidenced by selectivity in the presentation of research findings. Thus academics normally feel constrained to suppress publication of facts the general knowledge of which would be distasteful to employers. For example: an expert on industrial relations in a major British industry will, in the intimacy of seminar discussion, reveal substantial evidence that certain managements tap the telephone calls of their shop stewards. Yet this information – which throws a most significant light on the basically antagonistic quality of employer-worker relationships – is excluded from his published works. For academics to report such findings would threaten both their established relationships with employers and also their own image of industrial relations as based ultimately on a community of interest.

Many academics, it is true, may disavow any intention to buttress managerial control over employees. On the contrary: they may define their involvement in 'public policy' as 'serving the national interest', or even, in some cases, as furthering the interests of workers.

Academics are as susceptible as anyone to ideological influences; they may be happily unaware of the repressive implications of their practical and theoretical activities. Yet as Fox (1972) has demonstrated – in a discussion in which he disavows his earlier enthusiasm for the pluralistic perspective – academics with a genuine desire to 'improve the lot of the underdog' may effectively 'help to maintain the stability and continuance of the system which produces underdogs'. What is at issue, in other words, is not their subjective intentions but the objective consequences of their activities.

The intimate attachment between academic research and managerial preoccupations receives powerful ideological and practical support. The use of academic techniques and theories to facilitate managerial manipulation is sanctified by such descriptions as 'a fruitful exercise in applied social science'. As Merton indicates, companies asked to admit researchers to their premises and their records are liable to be influenced by their assessment of the orientation and likely results of such studies. Those with control over the allocation of government and private research finance – being, in general, managers of one sort or another themselves – are likely to regard with special favour projects promising a practical pay-off. Professors with a record of 'useful' research may well be more likely to attract research finance than others with a different record; and conceivably those who endow university chairs or appoint their incumbents might take such factors into consideration.

Conversely, it is considered academically somewhat disreputable to research into industrial conflict with the primary aim of assisting *workers*. To examine how a strike might be timed and organized for maximum effect; how management plans which threaten conditions of work or the autonomy of shop-floor organization might be frustrated; in what ways the structure of managerial control might be challenged and disrupted: to ask such questions is to display an 'irresponsible bias' which, strangely, is not noticed in managerially-oriented studies. Research which raises the *level* of inquiry – asking what general features of the existing organization and control of industry act as mainsprings of conflict, and in what manner and by what means these might be altered – is likely to be dismissed as 'patently ideological'. Again, an approach is not 'ideological' if the ideology is management's. And the academic who offers direct and practical advice to shop-floor workers in their struggles is likely to provoke apoplexy among vice-chancellors and those industrialists who figure prominently on the governing bodies of institutions of higher learning.

Such processes must not be exaggerated. A few eccentrics are acceptable within universities as evidence of their traditional liberalism, and some research and analysis into strikes and industrial relations generally rejects the dominant managerial orientation. But that this orientation *is* dominant remains unquestionable. The practical assistance which, on balance, academics render to employers is substantial. But their most significant contribution is at the ideological level: they fail – some might say, refuse – to question the social values which assign legitimacy to minority control over our working lives, but rather underwrite (in more elegant and sophisticated formulations, indeed) such values powerfully.

Whose strike problem?

It is not enough, it was shown earlier, to accept uncritically the conventional definition of any social phenomenon as a 'problem'. What is assigned problem status by one group in society may not constitute a problem for some other group – or may do so for quite different reasons. This final section considers this aspect of strikes from the contrasting perspectives of managements and workers.

Management's strike problem

Strikes appear as a problem to employers for three main reasons. The least important, as has been seen, is that they disrupt the process of production – though this is the reason most frequently cited. What is far more important is the fact that through their actual or potential use of the strike weapon, workers can impose limits to management's control over them. And thirdly, the occurrence of strikes is a persistent practical contradiction of the ideology of harmony of interests which assigns legitimacy to managerial power.

While strikes have always represented a problem for those in control of industrial enterprises, the seriousness of this problem is increasing. But the recent rise in the number and duration of stoppages is only marginally responsible for this. Far more important are contemporary trends in the very nature of industrial organization and production. The development of large-scale multi-national companies; the integration of diverse productive activities; the decreasing life-span of capital which is itself escalating in complexity and cost: all these create a need for long-term centralized planning within modern corporations. And effective planning requires company control over all factors which might otherwise interfere with manufacturing and marketing programmes.

The implications for industrial relations are obvious.

Planning is not easy, not even for the biggest. One element in particular is intractable – labour. It has a will of its own and more or less independent organizations. It can, and does, take advantage of its own scarcity. Its behaviour, and therefore cost, is fundamentally unpredictable. Yet the big corporation has not given up. It cannot (Kidron, 1970: 29).

The need for planning has created urgent pressures for new levels of predictability in labour costs and intensity in labour utilization. The passive subjection of workers to managerial control becomes increasingly the key to continued company profitability. Strikes however raise wages, limit managerial autonomy, and represent expressions of working people's self-activity. Not surprisingly, then, they appear increasingly intolerable to managements. Nor is it surprising that companies which have long abandoned the old ideology of *laissez faire*, and have come to welcome government assistance in all areas of economic life, should turn to the state for aid in combating the strike.

The government's strike problem

The state is widely regarded as a 'neutral' agency, over and above all internal social conflicts. It is scarcely popular to suggest that governments act predominantly in the interests of one particular class within society. The prevalent view of the state tends to match the ideology discussed earlier: governments serve not mere sectional interests but 'the country as a whole' and 'the national interest'.

There are three main reasons why this view is mistaken. First, those who own and control industry are able to exert a crucial influence over the activities of the state. Governments of whatever political label may be expected to give explicit assent to a system of industry geared to producing profits for a wealthy minority. Those who administer government policy – the professional civil servants – also accept this state of affairs as natural and proper. In short, the policies of those with official charge over state power normally derive from an unquestioned assumption that capitalist interests and 'the national interest' are one and the same.

Secondly, even governments which profess some detachment from business interests are in practice obliged to attend to the expectations of those with economic power. 'The control by business of large and crucially important areas of economic life makes it extremely *difficult* for governments to impose upon it policies to which it is firmly opposed' (Miliband, 1969: 147). The strategy of working within the confines of the existing economic system – which forms part of the consensus of all main political parties – thus entails a critical constraint: the need to maintain the 'confidence of industry', or more accurately of industrialists. Such confidence is necessary since the government's domestic economic policies may otherwise be sabotaged, while speculative pressures may engineer a trade or currency crisis. The experience of the Labour government of 1964–70 bears eloquent witness to the ransom to capital which may be demanded of any would-be reforming administration.

This leads directly to the third point. 'If the social process of investment and accumulation is left to private ownership then the fate of society as a whole is inextricably bound up with the fortunes of the rich. . . . So long as productive resources are in private hands, they must be allowed to produce a sufficient reward to maintain growth' (Blackburn, 1967: 19, 37). As long as the capitalist structure of industry is unquestioned, any government is bound to encourage profits. This point has been clearly stated by Michael Shanks, a leading economic commentator and industrialist:

The need at present is for prices to be allowed to rise, while wages are held back. . . . In other words, what is urgently required in the

United Kingdom's economy at the present time is a redistribution of national income away from wages and in favour of profits. It is not perhaps surprising that neither party is very anxious to spell out this awkward but inescapable fact of economic life (*The Times*, 16 June 1970).

If government policies directed towards the welfare of 'the' economy are in fact directed towards the welfare of a capitalist economy, then any action which benefits the owners of capital – making the rich even richer – must seem perfect economic sense.

Such pressures inevitably shape government attitudes towards strikes. Insofar as strikes are a challenge to managerial interests, they must represent a threat to 'the' economy. The consequences have long been manifest.

On innumerable occasions, and in all capitalist countries, governments have played a decisive role in defeating strikes, often by the invocation of the coercive power of the state and the use of naked violence; and the fact that they have done so in the name of the national interest, law and order, constitutional government, the protection of 'the public', etc., rather than simply to support employers, has not made that intervention any the less useful to these employers (Miliband, 1969: 80).

Recent dramatic examples of government involvement can be seen in the seamen's strike of 1966, or in subsequent systematic efforts to hold down wages in the public sector. Such confrontations reflect heightened economic pressures on the state as well as on individual companies. Virtual stagnation has meant that improved wages can no longer be financed painlessly out of economic growth; foreign competition limits the extent to which money wage increases can be clawed back through price inflation. The goal of accelerated investment and the pressures of international capital mobility rather necessitate, as Shanks suggests, a redistribution of income away from wages and salaries and towards profits; while concern for increased 'productivity' of labour creates a parallel interest in the consolidation and extension of managerial control at the place of work. Thus governments, like employers, have strong practical reasons for increasing intolerance of strikes. And in addition, striker-baiting is regarded as a fruitful form of party-political capital; strikers also serve as a convenient scapegoat for the abysmal economic records, in international comparative terms, of all recent British governments.

The idea that the state is 'above sectional conflicts' and plays a 'neutral' role in industrial relations is therefore mistaken; but it is of great ideological importance. When the government intervenes in a dispute, on the side of the employer, any attempt by the union concerned to stand firm can be presented as 'undemocratic' and 'a challenge to the constitution'. Where trade unionists themselves regard the state as 'neutral', their resolve is likely to crumble before such an ideological offensive.

The workers' strike problem

Managers and politicians are accustomed to articulating and publicizing their definitions of those areas of social reality which are of concern to them. This is of course not the case for the vast majority of ordinary people, who in any case lack comparable access to the media of communication. For the reasons argued earlier in this chapter, surveys of 'public opinion' are unreliable guides to people's thinking on social questions; they do not indicate, for example, whether people have given such questions serious consideration at all, and thus whether views expressed are likely to be altered by further thought or by practical experience. So statistics which purport to show the attitude to strikes of the general public, or of trade union members, should not be given excessive credence.

It follows however from what was said earlier concerning social values and ideology, that the definitions of industrial conflict constructed by those in positions of social control are likely to exert extensive influence. It follows that workers will tend to use such concepts as 'the country as a whole' or 'the interests of the firm' as part of the frame of reference through which they perceive and evaluate the strikes of other trade unionists. Most workers most of the time may be expected to share in part at least the managerial definition of strikes. This is particularly likely given the defensive and apologetic attitude taken by most trade unions towards strikes, and the open hostility of many of the alleged political representatives of labour.

Strikes are a more immediate problem to those indirectly affected by stoppages. In the car industry, for example, there are signs that workers with experience of lay-offs during strikes unrelated to their own immediate interests have a tendency to react antagonistically towards strikes in general. This is understandable. Since strikes involve initiative by the workers involved, the natural assumption is that they must be the aggressors: natural, that is, unless viewed with a sophistication or class-consciousness which insists that management action may well have precipitated the dispute. Car workers, it has been suggested, may be particularly lacking in 'solidaristic' class-consciousness: when aggrieved at losing money through lay-offs they may regard the strikers as the obvious culprits – particularly since the true causes of the dispute are unlikely to be widely publicized. This in turn may induce some employers to use the 'sympathy lock-out' as a deliberate tactic for putting pressure on strikers to return to work.

Not all trade unionists, however, blame fellow-workers in whose disputes they become indirectly involved. Indeed, the occurrence of sympathy stoppages, collections for strike appeals, and refusals to touch 'black' work indicates that feelings of solidarity remain widespread. The Devlin Report on the docks referred to 'an exaggerated sense of solidarity or loyalty': men accepted without question a policy of 'one out, all out', adopting the 'principle that the man who wants to strike is always right' (1965: 8). Such attitudes, condemned by Devlin as 'irresponsibility', may be viewed in the situation as a perfectly natural extension of trade union ethics. Dockers have learned that strike action is seldom taken frivolously, but reflects an accumulation of grievances; they are therefore willing to support their fellows in dispute without question, knowing that they themselves may some time depend on similar support. The absence of so firm a tradition of solidarity in some other industries may in part indicate a lesser need; under mass-production technology, a sectional group can achieve a similar effect by strike action whether or not other workers in the factory give active support. Nevertheless, an attitude of solidarity towards other workers' strikes can be found even in the car industry: witness the rapid preparations for support at other Ford plants before the Halewood strike was settled. Government attempts to outlaw sympathy strikes and similar action indicate the continuing significance of solidarity.

In any case, however ambivalent – or even downright hostile – some workers may be towards *other* strikers' actions, their views will be quite different when they themselves feel obliged to strike. 'He is an irresponsible wildcat; I am taking legitimate action to defend my rights' – such a viewpoint, probably quite widespread, reflects not so much double standards as the totally different definitions of the situation of the outsider and of those personally involved. Participation in a stoppage can thus transform a worker's viewpoint: the conventional stereotypes and values lose their grip.

> To go on strike is to deny the existing distribution of power and authority. The striker ceases to respond to managerial command; he refuses to do his 'work'. A new dimension of living can thus be revealed to the striker; an existence in which 'ordinary' people are able to control events and command the attention of 'them'. The experience of this new reality can transform the striker's perceptions of normal life. What was 'normal' can no longer be regarded as 'natural'. Attitudes towards work and authority become critical as opposed to acquiescent (Lane and Roberts, 1971: 105).

While such a transformation of attitudes normally weakens after a return to work, the effect is unlikely to disappear entirely. Since the inhibiting effect of the dominant social values on potential strikers appears to be weakening; since the statistics suggest that a growing proportion of employees are willing to discard their industrial virginity and turn to strike action as a solution to their grievances; so the effect of such experience on attitudes prevalent among workpeople is likely to extend.

For strikers, clearly, it is not strikes which are the 'problem'. The actions of management which violate their expectations; the features of the employment relationship which degrade and oppress them, generating deprivations and conflicts; the social values which deny the legitimacy of their struggle to defend or improve their conditions; these are the real strike problems for the actual striker. And most of all, attempts to put legal shackles on workers' freedom to withdraw

their labour create an intense and urgent 'problem': 'the strike is
strike is Labour's expression of free will; surrender that, and the
worker becomes the merest wage-slave' (Cole, 1913: 319). For those
who are concerned with human freedom, this is today's most burning
strike problem.

Alternative solutions

If the nature of the strike problem varies according to the perspective
from which it is viewed, so necessarily does the appropriate solution.
From the managerial viewpoint analysed above, such a solution is
increasingly urgent. And given the convergence of the economic
interests of the employers and the state, the same is true of the
government also.

The managerial response may take either of two forms. The first
is the method of outright coercion. As was seen earlier, the
government has on various occasions offered obstinate resistance to
unions representing its own employees – often with strong
encouragement from industrialists and the press. But the
government's writ does not extend to the private sector; and car
manufacturers, for example, have felt obliged to adopt a more
compromising stance – despite ministerial exhortation to 'stand firm'
– when faced by determined action from their own workers. So
government policy has extended to a more generally coercive strategy.
The deliberate creation of mass unemployment – which rose steadily
through the 1970s and escalated after 1980 – is one aspect of this
approach. This partly explains the fall in the number of strikes from
the peak in 1970 (though their average size and duration has
increased). Yet a policy of mass unemployment while eventually
reducing union bargaining power, obviously conflicts with the
objective of economic growth.

Hence the use of penal sanctions against strikers has become
peculiarly attractive to managerial interests. Such bodies as the
Confederation of British Industry and the Engineering Employers'
Federation urged this course on the Donovan Commission While the
latter was unpersuaded, both Labour and Conservative governments
proved more amenable, and the Industrial Relations Act is the result.
Yet as Donovan recognized, the prospects of success for a policy of

legal coercion are somewhat doubtful. Sanctions may be directed against trade unions; but since these are so detached from shop-floor industrial relations such sanctions will be largely irrelevant. They may be directed against shop stewards; but since these are rarely the agitators of popular imagination, this may if anything increase conflict. They may be directed against strikers as a whole; but British gaols are already too overcrowded to make such a deterrent credible. Certainly most employers, when confronted by a strike, will be more concerned to negotiate a resumption of production than to compound the conflict by dragging employees before the courts. It is possible that the mere existence of anti-strike legislation may intimidate potential strikers; but given the largely spontaneous origins of most stoppages, this effect will probably be limited. And in any case, while action against strikes is pursued as a means of securing a more compliant labour force, it is more likely to create a body of resentful employees whose resentments are expressed in less overt and less manageable forms of conflict.

The alternative managerial solution is that of manipulation. One example of this strategy goes by the name of 'incomes policy', an increasingly popular device in recent years. Great efforts are devoted to persuading trade unionists to acquiesce in self-emasculation, by agreeing to negotiate pay increases only within rigid limits, or by tying higher wages and salaries to increased 'productivity'. Within the perspective of the ruling ideology, such a policy is manifestly 'fair', since if trade unions hold back 'excessive' pay claims the employers express their readiness to hold back price increases. But any 'incomes policy' of this sort means, at best, that the relative shares of rich and poor – labour and capital – will be frozen; that the privileged position of the wealthy minority will be consolidated; and, if the 'productivity' criterion is rigorously enforced, that workers will have to pay for their own pay improvements through more dehumanizing conditions of labour. Not surprisingly, experience appears to have left many trade unionists unwilling to co-operate in any future exercise of this nature.

There are, however, other possibilities of manipulation. At the level of the individual firm, managerial policy can be adjusted along the lines recommended by human relations theorists or by subsequent breeds of industrial sociologists. At a different level, the type of proposals put forward by Donovan can be adopted: the reform of bargaining procedures, the formalization of industrial relations at factory or company level, the incorporation of shop-floor bargainers within the official institutions of trade unionism. Such a strategy will have genuine pay-offs: undeniably, some strikes are attributable to managerial incompetence, chaotic pay structures, or procedural inadequacies, and such causes are remediable. No doubt the integrating pressures on shop stewards can be stepped up to some effect. Yet as was seen in Chapter 4, there are limits to the extent to which conflict can be institutionalized and workers' representatives incorporated, without other types of action emerging. Moreover there are increasing signs of resistance from within the trade union movement itself to a policy of 'reforms' designed to intensify managerial control over trade unionists.

It is in any case central to the argument of this book that conflict is generated by the basic structure of industry in our society. If this is so, strikes are unlikely to yield substantially either to manipulation or to legislation. The example of West Germany – often presented as a case of model industrial relations – is illuminating. Free trade unions were smashed by the Nazis and replaced by authoritarian control of labour relations by managements and the state. With the tradition of independent worker organization destroyed, it was possible in the post-war period to establish a system of industrial relations deliberately designed to minimize overt conflict; and until very recently at least, West Germany has had by far the lowest strike figures in any major Western industrial nation. Yet the implications have been clearly stated by an eminent German sociologist: 'the translation of a collective situation into a mass of individual reactions'.

We find instead of work disputes, individual actions whose connection with social conflicts is barely recognizable at first sight. Sinking work morale, growing fluctuation, indeed even sickness and accident rates may be indicators of such redirections of industrial conflict. In these manifestations, the redirection of conflict . . . approaches repression of its energies. Some of the workers . . . display an attitude of almost hopeless resentment; this may become manifest unannounced and in ways removed from all chance of control (Dahrendorf, 1968: 178).

In the state capitalist societies of Eastern Europe, where the totalitarian control of a bureaucratic ruling class is used to suppress strikes, there is evidence of a similar redirection of conflict. In Britain today there is little chance that open industrial conflict could be prevented in this way; but if it were, the same result could be predicted: the expression of workers' grievances in less organized and less manageable forms. To this extent management's strike problem, however urgent, can never be satisfactorily resolved.

But equally, the problem as it confronts trade unionists cannot be resolved, so long as their definition of the causes of their grievances and their selection of responses remain at the present level of rationality. The argument of Engels nearly a century ago remains true still: 'the British labour movement is today and for many years has been working in a narrow circle of strikes for higher wages and shorter hours without finding a solution' (letter to Bernstein, 17 June 1879). Grievances are channelled through collective bargaining into demands which accept the legitimacy of the employment relationship and the status of labour as a commodity; discontent at managerial domination, which seems to underlie many disputes, is thus kept below the surface. This sublimation of workers' resistance to coercive control is, indeed, the most fundamental and persistent indication of the institutionalization of industrial conflict. So long as strikes are directed against the immediate manifestations of workers' deprivations, rather than their underlying causes, strikers will achieve only temporary relief; and they must expect to attract increasing social hostility and recurrent efforts at repression.

For the striker, then, the only real solution to the strike problem lies in a transformation of the status of labour and the whole structure of control in industry: replacing minority domination and the pursuit of profit by democratic control and the satisfaction of human needs. (By abolishing management in its present form this will, of course, also provide a radical solution to *management's* strike problem!) As was argued in the last chapter, the idea that strike activity might lead spontaneously to such a social transformation seems utopian. This is particularly true because the increasing intervention of the state on the side of employers in industrial relations means that the traditional trade union segregation of 'industrial' from 'political' activities has become largely meaningless. Every important trade union struggle over wages or conditions has today a political dimension, since it impinges directly on government economic strategy. And quite clearly, any attempt to change the organization and direction of individual enterprises or the economy as a whole would represent a highly political act – which would presuppose consciously articulated political aspirations on the part of working people.

Is such politicization of industrial conflict a serious possibility? It is important to remember that industrial disputes are only one aspect of contemporary resistance to the goals and structure of the political economy of modern capitalism. Recent years have seen the widespread questioning of all forms of established authority, a growing disillusionment with the charade of formal party politics, an increasingly articulate concern at the depredations which technology, directed only by the dictates of profit, inflicts upon the 'quality of life'. Such challenges to the logic of contemporary capitalist society have so far been isolated from the collective actions of industrial workers; so too have such movements as women's liberation, the struggle against racism, student activism, or the revolt of depressed regions. But should such movements intermesh, and should broader political questions spill over into the consciousness of workers *in their industrial actions*, the basis would exist for explicit and comprehensive demands for the democratization of industry and society as a whole.

There are already indications of such a development. Theories of workers' control, almost defunct for half a century, have in the last few years been revived and elaborated to meet the conditions of large-scale, technically sophisticated industry. In this process a small but increasing number of active trade unionists have played an important part. This is no intellectual accident: the growing demand for workers' control is a natural response to the problems which technological development, in the context of a capitalist economy, creates for organized workers. Ideas of industrial democracy articulate the experiences and aspirations which, in however confused and distorted a form, may be seen as underlying workers' day-to-day struggles on the shop floor. As Raymond Williams has argued:

> What is now called Luddism, or wildcat militancy, is very often, at root, a fight . . . to use the machines, rather than to be used by them; to impose a new social organization, where decisions are

made by the men actually doing the work, as against an old organization in which decisions are invariably made elsewhere; to learn, if only in the first instance by the co-operative revolts that we call strikes, the means of a new human order (1968: 297).

It should be clear that unless the educative potential of workers' struggles is realized – unless the demand for control becomes increasingly explicit – the efforts of managements and strikers to resolve their respective strike problems will continue to be mutually neutralizing. Disputes like that described at the opening of this book will remain a central feature of industrial relations. Managements will fail to suppress the often violent expression of workers' collective experience of deprivation. Workers will still be confronted by the *temporary* nature of whatever victories they achieve, and will continue to *react* to situations rather than exercising positive control over their industrial destinies. The crucial, and necessarily open question is whether workers themselves, in the course of their sectional conflicts, will succeed in transcending the conventional definitions of their own activity and of the industrial system which underlies it, and will thus raise their struggles to a new level of rationality. If this book has indicated the possibility of a more adequate interpretation of strikes than that popularly accepted – by showing how industrial conflict is inherent in the structure of capitalism – it may have contributed something to such a heightening of consciousness.

7. Strikes in the 1980s – and Beyond

The aim of this book has been, first and foremost, to assist the sociological understanding of industrial relations and in particular of industrial conflict. A major focus of analysis has been the antagonistic relationship between labour and capital: between workers of every kind (manual, technical, clerical) on the one hand, the employers and their agents who seek to control their work activities on the other, and the social and economic system which structures the world of work. A basic argument has been the *dialectical* character of industrial relations. What occurs is not simply the mechanical outcome of large-scale social forces, and can be understood only by reference to the perceptions, intentions and strategies of the men and women involved. Yet at the same time, people's consciousness and wills are the product of material social conditions, and these conditions set limits to what can be achieved through individual or collective action.

Because the main focus is on relations of employment which are general in character, the book's analysis should be of relevance wherever a capitalist structure of employment operates. In this sense it is of secondary importance that much of the book's discussion refers to industrial relations in Britain in the early 1970s; if valid, the argument should apply equally at other times and in other places. But since this book is designed to be of use to students of current British industrial relations, the changes since the first edition appeared have been so significant as to require explicit discussion and evaluation. In the following pages I will undertake two tasks: to take account of analytical advances (and my own intellectual development) during the past dozen years; and to provide a more extended perspective on the course of industrial struggle in post-war Britain.

Change and continuity in sociological analysis

Sociology is, above all else, an attempt to comprehend relations and interconnections. 'People make their own history,' wrote Marx, 'but they do not make it just as they please; they do not make it under circumstances chosen by themselves, but under circumstances directly encountered, given and transmitted from the past.' Throughout this book (particularly in Chapters 3 and 5) there have been frequent references to the tension within sociology between accounts which stress the determinant operation of objective forces, and those which focus on subjective meanings and motives. This tension all too easily results in the separation of two distinct sociologies: a sociology of structure and a sociology of action. But such fission is highly dangerous, for both levels of analysis are essential for understanding. Social structures contain and condition human action; but human action itself constitutes and in some circumstances transforms social structures. It is the reciprocal conditioning of structure and action which is – or should be – sociology's central focus.

This book was written at the moment of disintegration of the structural-functionalist orthodoxy which had dominated post-war sociology. This approach had *reified* social structure, treating abstract categories rather than real people as the active forces in social existence; it had viewed society as a harmoniously integrated organism; and its model of social life was timeless and static rather than historically evolving. By the late 1960s the obtrusive reality of wide-ranging social conflicts (particularly in the USA, the heartland of academic sociology), the evident fragility of the post-war world economic order, and the experience of revolutionary struggles in the Third World, robbed this orthodoxy of whatever plausibility it may once have held. A multiplicity of exotic 'sociologies' blossomed in its place.

The crass inadequacy of structural-functionalism requires no emphasis today. Rather, it is necessary to stress that the old orthodoxy did correctly identify as an object of analysis the structural regularities of social life; the systemic interconnections of different milieux and different spheres of activity; the patterns and principles which, though themselves the complex cumulative product of human action, nevertheless often transcend people's awareness and understanding and frustrate their projects and intentions. In rejecting structural-functionalism, many sociologists rejected the very notion of structure. Thus there arose various schools of phenomenological sociology preoccupied with subjective meanings and interpersonal relations in everyday life: intricately analysing a world untroubled by wars or famine, judges or politicians, banks or multinational corporations.

Other 'radical' sociologists did seek to relate their analyses to urgent national and global issues; but in rejecting the functionalist model of a beneficently integrated social system they all too easily reduced the idea of structure to the power and interests of privileged individuals and groups. They explained how NATO generals, corporate bosses, top civil servants and politicians, newspaper proprietors and others of their ilk dominated the running of society and benefited greatly from their dominance. Such analyses – often developed in painstaking detail – were not so much inaccurate as inadequate. They seemed to imply that at the top of society was an élite that *could* make their own history just as they pleased. Yet many studies of top decision-makers suggest that the perceived options open to them are often very limited indeed; that the strategies and policies of the economically, politically and militarily powerful are far from a closely integrated, conspiratorial unity; and that many key events are nowhere willed and initiated in the form in which they occur.

The question remained: what explained the course of a historical process seemingly recalcitrant to the direction even of the powerful? Marx's original analysis of the 'external coercive laws' of capitalist production was addressed to precisely this problem. What Marx produced was however a largely abstract model of the contradictory dynamics of a pure capitalist economy; his theories were not systematically adapted to the more complex realities of existing economies, nor was he able to explore in general terms the patterns of interconnection between relations of production and social life more broadly. Elaborating on Marxian political economy, and adequately integrating the changes in capitalist societies in the century since Marx's death, are tasks on which much has indeed been accomplished; but the controversies, uncertainties and silences remain intimidating. Unfortunately the most confident and influential Marxist attempts at general social theory during the 1970s, the structuralism of such French writers as Althusser, replicated many of the deviations of structural-functionalist sociology. Its reification of conceptual abstractions, the mechanical determinism of its analysis, even its predilection for pretentious jargon, all constituted a rigorously dehumanized vision of society. And this in turn stimulated the development of various forms of 'humanistic' Marxism in which creativity and agency were stressed and attention to structure largely evaporated.

The previous chapters must therefore be viewed in the context of their production. The emphasis is more on action and initiative than on structure and constraint. Some critics (particularly those whose political dispositions differ from my own) have argued that the whole analysis betrays a romantic exaggeration of rank-and-file militancy. Both on the general issue of subjective initiative as against structural determinacy, and on the specific question of 'rank-and-filism', I regard my treatment above as more balanced and more nuanced than some critics have implied; the changes I might make today would be primarily ones of emphasis. A more profound criticism would be that while I stress the need to integrate distinct levels of analysis, to relate action and structure, to take account of the scope for creativity which results from the contradictory character of social forces, it is not rigorously demonstrated how this can be done. The call at the conclusion of Chapter 3 for a dialectical approach may be considered an evasion (Edwards, 1979: 212): 'although the notion of dialectics is intuitively appealing, it is unclear what it involves in practice'. The answer is surely that imprecision is inherent in social reality itself: if the historical process reflects reciprocal conditioning rather than unilinear determination, contradiction rather than systemic integration, what happens is unpredictable before the event and only partially explicable afterwards. This is certainly the case when one considers the trends in British strikes over the past dozen years.

Beyond 'industrial conflict'

At the end of Chapter 4 the question is raised: why are there so *few* strikes, given the existence of so many cogent reasons for striking? A recent Department of Employment analysis of manufacturing plants in the early 1970s (Smith *et al.*, 1978) concluded that only 5 per cent experienced a strike during a three-year period when aggregate strike activity was high; in any single year, only 2 per cent were affected. This finding has been questioned (Kelly and Nicholson, 1980; Edwards, 1983) since there is evidence that only a minority even of those strikes which meet the official criteria are included in the statistics. Yet even allowing for unreported stoppages, it is still the case that most workers strike rarely if at all.

Part of the explanation is that there exist other forms of collective action at workers' disposal: what in Chapter 3 were termed 'cut-price sanctions'. Clegg (1979: 258) has recently commented that 'there can be little doubt that the overtime ban is now the most common form of industrial action'; and Edwards (1983: 229) has added that 'non-strike sanctions are a popular form of pressure, for their deployment can be varied to meet tactical needs and can put pressure on management while involving few costs for workers'. But he goes on to insist that 'their use is far from universal'.

It was suggested previously (page 56 above) that discontent and even resistance can be expressed in the form of 'unorganized conflict' which is not explicitly pursued as a sanction against the employer. There are however problems with this line of argument. Certainly considerable evidence exists that the suppression of open forms of collective struggle – through legal curbs, management repression, or fear of unemployment – often results in increased absenteeism and labour turnover. But firms and industries with high absence and turnover rates may also be relatively strike-prone – without workers' conditions being evidently worse than in far more quiescent areas of employment.

In fact the very concept of 'unorganized conflict' is defective. First, the 'organized'/'unorganized' distinction conflates a range of separate factors: overt and covert action, collective and individual, planned and spontaneous, oriented to collective bargaining and serving other purposes. The simple dichotomy seriously oversimplifies the complex issues which are discussed in Chapter 5. A further problem is that the underlying notion of 'industrial conflict' is analytically unsatisfactory (see Hyman, 1982). The various types of action or behaviour typically included under this label have little obviously in common beyond one fact: they all represent 'labour problems' for managements by interfering with the goals of control, productivity and profitability. In other words, the concerns of industrial sociologists who employ the notion of industrial conflict typically reflect a *managerial* definition of problems. 'Industrial conflict' is something done by workers which inconveniences employers. . . . Consider the quotation from Kerr on page 56. It would seem odd to read an academic discussion which noted that as well as the lock-out, conflict with the *employee* can take the form of plant closure, sackings, victimization, blacklisting, speed-up, safety hazards, arbitrary discipline and so on. The routine practices of employers do not *count* as 'industrial conflict'; they are part of the normal, repressive reality of work.

Making 'industrial conflict' the object of inquiry – or, one might add, taking a narrow view of strikes as discrete incidents in the conduct of industrial relations – is also unhelpful if it suggests that what is at issue is a discontinuous set of individual events, each with a clear point of commencement and termination. For to explain convincingly why there are so few strikes, or why disputes occur when and where they do, it is important to regard them not merely as incidents of industrial relations but as part of a continuum of practices and relationships inherent in any work situation. As Edwards comments (1982: 229): 'in explaining why strikes, as well as non-strike sanctions, emerge in some situations and not in others it is essential to have some understanding of the broad pattern of workplace relations'. His own empirical research (Edwards and Scullion, 1982) offers important insight into the ways in which the patterns of workers' relationships with each other and with management can assist or obstruct an awareness of collective grievance and its expression in different forms of action. Similarly, the studies of Burawoy (1979) have indicated how 'relations in production' can at times encourage, but far more typically inhibit, resistance to the employer.

It is now generally recognized by sociologists of industry that an understanding of the *labour process* is essential in order to make sense of the trends in work-centred relationships and the dynamics of collective bargaining. (For a useful survey of recent literature on this theme see Thompson, 1983.) The capitalist labour process is at one and the same time a co-operative and a conflictual activity. The diverse activities which are fragmented by the capitalist division of labour must be re-integrated; different phases of the production cycle must be co-ordinated; machines appropriate for the various operations must be procured and maintained in working order; materials and components must be available at the correct time and place; finished products must be despatched. In a society which divides and confines workers' understanding of the overall process of production, a privileged and hierarchical stratum of management performs an indispensable productive function. Yet at the same time, management's role as servants of accumulation means that there is a constant drive to reduce labour costs, to intensify the pressure of work, to render existing workers 'redundant'. And a notable feature of the past decade has been how far the same principles of economizing characteristic of private industry have been extended to public employment, subordinating notions of public service to the dictates of capitalist accountancy.

The contradictory position of management – co-ordinator of a complex and often baffling productive operation, yet at the same time a vehicle of discipline, control, and often disruptive pressure – evokes contradictory responses. The pattern of strikes must be understood against this background. How far in any situation the conflictual or the co-operative aspects of management-worker relations are seen as predominant is inevitably affected by a dense network of unique and detailed relationships. Perceptions of management control as legitimate or illegitimate, reasonable or unreasonable, technically necessary or arbitrary, develop in a continuous process of experience and adaptation. This process is strongly influenced by the fact that people who work together – whether as equals or as superiors and subordinates – naturally attempt, if only to make life easier for themselves, to minimize unpleasantness and aggravation. Typically there occurs a process which some sociologists have termed the 'negotiation of order';

whether or not a workplace is unionized, working relationships involve a large amount of give-and-take, of tacit informal bargaining, which normally smooths the rough edges of management discipline and control (Hyman, 1980). If such a relationship exists a strike may be unlikely to occur unless managers are unusually inept, bloody-minded, or responding to disruptive external pressures (which are indeed inherent in capitalist production). Just as any adequate sociology must comprehend both structural constraints and forces *and* purposeful initiative, so any adequate analysis of strikes must take account of the general dynamics of capitalist production but also the specific patterns of relations in the immediate work situation through which these are necessarily mediated.

The social organization of collective struggle

In Chapter 3, it will be recalled, the popular view of industrial conflict as the work of 'agitators' was examined and found unconvincing. This interpretation presupposes that ordinary strikers lack serious grievances of their own and must therefore be manipulated by 'tightly knit groups of politically motivated men'; if it is accepted that workers can strike for rational purposes then there is no need to seek an explanation for their action in terms of sinister manipulative agents. Nevertheless it has also been seen that stoppages do not normally occur totally spontaneously: some form of initiative and organization is normally required before men and women act collectively. The larger the scale of an industrial dispute, the greater is usually the need for leadership to focus the workers' varied grievances upon common objectives and to ensure united action; and this may often involve a protracted process of communication and argument to overcome possible doubts and reinforce the workers' determination (Batstone *et al.*, 1977 and 1978). In some cases this leadership is provided by full-time union officials; in others it devolves upon shop stewards and other 'unofficial' activists. Thus the extent of the strikes against the Industrial Relations Act owed much to the influence of politically conscious activists, who readily appreciated the dangers contained in the legislation and could communicate their understanding to fellow-workers. The campaign for 'parity' in lower-paid car factories owed much to the arguments of stewards with a detailed knowledge of earnings levels elsewhere. In many public sector unions, rank-and-file pressure for a more militant official line could not easily have succeeded without some *generalization* of the localized discontents of disparate groups of members; in the absence of official sponsorship this has at times required resources of communication and co-ordination which are most readily available to activists attached to a political grouping.

More generally it can be argued that *successful* struggle, particularly if confronting an employer possessing skill and sophistication, requires an appreciation of strategy and tactics which is normally acquired only through experience. Strikers are more likely to win – and will thus be more disposed to repeat the exercise – if they can draw on the accrued experience of the wider union movement. Not surprisingly, then, those whose background and commitment involve special familiarity with the organization of struggle are most likely to provide leadership and co-ordination when workers' discontents erupt into open conflict. This is indeed the single grain of truth in the 'agitator' thesis: industrial conflict occurs only where real grievances exist, but to take an organized form it may require the articulation of trade union activists whose commitment to unionism often stems partly from their political awareness.

Yet the notion of 'agitation' is so wide of the mark because those who articulate in organized collective form the diverse and perhaps inchoate grievances of an employee group may as often restrain as encourage militancy. This tendency was noted in Chapter 4 in the discussion of trade union leadership. However, the reference there to 'goal displacement' (pages 84–5) is not altogether satisfactory, in that it follows Michels in attributing the conservative tendencies within unionism primarily to *internal* organizational dynamics. This diverts attention from the potent *external* forces which lead union representatives to moderate both aims and methods. As I have argued elsewhere (1975: 89), the often overriding concern to maintain stable bargaining relationships and a legitimate status within capitalist society 'should be interpreted as an *accommodation to external power*'. The negotiation of order which occurs in unions' relations with employers and the state, as well as that involved in the informal relationships at workplace level, requires that both unions and the workers they represent should 'know their place'. The game of give-

and-take must remain essentially one-sided, or those who set the rules will no longer be prepared to play. Demands or action which go 'too far' would put at risk trade unions' acceptability to those whose displeasure can have dire effects. If such considerations particularly influence the central leaders of the movement, they are nevertheless important also at the level of 'unofficial' activists and representatives; we may recall the Donovan view of the shop steward as 'more of a lubricant than an irritant'. Certainly this verdict remains relevant today; indeed it can be argued that the increasing integration of shop steward organization within the formal institutions of industrial relations in the 1970s has been one cause of the recent dampening of collective struggle (Hyman, 1979).

To bring together these brief comments on the analysis of strikes: any theory or explanation of variations between different contexts, of secular trends, or of short-term fluctuations needs to take account of three distinct levels of social reality and the interconnections between them. The first encompasses the material factors which can serve as both provocations and resources for strike action: the physical situation of workers within production and in their wider circumstances, the patterns of management-worker relations, the nature of the employing organization and its setting in the broader political and economic system. The second involves the representation of this material situation (and hence its actual or potential transformation) through subjective consciousness: the strength and boundaries of collective identity, the salience of grievances, the perception of opportunities for remedy. Such issues were central to the discussion in Chapter 5. The third comprises the mediating activities of leaders and representatives: those whose official and unofficial influence helps collectivize workers' discrete experiences and aspirations, in forms which may either encourage or discourage assertiveness and struggle. The social relationships involved at all three levels are in large measure conditioned by structural forces; yet their complex and contradictory interconnections always contain space for unpredictability and initiative.

Recent trends in British strikes

The major changes in recorded strikes since the main text was written may be briefly summarized. The official records show the total number rising to an unprecedented peak of 3,906 in 1970; then declining, but for the next decade fluctuating around an average somewhat higher than in the 1960s. Desite the rising level of unemployment – historically associated with a sharp decline in the number of stoppages – in no year did the total fall below 2,000. But from 1980 the figure tumbled, the total for 1985 being the lowest since 1938. Since the late 1960s the number of workers involved has in almost every year been well above the average for the two previous decades. And the number of striker-days rose even more dramatically above the post-war norm, with peaks in 1972, 1979 and 1984 – the highest figures since 1926.

Secondly, official trade union involvement in disputes has become far more intimate than in the 1960s. The Donovan Report, it will be recalled, diagnosed a lack of articulation between what it called the 'two systems' of British industrial relations; and the present study also emphasizes (though in very different terms) the detachment between the official hierarchies of trade unionism and the majority of stoppages. Numerically most strikes still begin and end independently of the machinery of trade unionism outside the workplace; but the number of disputes in which outside union committees and officials are implicated has increased considerably, and it is strikes of this kind which have been of key political and economic significance in recent years.

A third development of vital importance is the changing role of the state in British industrial relations, and the impact of this role on the nature of conflict in industry. Government ministers, the courts and various statutory agencies have become far more actively and overtly implicated in the field of labour relations than ever before in peacetime. The distinction between 'industrial' and 'political' issues, always artificial and misleading, has in the process become increasingly unconvincing; and strikers themselves have on occasion viewed their actions in a far more directly 'political' light than in the past.

All these tendencies (some of which were apparent though less prominent in the 1960s, and have been noted in the preceding text) are interrelated. As is shown in the following pages, they stem partly from the developments affecting the whole capitalist world, partly from factors peculiar to the British context. Their cumulative effect has been to make it even less possible than previously to treat strikes as an isolated social phenomenon: they can only be understood within a broader political economy of industrial relations.

Statistical patterns

Table 2.1 (page 28) has been updated to take account of officially recorded strikes up to 1983. The number of stoppages reached an all-time peak of almost four thousand in 1970, and has since fluctuated around an average similar to that of the 1960s. Striker-days have oscillated considerably from year to year, but the average has been far higher than the post-war norm. Only once between 1933 and 1968 were over 6 million striker-days recorded (in 1957); this total was exceeded in every year between 1969 and 1975, and again in 1977 to 1980. The average size of strikes – involving roughly 500 workers – has increased marginally since the 1960s. In the 1970s the average length rose markedly: normally somewhat over three days for most of the post-war period, the figure was above four days in every year since 1969 – often substantially so – with a peak of fourteen days in 1972, and again in 1980. But since then the average duration has fallen sharply.

It is important to bear in mind an earlier caution: averages can be misleading, the figures in some years being dominated by a few exceptional stoppages. Recent trends in the size and length of strikes can be deduced with more confidence from Table 7.1. Throughout the period covered by the table, roughly half the recorded strikes have been of medium size, involving between 50 and 500 workers; it is not therefore surprising that the average size has remained stable. In the late 1960s there was however a modest but distinct decline in the proportion of stoppages involving less than 50 workers, and a similar increase in those involving over 500. The trend in duration was far more clear-cut: the proportion lasting less than one day was roughly halved in the ten years following the mid–1970s, while the proportion lasting over a week (i.e. five working days) more than doubled. But more recently the proportion of short strikes has returned to its previous level, while long strikes have declined in parallel.

Table 7.1
Percentage breakdown of British strikes by size and length, 1965–87

	Workers involved			Duration in days		
	Under 50	50–500	Over 500	Under 1	1–5	Over 5
1965	38·2	48·8	13·0	34·3	47·8	17·9
1966	42·2	45·0	12·8	33·3	52·6	14·1
1967	36·1	48·8	15·1	29·1	50·5	20·4
1968	31·6	53·1	15·3	28·6	46·4	25·0
1969	28·4	52·7	18·9	29·9	46·4	23·7
1970	29·1	53·8	17·1	24·6	45·4	30·0
1971	32·9	50·8	16·3	21·3	46·3	32·4
1972	29·9	51·5	18·6	22·7	39·2	38·1
1973	30·3	52·9	16·8	19·7	46·3	34·0
1974	29·7	53·0	17·3	14·9	43·9	41·2
1975	31·4	53·6	15·0	17·5	38·4	44·1
1976	34·9	51·1	14·0	19·7	43·3	37·0
1977	28·5	55·6	15·9	17·1	40·4	42·5
1978	29·2	55·1	15·7	18·1	40·9	41·0
1979	29·8	52·1	18·1	19·8	36·9	43·3
1980	34·1	49·1	16·8	26·8	38·8	34·4
1981	30·5	49·4	20·1	31·0	37·1	31·9
1982	34·1	47·6	18·3	37·0	33·4	29·6
1983	37·4	46·7	15·9	34·5	33·5	32·0
1984	24·6	52·4	23·0	29·6	36·1	34·3
1985	25·6	54·2	20·3	36·3	32·6	31·1
1986	32·3	48·9	18·9	48·6	29·3	22·2
1987	30·8	50·5	18·7	43·3	33·8	22·9

Source: Employment Gazette.

It follows that the increase in striker-days in the 1970s reflected a shift in the character of strikes in general, and not merely the impact of one or two massive stoppages such as the miners' strikes of 1972 and 1974. One aspect of this shift is indicated by the incidence of major disputes involving over 50,000 striker-days. Such strikes were rare during the first two post-war decades, occurring on average only five or six times a year in the 1950s and much of the 1960s. But in the years 1969–79 there were over 260 stoppages of this magnitude – a more than fourfold increase in annual incidence.

Despite these considerable changes in the overall statistics of strikes, their industrial distribution has altered little – with one exception. Table 2.2 (page 31) shows trends since the 1960s. The highest number of strikes in relation to size of labour force was recorded by the same five main industry groups: docks, coal-mining, motor vehicles, shipbuilding, and iron and steel. The trend towards a broader industrial distribution of strikes (see page 32) has continued. Excluding mining from consideration, the five industries with the greatest number of recorded stoppages – which until the mid-1960s accounted for the majority of disputes – averaged roughly 45 per cent in the 1970s, and only 40 per cent in the early 1980s.

The major exception to the record of gradual change has been coal-mining. As was seen earlier (page 32) there was a massive decline in the number of mining stoppages after the mid-1960s, but the national disputes of 1972 and 1974 brought the industry to the top of the league table for striker-days. Table 7.2 illustrates these changes, but also shows that more recently the pattern has altered

Table 7.2
Strikes and striker-days in coal-mining: annual averages 1948–87

	Number	% of total	Striker-days ('000)	% of total
1948–52	1,026	64·5	288	10·1
1953–57	1,771	75·9	598	15·8
1958–62	1,520	62·7	470	11·4
1963–67	746	33·6	253	10·4
1968–72	185	6·5	2,608	21·7
1973–77	240	9·4	1,185	15·0
1978–82	329	18·8	214	1·8
1983	355	26·2	484	12·9
1984	79	6·5	22,483	82·2
1985	160	17·7	4,142	64·7
1986	351	32·7	143	7·4
1987	296	20·9	217	6·1

Source: Employment Gazette.

once again. Since the introduction of pit-based incentives in 1977 (see Handy, 1981) there has been a revival of short local disputes, followed in 1984–5 by the most protracted national struggle in the industry's history. Though the industry no longer dominates the national total of strikes as it did in the 1950s (when the mining labour force was far larger than today), it still provided almost a third of all recorded stoppages in 1986.

One final aspect of recent British strikes deserves mention: the official classification of their 'causes'. It was argued in Chapter 5 that any assessment of strike causes – or even, using the more judicious wording of the official statisticians, of the 'reasons given' – can involve misleading oversimplification. This is evident from the treatment of the national engineering dispute of 1979, when a series of one- and two-day stoppages produced 16 million of the year's record total of striker-days. According to the Department of Employment the principal issue was a pay increase; but of the package of demands submitted by the unions the most contentious, and the reason for the struggle's significance for British industrial relations more generally, was the attempt to reduce the working week to 35 hours. Hence the need for caution in the use of official statistics is obvious. Nevertheless it is interesting to examine the pattern set out in Table 7.3, showing the distribution of stoppages between those centring on pay questions and other issues. It was noted earlier (pages 120–2) that some analysts discerned a trend away from wage-centred strikes in the 1950s and early 1960s – though they tended to neglect the special features of coal-mining disputes in this period. Since 1968 the majority of strikes (according to the official classifiers) has in every year primarily involved questions of pay, and these disputes have accounted for over five-sixths of total striker-days. A notable feature of the period since 1967 is the stability in the incidence of stoppages primarily involving questions *other* than wages and salaries, ranging between 542 and 1,411 a year. Striker-days fluctuated more, but still within a relatively narrow gauge. (It is worth commenting that in 1969, when very high striker-days in non-wage disputes were recorded, the two largest such stoppages both arose in the context of national negotiations involving 'packages' of pay and other conditions.) Pay disputes have proved far more volatile in both incidence and severity.

Indeed these account for virtually all the fluctuations in the overall statistics in recent years – with the crucial exception of the 1984–5 strike against pit closures, which dominated the annual figures.

Before seeking to interpret these developments, it is interesting to compare British experience with that in other countries. Table 4.1 (page 88) gave gross statistics of disputes in fifteen countries, indicating that all had been affected by a 'strike explosion' in the early 1970s. To bring out the significance of these trends it is necessary to relate the gross statistics to the size of the labour force in each country. The Donovan Report, as was seen in Chapter 2, used data from sixteen countries to argue that the relative number of stoppages in the United Kingdom was above that in most other

Table 7.3
'Causes' of strikes: pay and other items, 1967–87

| | Strikes | | Striker-days ('000) | |
	Pay	Other	Pay	Other
1967	992	1,124	1,660	1,123
1968	1,283	1,095	3,636	1,083
1969	1,850	1,366	4,113	2,812
1970	2,510	1,396	9,277	1,631
1971	1,177	1,051	12,306	1,283
1972	1,481	1,016	21,679	2,244
1973	1,462	1,411	5,147	1,998
1974	1,922	1,000	13,109	1,536
1975	1,318	964	4,448	1,466
1976	875	1,141	1,831	1,678
1977	1,558	1,145	8,223	2,155
1978	1,510	961	7,414	1,977
1979	1,230	850	27,139	1,912
1980	634	686	10,611	1,354
1981	628	710	2,630	1,614
1982	654	874	3,498	1,778
1983	548	804	2,311	1,670
1984	543	663	2,546	28,505
1985	361	542	1,588	4,814
1986	403	671	1,128	792
1987	367	649	2,919	627

Source: Employment Gazette.

Table 7.4
International trends since Donovan

	Stoppages per 100,000 employees			Striker-days per 1,000 employees		
	1965–9	1970–4	1975–81	1965–9	1970–4	1975–81
United Kingdom	9·5	12·0	9·1	156	585	467
Australia	31·4	45·2	46·1	217	581	641
Belgium	1·9	5·1	6·9*	73	242	215*
Canada	7·6	8·8	13·8	659	773	936
Denmark	1·2	4·1	10·1	30	360	119
Finland	4·2	44·7†	103·2	84	600†	511
France	9·6‡	17·7	18·5	126‡	166	178
German Fed. Rep.		Not available		6	49	22
Ireland	10·2	15·4	17·8	543	434	791
Italy	16·3	25·6	15·9	817	1,070	1,151
Japan	3·0	6·2	4·8	68	115	64
Netherlands	0·6	0·7	0·6	5	48	22
New Zealand	12·8	30·4	39·3	103	187	323
Norway	0·4	0·8	1·3	8	52	34
Sweden	0·5	1·9	2·9	25	56	194
United States	6·4	6·7	5·6	492	531	419

* 1975–80.   † Official criteria for recording strikes changed during this period.
‡ 1968 excluded from average.

Source: International Labour Office, *Yearbook of Labour Statistics*, and *Employment Gazette*.

nations, though in terms of striker-days this country occupied a
lower position. Table 7.4 indicates subsequent trends in the countries
of the Donovan survey; the data are not directly comparable with
those in Table 2.3 (page 34) since they cover all employees, and not
merely those in manufacturing industry. (In particular it should be
noted that strikes are rare in agriculture, and that Britain has an
unusually small agricultural sector; if non-agricultural employment
alone were considered, the UK would rank lower in the 'league
tables'.) It is important to bear in mind the previous warning of the
difficulty of comparing international data of this kind: different
methods and criteria for recording disputes can distort the picture,
particularly when comparisons involve the *number* of stoppages.
Changes in official criteria can likewise distort trends over time:
such alternatives partly explain the upsurge in recorded strikes in
Finland, and are the main reason for the sharp fall in the USA.

Despite these reservations, the clear implication of Table 7.4 is
that the situation identified by Donovan has been reversed: the UK
is now near the top of the 'league table' for striker-days per employee,
but only mid-way up the table for numbers of stoppages. The table
also confirms, in different form, the conclusion drawn on page 88 –
that internationally, strike activity in the past decade has been
generally higher than in the 1960s.

Strikes, trade unions and the state

The previous chapter ended on a deliberate note of uncertainty: the
aim was to stress the contradictory character of industrial conflict at
the outset of the 1970s, and in consequence the radically different
possibilities of subsequent development. In the 1980s it is clear
that this caution was justified: for the trends in strike activity since
this book was written derive far more from the impact of external
economic and political forces than from the internal operation
of those processes conventionally (and narrowly) understood as
'industrial relations'. The sociology of industrial conflict has become –
far more than in any other period of recent British history – subsumed
within a much broader pattern of national and international
developments. It has become correspondingly important to locate

the analysis of strikes within a more general conception of political economy. Inevitably this greatly increases the complexity of any explanation – let alone prediction – of trends in industrial conflict.

What is now clear is that over the past decade there has occurred a remarkably rapid transformation in the relationship between workers, their unions, and the state; and that this is the primary explanation of the upsurge in strike activity at the beginning of the 1970s; the fluctuations of the rest of the decade; and the sharp decline in the early 1980s. Both the direction and the pace of this changing relationship have to be understood in terms of the crisis of British capitalism in this period and the implications of this crisis for collective labour organization and action. This then defines the theme of the remainder of this chapter – though it is impossible in the space available to do more than outline some of the key factors at issue.

Confrontation in the 1970s, collapse in the 1980s?

It is evident that the trends in recorded strike activity in post-war Britain have been complex and uneven: a reflection of underlying diversity and fluctuation in labour markets, the organization of the labour process, the structure of capital, and the economic role of the state.

A recent detailed study of statistical patterns up to 1973 (Durcan *et al.*, 1983) has suggested that these years represent four distinct phases. They term the period up to 1952 the 'post-war peace'. The pressures and restrictions which had created flashpoints during the war were gradually eased, there was a strong mood of joint employer-worker commitment to social and industrial reconstruction, and this ideology of harmony was buttressed by official union willingness to restrain militancy to assist the Labour government which held office until 1951. Probably also of importance at this time is what Cronin (1979: 138) has called a continuing 'depression mentality': most union activists and leaders had learned their trade unionism during the unemployment and demoralization of the 1920s and 1930s, when collective struggles were overwhelmingly defensive; they had not yet developed the ambitions to match changed economic circumstances.

It was this period directly following the end of the war which led

Ross and Hartman to propose their thesis of the 'withering away of
the strike'. But as has been seen, circumstances changed abruptly.
In Britain, Durcan *et al.* identify the years 1953–9 as the 'return of
the strike'. The number of stoppages increased, particularly in
mining; while striker-days also rose, partly because of the return for
the first time for a quarter of a century of industry-wide
confrontations. The change owed much to a growing assertiveness
from below: already by 1950, rank-and-file discontent in many
unions caused the breakdown of wage restraint. The defeat of the
Labour government removed the political framework for
collaborative industrial relations, while the surge in price levels
associated with the Korean war inevitably stimulated wage militancy.
It was in the 1950s that the 'depression mentality' finally gave way
to the expectation of regular improvements in pay and living
standards; conflict was raised to national level when the Conservative
government sought to curb public sector pay, or encouraged private
employers to resist union demands.

Durcan and his colleagues label 1960–8 the 'shop-floor revolt'.
The experience of the 1960s frames much of the analysis of
the preceding chapters: the spread of workplace bargaining, the
increasing self-confidence of shop steward organization, the rising
strike activity in virtually every industry outside coal-mining. But
large-scale stoppages remained very exceptional; and major
confrontations were further inhibited, initially at least, by official
union support for the new Labour government elected in 1964.

Finally, the authors characterize 1969–73 as the 'formal challenge'.
Large-scale and at times protracted conflicts became more common,
particularly in the public sector, often involving occupational groups
with little or no previous record of militancy. As has been seen,
disputes of this nature necessarily involved the official trade union
machinery in a manner contrasting starkly with the tradition of
largely autonomous workplace bargaining and struggle. The political
character of major conflicts was heightened by the abrasive policies
of the Heath government elected in 1970. Striker-days reached
record levels.

This periodization helps underline some of the key fluctuations
in the quarter-century before the first edition of this book appeared,
even though it is misleading to suggest that developments were so

clear-cut. The 'post-war peace' was gradually eroded, partly by pressure from below, partly by force of external circumstances. The 'shop-floor revolt' – which was itself only infrequently a conscious challenge to established institutions and practices – developed slowly and evenly, and continued to unfold into the 1970s. Rather than distinct phases, it may be more accurate to speak of overlapping and at times contradictory tendencies, each dominant to a greater or lesser degree at particular points of time.

In the decade after the conclusion of these authors' analysis, the discontinuities in strike trends have become sharper and more rapid. Again simplifying, it is possible to identify three main phases. The years of the 'social contract' – 1974–6 – saw a new attempt by a Labour government to curb the confrontation and wage militancy of the Heath era. The decisive transition came in the summer of 1975 with TUC agreement to rigid pay restraint. This phase of union-government co-operation appeared to receive significant support at workplace level, reinforced by fear of the political alternative with the emergence of an even more reactionary Conservative leadership under Thatcher.

The following three years, 1977–9, saw a revival of struggle, as many union leaders suffered a decline in real incomes while disillusionment spread at the economic and social record of the Callaghan government. New public sector conflicts were provoked, particularly with the attempt to impose remarkably parsimonious pay limits in autumn 1978 against TUC opposition.

Finally, the early 1980s may be termed the years of coercive pacification. Unemployment, which had risen for much of the period of the Labour government, actually doubled in Thatcher's first two years; the official level of 3 million which was reached in 1982 undoubtedly understated the true number of jobless. A quarter of all jobs in manufacturing have been destroyed, while public sector employment (which in the previous decade took up some of the 'slack' in the labour market) has been rigidly curbed. The economic policies which created this devastation were deliberately intended to undermine workers' collective stength and confidence, and in large measure they succeeded. This effect has been reinforced by legislation of 1980, 1982 and 1984, which imposed far more severe restrictions on strike action than was achieved by the Industrial Relations Act.

Employers, too, have exploited the new opportunities to challenge the former balance of power in industrial relations – sometimes brutally, sometimes with sophistication.

The changing context of strikes in Britain during the past decade, and in particular the evolving relationship between the state and industrial relations, is explored in more detail below.

The decline of 'free collective bargaining'

From the 1960s, government incomes policies have been a persistent feature of British industrial relations. The introduction of 'a policy for productivity, prices and incomes' was one of the commitments of the Labour government elected at the end of 1964, and was initiated within a few months. A percentage norm for pay increases was specified, to be exceeded only in a defined range of exceptional circumstances. The policy was endorsed by the TUC and CBI, and was to be observed voluntarily by the parties to pay negotiations; but it had little apparent effect as a mechanism of wage restraint. Then in 1966 the Prices and Incomes Act attached legal sanctions to a six-month pay freeze, followed by a further six months of 'severe restraint'. Subsequently the statutory powers were relaxed, though the government retained (and on occasion exercised) the right to delay the implementation of pay agreements for several months pending reference to the Prices and Incomes Board. The TUC, which 'reluctantly acquiesced' in the Prices and Incomes Act but later demanded its repeal, continued to support the principle of incomes policy. For a time it endeavoured to monitor and control the claims submitted and settlements reached by member unions. But by 1970 neither the unions nor the government gave serious attention to the incomes policy still nominally in operation.

The Conservative government elected in that year was pledged to end pay controls, and abolished the Prices and Incomes Board. But it was no less anxious than its predecessor to limit wage and salary increases by *indirect* means. (The Industrial Relations Act, which imposed severe curbs on trade union action, and monetary and fiscal policies resulting in mounting unemployment, can be seen as in part directed to this end.) Moreover, it sought to impose restraint directly on public sector employees through the so-called 'n minus 1' formula:

insisting on a lower percentage increase in each successive pay agreement. This attempt collapsed with the miners' strike in 1972, and at the end of that year a statutory pay policy was enacted. The three-stage controls lasted into 1974, involving first a total freeze and then two sets of rigid ceilings to wage and salary rises.

The cycle was repeated under the Labour government which came to office in 1974. As one of its election pledges it abolished (though not immediately) the Conservative controls and the Pay Board which had administered them; instead it was to rely on the voluntary commitment of the unions, as part of the so-called 'social contract', to 'take account of the general economic and industrial situation' and seek pay increases normally no greater than the rise in the cost of living. But ensuing wage increases were at a record level (as, indeed, was price inflation); and in the summer of 1975 the government enforced a £6 limit on pay settlements, on the proposal of the TUC itself. A year later it was replaced by a limit of 5 per cent with a £4 ceiling, again by agreement with the TUC. By 1977 most workers' earnings were falling below the rate of price increases, and opposition to the 'social contract' controls was mounting within many unions – notably the Transport and General Workers, whose conference voted against continued pay restraint despite the pleas of the general secretary. The government responded to the growing unrest (reflected in a sharp rise in strike figures) by proposing a less stringent pay limit of 10 per cent. This was not approved by the TUC, but neither was it actively opposed; and when the firemen came out on a two-month strike at the end of the year they received little real support from other unions. In the autumn of 1978 a fourth phase of restrictions was imposed; the limit of 5 per cent was well below the rate of inflation. This time opposition was more widespread, and involved major stoppages at Ford, among lorry drivers, and in the public sector – notably the health service and local government.

The collapse of the relative industrial harmony promised – and at first seemingly realized – by the 'social contract' led hostile press commentators to speak of a 'winter of discontent'. Fearful of the electoral implications of this resurgence of confrontation, the government and TUC in February 1979 agreed to a 'concordat' defining procedures for the calling of strikes, the maintenance of emergency services and the conduct of picketing. More substantively, an attempt was made to defuse the mounting anger among public employees by the appointment of a Comparability Commission the following month. Neither initiative saved Labour from heavy electoral defeat in May 1979.

As a decade earlier, the new Conservative government abandoned the formal machinery of incomes policy, and quickly abolished the Comparability Commission. But in the public sector, pay curbs became a practice even more stringent than before, with the rigid enforcement of 'cash limits'; while private employers were stridently encouraged to respond to 'market forces' and use mass unemployment as the opportunity to hold down wages. The last major struggle for a real advance was the sustained but largely unsuccessful campaign in engineering towards the end of 1979. Thereafter most disputes were defensive: against redundancies, attacks on workplace union organization, speed-up, or falling real incomes. Major instances were the national steel strike of 1980, involving almost 9 million striker-days; the long campaign of selective stoppages by civil servants the following year (1 million); the railway footplatemen's resistance to flexible rostering in 1982 (1 million) and the health service dispute the same year ($1\frac{1}{2}$ million); and the water workers in 1983 ($\frac{3}{4}$ million).

Overshadowing all these confrontations was the year-long stoppage against pit closures in 1984–5. Here the clash between opposing philosophies of work and society was starkly revealed. On the one side was a narrow pursuit of balance-sheet profitability, irrespective of *social* costs and benefits; indeed under government pressure, the Coal Board arguably embraced an even more ruthless and restrictive capitalist logic than is customary among private employers. On the other side, those miners who sustained the strike were resisting a form of economic accounting which treats not only jobs and workers, but whole communities, as disposable in the interests of short-term profit. Faced by a ruthless adversary and internally divided, the miners suffered a shattering defeat; and in few of the other major confrontations of recent years have strikers achieved more than token success. This does not necessarily mean, however, that their efforts have been futile. The fact that many workers are still willing, despite hostile circumstances, to take determined action to defend their conditions has imposed real constraints on the actions of government and employers. Without such resistance the rout could have been far worse.

Incomes policy, bargaining structure and the pattern of disputes

The discussion in this book does not give primary attention to official trade union involvement in strikes. Rather the focus has been on the great majority of disputes which 'are over before the unions which might have members involved have even heard of them' (Turner, 1969: 27). This emphasis reflects the predominant post-war pattern of stoppages, particularly in the main strike-prone industries, the major proportion having their origin in the 'informal' processes of workplace industrial relations and necessarily lacking prior official union sanction. Certainly some disputes of this kind in the 1960s were larger or more protracted than the average, and became a subject of official concern. In some cases, formal authorization was accorded retrospectively. In others, union officials attempted a role of detached neutrality. They might feel obliged 'for the record' to dissociate their organization from unconstitutional action by their members and to 'advise' a return to work; but it was uncommon for them to *instruct* members to end a strike. Such intervention was most likely to occur when, as in the motor industry, a small-scale stoppage seemed likely to lead to multiple lay-offs (evidence, perhaps, of the power of the employers' 'sympathetic lock-out').

It is still the case that 'most strikes remain extremely short and limited affairs, of significance only in the workplaces in which they occur' (Edwards, 1982: 14). In the early 1970s there was a slight rise in the proportion of stoppages 'known to be official'; but as Edwards comments, this increase was 'hardly dramatic'. Nor, in most years, has there been a significant growth in the proportion of striker-days resulting from official disputes. Nevertheless, there is reason to argue that the official institutions of trade unionism and collective bargaining have been far more closely connected with the strikes of the past decade than was previously the case. Often this has involved informal advice and guidance or tacit support without formal endorsement; at other times, explicit opposition by union leaders and executives. The official attitude to particular strikes is far more than in the past a matter of contention; as Edwards suggests (1982: 15), 'intra-union conflicts over strikes have been forced more into the open'. Again, the miners' strike was a forceful demonstration of this point: existing regional and political rivalries were further polarized over the decision not to hold a national strike ballot, and the eventual outcome was a breakaway union based on the Nottinghamshire coalfield.

To an important extent this reflects the trends indicated in Table 7.1. From the late 1960s there was some rise in the number of large-scale stoppages, and a substantial increase in the proportion of prolonged disputes; and it is precisely in such cases that strikes are likely to come to the notice of union officials and to require the enunciation of an explicit attitude, either in support or in opposition. This trend is in turn partly attributable to changes in the character of collective bargaining. The central emphasis of the Donovan Report, it will be recalled, was the lack of adequate machinery to integrate fragmented workplace bargaining with the structure of national negotiation and agreement in engineering and other manufacturing industries; its major recommendation was accordingly the formalization and centralization of domestic bargaining at plant or company level. This was to endorse a development already in process in a number of major enterprises. One of the aims of companies in pursuing productivity agreements was to eliminate a situation in which a wide range of managerial decisions (on manning levels, task allocation, workloads, production speeds, overtime working and bonus payments) was largely shaped by piecemeal accommodations with shop stewards and by the expectations and pressure tactics of a multiplicity of sectional worker groups. Radical changes to payment-by-results systems, or the complete replacement of piecework by measured daywork, were similarly designed to eliminate decentralized bargaining and facilitate managerial control. Before the Donovan Commission reported, such changes had been strongly advocated by the Prices and Incomes Board; and they were powerfully encouraged by the favourable treatment accorded to agreements of this type within the framework of Labour's incomes policy.

By the 1970s the 'reform' of collective bargaining at domestic level had been carried through extensively within many major British companies. The consequences for industrial conflict were twofold. The *introduction* of the new arrangements was a potential source of serious conflict. While some agreements of this kind were negotiated peacefully, in other cases they were imposed only against bitter shop-floor opposition. (The abolition of piecework in the motor industry provoked several such instances.) Strikes which occurred in such circumstances were typically large and protracted. In a number of cases agreements which were accepted by full-time union officials were rejected by workplace representatives, resulting in explicitly *anti*-official strikes: the unofficial action against the reorganization of dock labour in 1967 was a notable example.

The changes in bargaining structure also had *longer-term* consequences not generally anticipated. Sectional demands or grievances could less easily be resolved through an understanding with the foreman or a brief and relatively painless stoppage. Many no doubt were suppressed (or else expressed in various forms of 'unorganized' conflict); others fed into major company-wide issues, and some generated protracted collective disputes. Official union involvement became almost inevitable in such circumstances. It might be argued that the prevalence of sectional 'do-it-yourself' action on the shop floor – so universally deplored in the 1960s – was in some respects a safety-valve; and that subsequent 'reforms', shutting this off, were potentially explosive in their effects. Not surprisingly, the emergence of the large plant-wide stoppage has been seen as one of the important features of recent years, attracting the label 'post-Donovan strike' (Durcan and McCarthy, 1972).

A number of more general contextual changes have reinforced such tendencies. With the wave of mergers and take-overs in the 1960s, multi-plant (and often multi-national) companies have become increasingly central to British industry. In the past decade, in an unfavourable economic climate, their industrial relations strategies have shown a new assertiveness and sophistication. Such strategies have often involved escalating localized conflicts, playing off workers in different establishments, and provoking disputes at moments of greatest tactical advantage. In some cases, managements have tried to involve union officials in their dealings with a militant workforce. In others, unions have recognized a need for co-ordination to match the concerted strategies of employers. At least potentially, small-scale disputes are seen to hold large-scale implications.

Official union policy has also become of new importance because of the unfavourable economic and political circumstances of the new decade. Deliberately created mass unemployment and anti-union laws are clearly designed to inhibit strikes and to ensure that those which do occur are likely to end in defeat. Another of the early actions of the Thatcher government was to end the speedy payment of tax rebates to strikers and to reduce supplementary benefit entitlements for their dependants. To sustain a strike for anything more than a token length of time, material and moral support has become more and more important. Through its ability to provide or withhold backing, official trade union machinery is today a decisive factor in any substantial dispute.

Incomes policy has had important implications for the pattern of disputes. Some have been generalized and diffuse. For example, an explicit aim of the Prices and Incomes Board was to specify principles which might guide judgements on the 'fair' level of pay for different occupations. One author had written of industrial relations between the wars that 'the abstract and unanswerable general problem, What is a fair wage? never came up; the problem was always the problem of a particular rate for a particular job' (Clay, 1928: 74). This remained true of post-war wage determination: 'fairness' was viewed pragmatically, employers and union negotiators alike tending to accept with little question that traditional relativities between different industries and occupations, with modest annual increases all round, were natural and reasonable. But in the incomes policy debates of the 1960s, traditional relationships *were* put in question; and it may be more than coincidental that a number of groups of workers began for the first time to challenge what they saw as inequities in their own pay position. Demands for equal pay for women took on a new urgency; car workers in low-paying companies or areas insisted on parity with wage levels elsewhere; manual workers in hospitals and local government began to ask why, given the social value of their employment, they earned so much less than was the norm in private manufacturing industry. In a period when *all* workers felt the effects of rising prices combined with a growing burden of tax and other deductions from wages (Turner and

Wilkinson, 1971), the weakening of traditional justifications for pay relationships gave many groups a rationale to fight for special treatment. It is plausible to see this as one factor behind the upsurge of pay disputes at the end of the decade.

More easy to identify have been the effects of the *uneven impact* of incomes policies. Without oversimplifying too much, wage bargaining in the 1950s and 1960s might be described as a two-stage process: the pace of earnings movements was set by strongly organized groups in private industry, often largely through shop-floor action; and increases were then generalized throughout the economy by national negotiations for groups of workers with less power at the point of production. In such negotiations, both parties normally accepted the principle of 'fair comparisons' with pay movements elsewhere; indeed there were agreed methods for applying this principle to some groups of public employees.

The incomes policy of the 1960s had only limited impact on sections of trade unionists able to negotiate effectively within the workplace. But national pay negotiations naturally came under close scrutiny; and the Prices and Incomes Board insisted that 'fair comparisons' should *not* normally be considered an acceptable reason for pay increases. Public employees thus tended to feel the most rigorous effects of wage restraint – particularly at the end of the decade, when observance of the pay norms in the private sector was relatively perfunctory. In the early 1970s the public sector unions were again the main victims when the Conservative government imposed its 'n minus 1' formula.

Mounting discontent was a predictable consequence; and given the central role of national bargaining, the official trade unions were directly implicated in this unrest. A common pattern was repeated in a number of different branches of public employment: expressions of dissatisfaction at the size of national settlements, given added force in some cases by unofficial protest strikes, more ambitious demands in subsequent national negotiations; finally an official strike, perhaps the first in the union's history. With minor variations, these stages were followed by postal workers, schoolteachers, local government officers, and civil servants. In 1969 there were large-scale strikes of local authority workers (most prominently dustmen) when deadlock was reached on a national claim for just under £1 a week increase. The strikers insisted on £5, a demand which was hastily taken up by the national negotiators, and agreement was finally reached for half this figure. The following year the unions' demands were from the outset more substantial, and a six-week official strike was called. The process was then repeated among hospital ancillary workers, who were mainly organized in the same unions. But the most outstanding example is that of coal-mining. As was seen earlier, the number of disputes in the industry fell sharply with the contraction in employment and the abolition of piecework; but the new importance of national pay negotiations made the main focus of discontent the National Union of Mineworkers itself. In both 1969 and 1970, a large proportion of the membership participated in unofficial strikes in protest at aspects of pay agreements negotiated with the Coal Board. The official strikes of 1972 and 1974 were the culmination of these movements, the national leaders (some newly elected) adapting to the mood of the more militant sections of the membership.

These developments can be quantified with some precision. In the years 1960–8 there were only six official industry-wide stoppages, and all but one of these were one-day token strikes. Between 1969 and 1974 (a shorter period) there were nineteen such stoppages, and of these only four were one-day demonstrations. While the small unofficial strike was usually defined as the main 'problem' of British industrial relations in the 1960s, the large official stoppage was not surprisingly so regarded in the early 1970s. But in most of these disputes, newspaper stereotypes of belligerent union leaders straining for confrontations with employers and the government were very wide of the mark. Union negotiators, as was emphasized in earlier chapters, normally seek stable bargaining relationships which a major conflict can seriously disrupt. Hence it is reasonable to assume (and the evidence suggests) that national officials normally entered stoppages only under intense pressure from the members – or at least their active representatives. The choice was often between sponsoring ambitious demands and aggressive action, or facing internal opposition and unauthorized outbreaks which undermined leadership authority. The one-day token strike – used as a futile gesture by the engineering unions on several earlier occasions – sometimes proved sufficient to satisfy such pressures. (For while a token strike *can* be a means of showing the employer that a union and its members mean business, of building up morale and determination among the rank and file, or of testing the union's organization in anticipation of a serious struggle, it is more often used to 'cool out' unrest by permitting resort to a strictly controlled form of militancy.) The conduct of the official health service dispute in 1982 was very largely a record of token gestures of this kind.

Official reluctance to become involved in major challenges to the government helps explain why incomes policies – though they probably helped generate the build-up of strike numbers to their 1970 peak, and certainly caused the record striker-days of the early 1970s – can also be associated with *reduced* strike activity. Pay controls have been a particular source of conflict when they have challenged established principles of wage determination; when their contents have been sufficiently unclear or ambiguous to permit divergent interpretations in particular cases; when they have been applied unequally, so that some groups have felt themselves victims of unfair discrimination; and when workers in individual occupations or industries have felt confident enough to insist on their objectives regardless of the limitations in force.

The consequences can be very different when relatively clear and unambiguous pay restraints are imposed uniformly on all groups of workers, and receive the endorsement – or at least the acquiescence – of most trade unionists. A combination of overt coercion and ideological influences can then lead to a diminution in disputes. A wage freeze or fixed pay limit permits little argument over interpretation. As long as employers are prepared to concede the maximum permitted (and this has normally been the case) a dispute will occur only when workers directly challenge the policy. But recent experience indicates that most unionists – encouraged by the insistent arguments of politicians, the media, and at times their own leaders – tend to accept (for a time at least) the fairness of any curbs which permit no exceptions. (Why it should be considered fair to impose uniform restraints on wages when profits – inevitably in a capitalist economy – are not so restrained is quite another question, and one which not surprisingly is rarely raised in the media.) In such circumstances only isolated groups of workers are likely to be motivated to insist on more than the policy permits; and because of their isolation, very few can feel confident of success in a serious confrontation with the powers of the state. The humiliating defeat of the postal workers in 1971 had an obvious deterrent effect on other groups of public sector trade unionists. Under the 'social contract', groups willing to challenge the norm – seamen, firemen, toolroom workers – found it difficult to win broader support. The same has been largely true of public sector resistance to Conservative 'cash limit' curbs – with the exception of the hospital workers, who were still defeated. Thus rigid pay limits typically sustain a vicious circle of isolation.

The pay freeze of 1966 to which the TUC grudgingly assented was almost universally observed; significantly, the number of strikes in that year was the lowest since 1953 (1,937, of which only 901 were officially classified as wage disputes). In the twelve-month period of freeze and severe restraint there were only 1,800 stoppages, a mere 641 of these on pay issues; and total striker-days were at the unusually low level of 1·7 million. The next experience of rigid pay controls was during the three-stage legislation introduced by the Heath government at the end of 1972. Despite vehement verbal opposition from the trade union movement, the first year's restrictions were challenged in national strike action by only three relatively minor groups. (And all three – civil servants, hospital ancillary staff and gasworkers – had special grievances, since the abrupt introduction of the curbs separated their pay increases from those of groups whose agreements they normally followed.) Not until the end of 1973 was the government's policy forcefully challenged, by the miners (their confidence boosted by their successful strike in 1972, and by the strengthening of their industry's strategic position in the wake of the oil crisis). The statistics indicate the effect of the government's previous success: while strikes on non-wage issues increased substantially in 1973 there was a reduction in those over pay; and striker-days fell to the lowest level since 1969.

Not only did the TUC initiate the restrictions introduced in the summer of 1975, it was also prepared to threaten dire sanctions against nonconformists (as the seamen discovered the following year); and the consequences for strikes were even more clear-cut. In 1974 there were almost three thousand strikes, two-thirds being pay disputes; and the figures for the first half of 1975 were closely comparable. But in the following twelve months, with the £6 limit in force, there were only 1,873 stoppages and a mere 859 on pay issues; striker-days were also down sharply.

The lesson is unremarkable: official trade union acceptance – explicit or implicit – of such policies of pay restraint creates conditions for a low level of collective conflict. But to state this simple point is scarcely enough. Experience in Britain and abroad shows that restrictions of this kind are not permanently effective: they may be eased by governments themselves (often for reasons of electoral advantage), eventually challenged by a determined and strategically powerful union, or eroded by the more diffuse and fragmented pressures of disenchanted sectional groups.

This argument is supported by developments after the first two years of 'social contract' pay controls: a renewed challenge from below, forcing its way through into official trade union policy. As was seen earlier, this process was demonstrated dramatically in the case of the TGWU: its 1977 conference rejected the appeals of the general secretary Jack Jones, the main architect of the 'social contract', and called for the abolition of wage restraint. The revolt from below was also manifested in a massive upsurge of pay strikes, increasing by almost 80 per cent to 1,558; and this level was sustained in the following year.* Hence the conclusion drawn by Davies (1983: 446) on the basis of a statistical analysis of strikes and incomes policies:

The imposition of incomes policy seems to have reduced the number of strikes over pay issues but, especially during its 'hard' phases, to have increased the number over non-pay issues. Moreover, the reduction in pay strikes is apparently achieved only at the expense of a sharp upsurge in such strikes as soon as the policy is removed. This result is consistent with workers and their unions attempting to make up lost ground and to rectify perceived

---

* It is impossible to resist quoting the following sentences from the second edition of this book, written just after the TUC in 1976 had overwhelmingly endorsed the second year of rigid pay limits: 'the moment of breakdown is rarely predictable; but when it comes, the characteristic result is an upsurge of previously suppressed collective action. There is little reason to assume that the relatively low level of strike activity of the mid-1970s will endure indefinitely.'

inequities and anomalies. Thus when an incomes policy is considered over its complete 'life cycle' . . . it appears to have been associated with a significant increase in the overall frequency of strike activity.

Do such conclusions hold true for the 1980s? As Table 7.3 shows, the policy of pay restraint inherent in Thatcherite economic strategy (even though not explicitly called an incomes policy) has been associated with another sharp decline in pay strikes. The highest number recorded has been 654 in 1982, while the 1985 figure of 361 was the lowest for several decades. But on this occasion there has been no compensating rise in non-pay strikes: these have fallen too, though less rapidly. This is the more significant in that these years have seen a brutal reassertion of the insecurity and subordination inherent in labour's commodity status. Plant closures and other forms of job loss, unilaterally imposed alterations in work organization and working practices, challenges to many of the established forms of shop steward representation, and the undisguised arrogance of newly confident 'macho management', all provide potential flashpoints which a decade ago would almost certainly have resulted in an explosion of strikes. That this is far less commonly the response today is evidence of an erosion of the will to resist. Obviously this reflects the extent to which the terrain of struggle has itself been transformed: mass unemployment and the politics of Thatcherism have ensured that in most disputes, the balance of advantage is overtly and overwhelmingly on the side of the employer. The nature and significance of this transformation in the broader environment of industrial conflict provide the themes of the concluding part of this chapter.

The political economy of strikes

The importance of the state

The main theme of this book has been the inevitability of industrial conflict in a society in which the main purpose of industry is profit, and in which the relationship between employers and workers is dominated by the drive to extract surplus value from the labour of men and women. The state in capitalist society is necessarily implicated in this process; but its involvement may be direct and overt or indirect and tacit. A key feature of recent years has been the increasing overtness of state involvement in British industrial relations.

Traditionally the law and the various agencies of government have intervened *directly* in labour relations in Britain far less than in almost any other country. The preference for 'voluntarism' – like the more general tradition of *laissez faire* in economic life – is often regarded as evidence of the state's neutrality; but it is only superficially so. For many decades 'voluntarism' operated in the context of insufficient numerical strength or cohesion on the part of British unions to pose a serious threat to the industrial priorities on which the stability of British capitalism rested. When trade unionism grew stronger it remained possible for 'voluntarism' to continue because unions showed little disposition in their objectives or their actions to challenge the economic goals of employers and governments. Yet on those occasions when a serious challenge to these priorities was discerned (as in 1926, for example), the mask of neutrality was abruptly discarded. But in the routine conduct of industrial relations the state was sufficiently detached from the main action to give credibility to the twin ideological postulates of the impartial state machine and the necessary separation of 'industrial' and 'political' issues.

From the 1960s – as was argued in the previous chapter – the traditional relationships have altered radically. Three main reasons may be noted. The first has already been discussed: the growing dependence of private capital on state support and sponsorship. This can take a multiplicity of forms: government 'demand management', state planning agencies, investment grants, lucrative public contracts, subsidized services from nationalized industries, research facilities and so on. This growth of 'interventionism' dates back several decades (Harris, 1972), but had become more systematic and intense at the time when this book was first written. The process was further accelerated in the 1970s by the unprecedented conjunction of double-figure inflation with a major recession: problems with which private capital alone cannot conceivably cope. As *laissez faire* has been replaced by growing state involvement in economic affairs, it would be remarkable indeed if labour relations were exempt from the effects of this trend; and of course they are not.

A second cause derives from the special problems of the post-war British economy: an often outdated industrial infrastructure, a low rate of investment, a heavy burden of arms spending, a financial system peculiarly vulnerable to short-term disruption because of the international role of sterling. These persistent weaknesses were overlaid in the late 1960s by what Glyn and Sutcliffe (1972) have termed the profits squeeze. They contest the assertion (which is too baldly stated on page 80 above) that the share of wages and salaries in the national income has remained constant throughout this century. On the contrary, they insist, trade union struggle has consistently raised labour's share until profit margins – and the very survival of British capitalism – were seriously threatened. The whole process, they argue, culminated in a crisis in the late 1960s. Glyn and Sutcliffe's thesis is open to challenge in certain subsidiary respects. (Their treatment of wages and salaries as a homogeneous category neglects the extent to which top salaries may represent an outcome of the performance of traditional capitalist functions rather than a payment for labour – the theoretically important though difficult article by Carchedi (1975) is relevant here. Their whole analysis in terms of factor shares loses some of its significance given the interpenetration of the state and monopoly capital, and also the differential impact of taxation on companies and employees. Arguably, Glyn and Sutcliffe also put too much weight on specifically short-run trends – see page 89 above.) Nevertheless, their analysis points to a major cause of the crisis of British capitalism and British industrial relations in the 1960s; and hence indicates why all subsequent governments have sought a regeneration of British industry through a defence of profits and an attack on the living standards of the majority of the population. Such policies have moreover achieved some effect; more recent analysis would show a partial reversal of the trend identified by Glyn and Sutcliffe.

The third factor is related to the other two: the rapid expansion of the public sector in a time of budgetary stringency. The traditional willingness of governments to apply to their own employees roughly the same wage rates as are negotiated for similar groups in the private sector developed in an era when public employment was relatively small. An interventionist state is necessarily a large employer (some 40 per cent of all British employees, and a majority of trade union members, are now in the public sector). A natural consequence is the decision to set the pace in collective bargaining rather than to follow the lead of others. Pressures to reduce costs and increase 'productivity' have become as urgent as in private industry, and are further intensified by the budgetary consequences of the worldwide economic crisis of the 1970s.

The contradictory politics of trade unionism

Trade unions are the collective instruments through which men and women in shop and office, factory, mine and mill, seek to increase their control over the conditions of their working lives. This purpose necessarily conflicts with the interests of employers and with the strategies of governments committed to the stability of an economy based on private capital. Yet in their day-to-day activities, trade union representatives – including those with some form of socialist aspiration towards a radically different social and economic order – are under intense pressures to behave as if capitalist relations of production are unalterable (except, perhaps, by gradual and piecemeal adjustment). The maintenance of orderly relationships with employers and governments can then easily become an overriding priority. In part this reflects an accommodation to the realities of external power: for a serious challenge to the established patterns of industrial relations (in which workers' organizations accept a subordinate and reactive role) would invite retaliation which in extreme circumstances could jeopardize union survival itself.

Such practical constraints coincide with the ideological pressures which were discussed in the previous chapter. Even committed trade unionists normally view society through a set of ideas and beliefs which reflect values antagonistic to their own needs and objectives. Hence workers' widespread acceptance that capitalist economic priorities constitute an overarching 'national interest' justifying sacrifices of their *own* interests; that even modest improvements in wages and conditions can properly be resisted as inflationary and disruptive; that organized collective action is a morally suspect deviation from the normal situation in which workers are divided and subservient to the employer's control; that 'fairness' exists if all progress uniformly from starting points which are themselves radically unequal. In practice, much trade union activity necessarily contradicts such assumptions: on occasions directly and dramatically, more usually through partial and tentative evasion of capitalist control or piecemeal pressure for objectives which imply divergent priorities. But the crucial fact is that such opposition is rarely sustained by a coherent counter-ideology. Trade union consciousness, as Parkin has argued (1971: 91–2), involves an 'uneasy compromise between rejection and full endorsement of the dominant order . . . what could be called a "negotiated version" of the dominant value system'. The consequence is that trade unionists can act collectively in ways incompatible with the aims and interests of those dominant in capitalist society; but the more serious and overt the conflict with the established order, the more likely is the hold of an alien ideology to prove inhibiting and demoralizing.

The point at which this occurs is neither precise nor unchanging. This is illustrated by the weakening in recent years of trade unionists' reluctance to strike for overtly 'political' purposes. The Industrial Relations Act of 1971 marked an important turning point in this process. Though union leaders attacked the 'penal clauses' contained in the legislative package proposed by the Labour government in 1969, most were almost equally hostile to the two protest strikes called unofficially. But in the case of the Conservative legislation of 1971 a series of 'Kill the Bill' strikes received first the acquiescence, then the official endorsement, of a number of union executives. In the following year the TUC itself was prepared to back a stoppage against the gaoling of five dockers by the National Industrial Relations Court (they were released before the date set); and in 1973 a TUC-sponsored one-day strike in protest against government pay restrictions did actually take place. (None of these disputes, being classed as 'non-industrial', are included in the official statistics for the relevant years. This underlines the argument of an earlier chapter: that the recording and classification of strikes is itself a 'political' process.) Equally notably, the miners in 1974 persisted in their strike in defiance of government wages policy despite a violent orchestrated campaign accusing them of placing 'constitutional government' in jeopardy.

The significance of these developments must be seen in perspective. In an important sense, all the confrontations with government have been primarily defensive: against legislative and judicial attacks on long-established rights of trade union organization and action; against statutory curbs or other forms of government interference with the traditional machinery and principles of wage negotiation. Most trade unionists would thus probably have argued that their own policies had not changed; rather the government itself had imported 'politics' into the world of trade union action. This attitude is understandable: the political meaning of trade union action has indeed become explicit because governments, themselves responding to major changes in the environment of economic policy, have demolished many of the foundations of the old ideological distinction between politics and economics. In no way do recent conflicts indicate – as some hysterical commentators have assumed – that union members or their leaders have determined to apply collective sanctions at the point of production as an instrument of radical social change.

Nevertheless the implications of these events are profound and complex. 'Free collective bargaining' has for over a century provided a centrepiece of British trade union consciousness, and it remains a slogan of enormous emotive potency. It follows from the whole argument of this book that the notion of 'free' collective bargaining is at any time misleading: the demands of trade union negotiators and their access to sanctions in support of these are subject to a whole array of constraints and influences long before the two sides reach the bargaining table. The cards are already stacked before the game begins. Yet in the traditional pattern of collective bargaining the prior constraints and influences are for the most part covert rather than overt, and are not so complete as to exclude all choice and unpredictability: the bargainers do not merely engage in a predetermined charade. The demand for free collective bargaining is an insistence on the preservation of this area of autonomy: a margin of independent action which – however circumscribed by the productive relations of capitalism and the ideological reflections of these relations – is of vital importance in providing British trade unionism with what has traditionally been regarded as its main reason for existence.

Yet in the political and economic context outlined above, even the traditionally limited sphere of trade union autonomy has cumulative effects (in terms of labour costs, restraints on managerial control of the labour process, obstructions to overall economic planning, disturbances to the 'confidence' of foreign and domestic financiers) which contemporary capitalism has a diminishing capacity to absorb. 'Free collective bargaining' may be regarded by trade unionists as a defensive and even conservative slogan, but its implications are increasingly disruptive and subversive.

Confrontation, containment and resurgence: the record of the 1970s

The previous chapter pointed to two alternative strategies available to governments and employers: the one overtly coercive, the other more sophisticated and manipulative. The simplicity of the coercive strategy appealed to the Heath government in its early years; the consequences were far from those intended. The Industrial Relations Act, viewed by most union representatives as a threat to their effective functioning, provoked a forthright (though highly constitutional) TUC campaign of opposition. This in turn helped legitimize more vigorous action by rank-and-file critics of the legislation. The cumulative effect was to generate a mood of resistance which inspired a TUC decision (going considerably farther, perhaps, than many of its leaders originally intended) to boycott many of the institutions of the Act. Two years after it assumed office, the government's industrial relations strategy was in ruins. The 'n minus 1' pay formula was destroyed by the mineworkers; the 'national emergency' provisions of the Act had lost all credibility with the railwaymen's massive vote in support of their leaders' recommendations; bizarre legal machinations had been required to defuse the crisis created by the imprisonment of the five dockers; while the use of the legislation in this case helped make a national docks strike inevitable. This experience pointed to three conclusions. There are limits to trade union self-restraint; when vital functions are considered at risk, union leaders may overcome their inhibitions against confrontation with the state. Secondly, government economic objectives cannot be effectively achieved in the face of persistent conflict with the unions, so long as union members are ready to follow their leaders' calls to action. Finally, official opposition to the government – however reluctant – encourages forms of unofficial militancy as disturbing to most union leaders as to government policy-makers.

These lessons reinforced the attractiveness – to both parties – of an accommodative strategy. That this was well understood was evident in the long round of Chequers and Downing Street talks in the second half of 1972, when the TUC was willing to discuss a detailed programme involving wage restraint – even though the execrated Industrial Relations Act remained on the statute book. In fact no agreement was reached, but it was seen earlier that despite verbal denunciations (and a token TUC-sponsored stoppage) most unions fell quietly into line with the ensuing statutory controls. Heath, according to a journalistic account, 'spent more time than any Prime Minister before him in seeking to bring the unions into the process of government. The fact that he failed – and that these talks ended in a freeze imposed against union will – is less important than the acquiescence which, in practice, the unions granted Stages I and II.' Throughout 1973, reports suggest, secret contacts and discussions between government and union leaders were regular and sympathetic. On this reading, the miners' strike which brought the government's downfall stemmed from a tactical blunder, after Stage III had been specifically drafted (with provisions for 'unsocial hours' and 'efficiency agreements') on the understanding that an acceptable settlement would be possible ('The Fall of Heath', *Sunday Times*, 22 February 1976).

Whether or not this interpretation is accurate in detail, the process of overt or tacit understandings between ministers and union leaders is in line with the logic expounded by the former General Secretary of the TUC almost a decade earlier. Supporting Labour's new incomes policy before a special conference of executives in 1965, Woodcock had argued that 'we cannot remain, whether we like it or not, in these days at arm's length from Government. . . . It is, I believe, the essence of modern trade unionism to get to grips with Government and to be bargainers. To be bargainers you have got to have something to give.'

The conclusion drawn from the dominating economic role of contemporary government was thus that collective bargaining must be raised to the level of the state. This explains the publication of a TUC Economic Review in every year since 1968, timed to appear shortly before the budget. In effect the Review constituted a programme of economic and social policy which, it was hoped, formed an agenda for negotiation with the government. Yet paradoxically, the 'something to give' in any such negotiation can be nothing less than the acceptance of curbs on the operation of 'free collective bargaining' at the level of traditional wage determination between unions and employers. The unpalatable implications of this paradox perhaps explain why bargaining with government has tended to be private and informal, in contrast to the more public and institutionalized relationships of 'social partnership' traditional in several continental countries. As a corollary, however, any agreement to exercise restraint in bargaining over wages and salaries has often been tacit and imprecise, and insufficient to withstand strong grassroots pressure from within unions.

The clearest expression yet of continental-style social partnership is to be found in the 'social contract' agreed between the TUC and the Labour Party before the first 1974 election. The terms of collaboration were explicit: there should be joint agreement on the social, industrial and fiscal policies to be pursued by Labour in government, and in return the unions should contain wage aspirations and settlements within margins compatible with government economic strategy. When voluntary restraint proved ineffectual – for the removal of the Conservatives' statutory controls at a time of unprecedented price inflation naturally resulted in record pay settlements – the TUC helped initiate the compulsory limits described previously.

The revival of the term 'social contract' was not without significance. The notion originally acquired currency in the context of seventeenth-century political philosophy, serving as an ideological device to legitimize a social and political order which sustained the existing (and highly unequal) distribution of property (Macpherson, 1962). In the 1970s the implications of the concept may at first have appeared very different: indeed a highly attractive arrangement for trade unionists. The government was to replace the Industrial

Relations Act by legislation agreed with the unions; maintain full employment and stable prices; sustain and improve welfare payments and social services so as to enhance the 'social wage'; and 'bring about a fundamental and irreversible shift in the balance of power and wealth in favour of working people and their families'. Some restraint in wage bargaining, it might plausibly be argued, was a small price in return for benefits of this order.

In practice the constraints within which the government's economic policies developed made nonsense of most of these commitments: the new social contract, like the old, appeared increasingly to function as a device for warding off attacks on an economic system founded on privilege and inhumanity. The Industrial Relations Act was indeed repealed in favour of the Trade Union and Labour Relations Act of 1974 and the Employment Protection Act of 1975. But prices continued to escalate while unemployment rose inexorably to levels far above the previous post-war maximum; curbs on public expenditure brought savage cutbacks in welfare services; the main concession towards the radical proposals for greater equality was the appointment of a Royal Commission – the traditional formula for avoiding serious action. Yet the TUC remained willing to give virtually unanimous backing to pay limits which entailed a fall in the real net incomes of most workers; and this policy was pursued with a rigour which, as has been seen, brought a major reduction in strike activity.

There would seem to be four main reasons for the persistent trade union commitment to the social contract. The first was the traditional attachment and loyalty of most unions to the Labour Party. Yet this can be only a minor part of the explanation, for sentiment alone has rarely caused British unions to tailor their industrial activities to the wishes of Labour governments; and with the growing white-collar coverage of the TUC an increasing proportion of its constituents in any case lacked the traditional political reflexes. The second factor was a more pragmatic desire to help sustain a Labour government for fear that the Conservatives (especially given their current leadership) would pursue industrial policies even more unpalatable to the unions. Thirdly there was a belief that the existing economic predicament allowed the government few policy alternatives; and that without TUC co-operation on wages, the rates of inflation and unemployment and the scale of the attacks on the 'social wage' would be even worse. The final factor was a generalized fear that, *whatever* the government and its policy objectives, a major confrontation with the unions might lead to a collapse of existing social and political institutions (perhaps a central reason for the pursuit of agreement with Heath in the summer of 1972).

Originally founded on optimistic aspirations for radical (though purely constitutional) social and economic transformation, the social contract thus survived increasingly for negative and pessimistic reasons: alarm at the prospects of even greater deterioration in the position of British workers, rather than a serious hope of significant improvement. Eventually, such motives proved insufficient. Continued restraint was first passively deprecated (1977–8, when only the firemen offered a sustained and large-scale challenge), then actively resisted (1978–9, the 'winter of discontent'). Strikes and trade unions were once again presented as a central 'problem' of British society. The scene was set for a radical return to a strategy of coercion under the Thatcher government.

Thatcherism: coercive pacification

All post-war British governments regardless of party (with the partial exception of Heath's first two years) had shared a commitment to the consensual management of a 'mixed economy' in which state and private capital both exercise important functions. The aim of maximizing agreement on questions of policy involved elaborate processes of consultation with representatives of employers and trade unions, and the proliferation of tripartite agencies and committees. The most prominent of such bodies, the National Economic Development Council, was formed by a Conservative government in 1962; its effect was typical of tripartism in making unions more responsive to government economic priorities, rather than allowing them genuine influence on these priorities. However the *form* of TUC participation in such machinery, particularly during the period of the 'social contract', contributed to an illusion of trade union power. The presentation of industrial relations in the media – which emphasizes trade union pressure for adjustments in the detail of government and company policy, while ignoring the far broader issues of economic strategy which unions seem powerless to challenge – of course reinforces this illusion.

The Conservatives in their 1979 manifesto made 'trade union power' a central issue. They blamed 'a minority of extremists' for the problems of the British economy, and denounced Labour's industrial relations legislation as a 'militants' charter' which had 'tilted the balance of power in bargaining throughout industry away from responsible management and towards unions'. Anti-unionism is closely linked to the faith in 'free market economics' which has come to dominate British Conservatism. The arguments of Thatcherism challenge the post-war consensus on which tripartite economic institutions have rested. Put simply, these arguments are that the Keynesian commitment to full employment has removed the discipline of labour market competition, allowed trade unions to pursue inflationary wage claims, and frustrated the efficient management of labour; that unions' damaging power was further enhanced by a privileged legal status, and by the fact that many of them negotiated collusively with 'public sector monopolies'; and that labour market discipline was also weakened by state welfare provisions. While Thatcherite anti-unionism is embedded in a visceral ideological hostility, it thus also reflects an integrated economic analysis. The succession of anti-union laws, the attacks on public welfare, the 'privatization' of state industries and services, the deliberate creation of mass unemployment, are all logical reflections of a passionate faith in the virtues of competitive capitalism.

Some would see the intention of this offensive as the 'de-unionization' of British industrial relations on the American model: a more radical objective than that of most major employers. At the very least, the aim is to overturn the assumption in British public policy (dating at least from the Report of the Royal Commission on Labour in 1894) that collective representation and collective bargaining are inherently desirable. By consolidating definitions of worker interests opposed to those of capital and the state, trade unions necessarily contradict a politics which extols individual initiative in the marketplace while also calling for universal sacrifice in the 'national interest'. Such a politics naturally addresses workers as individual citizens, not as members of collective organizations. The tradition of tripartism, of close consultative relationships with union leaders, is incompatible with such a politics. To attack the political legitimacy of unionism is thus to reinforce the politics of Thatcherism. At the same time, union-bashing is regarded as electorally popular (for reasons which are examined below), as well as appealing to the shopkeepers and small businessmen who form Thatcherism's social base.

In line with this perspective the government has developed a multi-pronged offensive. First, it has challenged, not merely the legislation of 1974–6, but the whole framework of labour law established between 1871 and 1913. The Employment Acts of 1980 and 1982 constitute a more far-reaching though more piecemeal attack on trade unionism than the ill-fated Industrial Relations Act, outlawing most forms of strike, picketing and closed shop, and exposing unions to heavy financial penalties. The 1984 Trade Union Act exposed unions to legal action for any strike called – however urgent the issue involved – without a prior ballot of the members affected. (The same Act also required secret ballots to elect union executive committees and to determine the maintenance of political funds.) Legislation before parliament in 1988 will impose further restrictions on collective organization and action. In less than a decade, the framework of British labour law has become the most anti-union of any major industrial country.

Secondly, many of the positive protections contained in Labour's legislation have been diluted or eliminated, as have such long-standing provisions as the 'fair wages clause' in government contracts. The Wages Councils, which have sought to provide some statutory minimum to earnings in the lowest-paid industries since the beginning of the century, face abolition. Most Industrial Training Boards have been closed down, and public funding for trade union education drastically reduced. These changes are the more significant in a hostile economic environment, with declining trade union membership (TUC affiliations fell from a peak of almost 12·2 million in 1980 to 9·3 million in 1987), and consequential financial problems.

Thirdly, Thatcher's ministers have been even more anxious than those of the early Heath years to discard the cosy etiquette of consultative relations with union representatives. Openly contemptuous of the whole philosophy of tripartism, one of the government's first acts was to initiate a review of the 'quango' system; this resulted in the abolition of a number of such bodies (though it proved impracticable to eliminate as many as had been expected). But in those that survived, TUC nominees could no longer pretend to exert any discernible influence; indeed their views were treated with such obvious disdain that for a time the TUC withdrew from the NEDC. More recently, there have been agonized debates as to whether the TUC should still participate in the Manpower Services Commission, whose activities increasingly concentrate on poorly paid 'training' schemes which the young unemployed are obliged to pursue on pain of loss of state benefits.

The fourth main challenge has occurred within public sector industrial relations. Like its predecessor in 1970, the Conservative government – as was seen earlier – has disavowed an incomes policy but has imposed rigid pay curbs for its own employees through cash limits. The system of budgetary controls initiated by Labour has been intensified, and percentage allowances for wage increases have been specified at levels considerably below the rate of inflation: the choice for unions has thus been falling real incomes or even faster job losses. In the nationalized industries, government willingness to fund investment programmes (or to offset operating losses) has been directly proportionate to management rigour in attacking established collective arrangements. Perhaps most notable has been the experience at British Leyland (now the Rover Group), where management forced through an extensive programme of 'rationalization' of production, plant closures and redundancies; overturned workers' collective job controls, speeding up the work process and intensifying discipline; launched a systematic attack on shop steward organization, withdrawing long-standing facilities and harassing union activists (even dismissing the senior union representative at the company's main factory); and regularly appealed over the heads of union representatives through postal ballots of employees (thus anticipating the government's current legislative initiative). Similar managerial aggressiveness has been displayed in British Steel, where employment has been cut by more than half since 1979; in British Rail, where a succession of disputes has been provoked over pay and working conditions; and in the National Coal

Board (now British Coal), where pit closures, disciplinary procedures and changed working practices have all provoked serious conflict.

Thus the political environment of collective organization and action has been radically transformed, at the same time as the economic context (partly as a result of deliberate government policy) has become so hostile. These factors go a long way to explain the rapid change in strike activity: when this book first appeared industrial struggle was at its height, while a decade later the level is the lowest since the war. The 'demonstration effect' identified during the strike 'wave' of the early 1970s seems to have been reversed. Then, the successful struggles of groups of workers with little record of militancy encouraged others to take action; today, each defeat discourages others from the risk of a strike. This negative demonstration effect is part of a process which may be termed 'coercive pacification': sustained mass unemployment and a governmental offensive have systematically undermined most workers' collective strength and confidence. Yet there is also a broader ideological dimension: the hostility of 'public opinion' identified in the previous chapter has clearly intensified, and this too is part of the explanation of the decline in strike activity. The erosion of the ideological foundations of collective action forms the concluding topic of discussion.

The problem of ideology and organization

The previous chapter identified a gap between activity and consciousness: trade union members and participants in strikes often endorse generalized criticisms of strikes and unions. For over a decade, opinion polls have regularly suggested that three-quarters of the population, including the majority of union members themselves, regard trade unions as 'too powerful'; only 5 per cent respond that they are not powerful enough. Surveys during the 1983 election indicated 72 per cent support for stricter laws to restrict union freedom. It was argued earlier (pages 152–3) that it is unwise to place excessive credence on facile responses to pollsters' superficial questions; workers may react very differently when faced with a clear attack on their material interests. Nevertheless, the elections of 1983 and 1987 demonstrated that such responses carried over at least into voting behaviour. Of trade unionists who voted in 1983, roughly three in five supported either Thatcher – despite the record of 3 million unemployed and the dismantling of the public services – or the SDP, which embraced a similarly anti-union platform. The result in 1987 was similar, with a continued trend to Conservative voting among the skilled manual working class. Ironically, this section was in the forefront of the fragmented wage militancy of the 1960s; but those still in jobs had in most cases enjoyed real wages rising in the 1980s, and their political perspectives were seemingly adapted to their immediate economic self-interest.

These political trends are relevant to any discussion of secret ballots in trade union decision-making and, in particular, strike ballots. The Conservative government has presented its legislation on this issue as a self-evidently desirable method of rendering unions more democratic; and survey evidence suggests that most trade unionists themselves agree. Why then have most union activists and officials strenuously opposed the legislation? In part the objection is to the state, and in particular a hostile government, imposing a specific model of government on trade unions – especially since other organizations such as employers' associations are not subject to these controls. Companies are not required to ballot their shareholders before donating to the Conservatives, or before threatening employees with a lock-out if they do not accept new conditions of employment. Thus the law is clearly one-sided.

Underlying the argument for secret ballots is a variant of the familiar 'agitator' view of disputes: strike-happy union leaders or militant shop stewards are assumed to impose their will on reluctant union members. As the whole of this book has tried to demonstrate, this is a bizarre inversion of the normal pattern of relations between membership and leadership in trade unions. Officials are typically reluctant to initiate strikes, and would be foolish to do so without strong membership support. (In the 1984–5 miners' dispute, when the refusal to hold a ballot as specified in the rulebook was arguably a serious tactical error, there was clearly a strong groundswell of support for the strike – which indeed commenced unofficially.) Part of the reason for the appeal of strike ballots to union members, however, is that they feel remote from the *process* of decision-making within their organizations – a serious problem which is examined further in the following pages.

There is reason to be sceptical, however, of Conservative claims to be defenders of workers' rights. The whole thrust of legislation since 1979 has been to weaken employee rights *against employers*; and the Thatcher government has strenuously resisted the most modest proposals for European legislation for employee rights of information and consultation in large enterprises. The enthusiasm for balloting in unions would seem to owe much to the clash between a *passive* and *individual* model of decision-making, and the *collective* and *participative* principles on which trade unionism depends. Conservative contempt for the idea of collective self-defence of employees through trade unions is made clear by the 1988 legislative proposals, which will prevent the application of collective discipline over strike-breakers *even when a dispute has the backing of most members in a secret ballot*. The aim is not to democratize unions but to disorganize them.

- Nevertheless, these initiatives cut with the grain of the current ideological climate. Labour's humiliation in 1983 and 1987 demonstrated the lack of influence, even on their own members, of union leaders and activists who campaigned in support of the party. This contrasted markedly with the success of all the unions which held political fund ballots as required by the 1984 Act; it is significant that most unions campaigned on the theme of a right to a voice in parliamentary affairs, and played down their association with the Labour Party. The traditional politics of the labour movement no longer evokes its former reponse. This reflects a major weakening of what may be called the moral basis of collective identity and of resulting collective struggles. Historically, trade unionism was deeply embedded in the culture and communal relationships of many sections of the working class: unions' strength rested primarily on a strong sense of collective identity expressed and reinforced by mass meetings, parades, banners, social activities. Today such manifestations of union commitment have withered; while workers' sense of class (or at least occupational or industrial) solidarity has been increasingly displaced by receptiveness to individualism and to notions of 'national interest' – which, as was indicated earlier, characterize the ideological appeal of Thatcherism.

These changes reflect in part far broader cultural transformations: the declining significance of traditional working-class communities with their tight-knit but often oppressive and introspective networks of social relationships; and the impact of new media of 'mass culture' owned and controlled by capitalists or those favourable to their interests. Also relevant are the shifts in the composition of employment and union membership which were noted previously. The work organization and work culture of manual labour in mine and mill, dock and railway, shipyard and engineering factory, were relatively conducive to a 'spontaneous' sense of solidarity. Shops and offices, schools and hospitals are significantly different work milieux, with labour processes which are often fragmented and isolated. Clerks and typists, nurses and teachers, supervisors and technicians, typically respond to a complexity of interests and pressures; and their responses are rarely informed by a reflex commitment to the ethics and traditions of the labour movement. Historically, 'making trade unionists' always depended on a deliberate effort of ideological struggle; this is even more necessary today.

But in large measure, British unions in recent decades have abdicated such a struggle. In fact, many have found it possible to boost membership without the need to win the active commitment of those recruited. It is a remarkable fact that the number of union members rose consistently and substantially throughout the 1970s, despite a particularly unfavourable economic environment and the climate of public hostility which has been noted. A major explanation is the growing extent to which union membership has become a condition of employment. In 1977–8 a survey of manufacturing industry showed 37 per cent of non-managerial employees covered by a 'closed shop'; a broader study in 1980 indicated that 27 per cent of the total workforce was so affected. The extent has, however, declined with the collapse of employment in many traditional trade union strongholds; a recent estimate suggested that employees covered fell from some 4·8 million in 1980 to 3·6 million in 1984 (Millward and Stevens, 1986: 107).

The closed shop is a traditional feature of British industrial relations, but as a social institution reflecting the strong trade union commitment of the vast majority of the workers involved. Seeing collective organization as a condition of their own standards and security, they refused to work with non-unionists, enforcing this principle often without the official recognition of either management or union. By contrast, the 1970s saw the elaboration of 'union membership agreements', often without reference to the workforce affected, and in areas of employment without strong union traditions. Many employers were happy to enforce such arrangements as a means of simplifying bargaining structure, preventing inter-union rivalry, and providing union officials with the disciplinary sanctions necessary to police agreements.

Recruitment through such mechanisms creates mere paper trade unionists. Workers whose entry to the union is a routine corollary of commencing employment, and whose weekly subscription is automatically deducted from their wages by the employer, do not normally object to the fact of their membership. But they relate to the union passively, as atomized individuals: *not* as participants in a living collectively. Not surprisingly, 'the union' represents a distant impersonal power, not an expression of their own identity and interests. The alienation of members from their own unions has almost certainly been accentuated by the 'reform' of industrial relations in the 1970s. The common (though far from universal) pattern of decentralized bargaining by shop stewards in close and continuous relationship with their members was transformed by the formalization of negotiating arrangements at plant or company level; by the increasingly hierarchical nature of workplace union organization; and by the developing involvement of senior stewards in high-level consultative relations with employers. A more bureaucratized shop steward organization often became dangerously isolated from the general membership: a situation which managements have proved quick to exploit.

Finally, unions' current ideological weakness must be seen in the context of the traditional sectionalism of British union practice. Though it would be wrong to dismiss the significance of appeals to a common movement in the language of British trade unionism, or to ignore the evidence of moments of wide-ranging solidarity, the typical constituency of collective identity and collective struggle is probably far narrower in Britain than in many other countries. Parochialism and sectionalism have clearly been reinforced, over the course of more than a generation, by the considerable *effectiveness* of fragmented militancy during the years of favourable labour market conditions. But not only is such fragmentation of struggle now often materially disabling, in the context of more co-ordinated and centralized strategies of capital and the state; its ideological effects are also damaging. Though there is little basis for an argument that sectionalism has significantly increased in recent years, its implications have certainly altered. This reflects the ever more elaborate division of labour which intensifies the interdependence of disparate productive activities; and the expanding area of our everyday subsistence which today depends upon the wage-labour of others, employed either in the private 'service' sector or by the state.

Sectional militancy (or even *defensive* action) now typically has disruptive consequences for workers not directly involved. Localized strikes commonly result in widespread lay-offs – often as a deliberate employer tactic of escalation. And disputes involving public service workers – an important feature of British industrial relations in the 1970s – have often had a particular impact on working-class households. The evident reaction of many workers (and indeed many trade unionists) is to regard themselves as *victims* of industrial disputes, and to express hostility to strikes – except their own. In a climate of strident press and television denunciation of strikes, it has been easy for the state to reinforce their ideological isolation in its role of defender of the 'public interest' and the 'rights of consumers'. Lacking a persuasive and principled link between their parochial demands and struggles and a broader vision of the interests and projects of the class, trade unions in Britain today are largely defenceless in the face of ideological attack.

Beyond the crisis?

The argument has returned to the point at which Chapter 6 concluded: strikes are a response to a problem which they are unable to resolve. But can there be a solution? Strikes are an inherent accompaniment to trade unionism and collective bargaining; their strengths and weaknesses as a form of action can be properly assessed only through a broader appraisal of the meaning and contradictory character of union organization. Hence it is necessary to review the 'state of the unions' in Britain today. The problem of strikes, it may be suggested, is closely linked to four distinct but related problems of current collective organization.

The first is that of bureaucracy. 'Trade union bureaucracy' has long been a popular condemnatory slogan of the left. Used to denote a particular stratum of officials, leaders of representatives, the term is virtually empty of theoretical content: not least in Britain, where so many of the 'bureaucratic' functions of trade unionism are performed by lay activists who are not on the union payroll. There is value, however, in conceptualizing bureaucracy as a *social relation* pervading trade union practice at every level: a social relation corrosive of the foundations of collective solidarity.

Despite the powerful pressures on trade unionists to behave 'responsibly', opposition and struggle are in reality essential for the very meaning and existence of unionism. The dominant ideological definitions in our society distort workers' interests and treat capitalist priorities as natural and inevitable; it is through self-activity and mobilization that workers can establish an alternative definition of distinctive collective interests and can formulate alternative objectives. But collective bargaining undertaken by 'specialist' negotiators *on behalf of* the broader membership consolidates a representative hierarchy functionally oriented towards accommodation and compromise with capital and its agents; committed to what has been called an 'industrial legality' which may permit some improvement in workers' conditions yet simultaneously endorses the legitimacy and security of the employer. Representation becomes detached from mobilization; the preservation of the bargaining relationship with the employer bespeaks a containment of 'unofficial' exercises in class struggle. Without resorting to Michelsian 'iron laws' it is possible to identify a contradiction: workers' organizations which are defined and constituted through struggle tend also to contain and inhibit such struggle.

Bureaucracy as a social relation is manifest in a hierarchy not only of control (which may be partially mitigated by various norms and traditions of union democracy) but also of activism. In Britain, as has often been emphasized, the largely unremunerated activities of a substantial cadre of lay officers and representatives are vital for the operation of trade unionism. Because the relatively small staff of full-time officials is in many respects dependent on the work of such activists, a lively process of internal union democracy is facilitated. What is increasingly evident, however, is the disjuncture between this internal political process and the majority of union members. The routines of branch agenda, district committee meetings, conference procedure, of motions, amendments and resolutions, involve a minority of enthusiasts distinguished by interest and understanding from the broader membership. In this respect lay activists – who often regard themselves as the authentic voice of the rank and file – may be as far (or even further) removed from the sentiments of their constituents as are the full-time officials. It is precisely this hierarchy of activism and involvement, and the detachment of the formal mechanisms of policy- and decision-making from the experience of most ordinary members, that have encouraged the recent legislation which displaces traditional forms of union democracy by the application of obligatory ballots.

It would be wrong to posit a crude dichotomy between 'active minority' and 'passive majority': there are many gradations of activism, and at certain moments or in certain contexts there may be a high degree of membership involvement in the collective relations which constitute trade union practice. Nevertheless, in most unions and at most times internal politics appear to operate as an esoteric pastime of exceptional enthusiasts. And it is not merely their activism which differentiates those so involved. Typically, activists and officials derive disproportionately from relatively advantaged sections of the workforce: male, white, higher-skilled, higher-paid, in more secure jobs. Such characteristics – commonly associated with greater self-confidence, familiarity with official procedure, standing with fellow-workers, and identification with work and hence work-related institutions – may be seen as encouraging involvement in trade unionism and a successful 'career' as union activist. Hence hierarchy within the working class is replicated within trade union organization. In identifying grievances, selecting demands, formulating strategies and determining priorities, the perspectives and interests of the dominant sections almost inevitably exert disproportionate influence. The consequential subordination (or even exclusion) of the concerns of women, immigrants, lower-skilled, lower-paid, less secure workers (not to mention the unemployed and casually employed) in the agenda of union action necessarily weakens their identification with 'the union'. In consequence, the bureaucratic-hierarchical tendencies of trade union organizational practice provide a material foundation for Conservative anti-union populism.

The problem of bureaucracy connects with that of the state. Within the British labour movement for the past century, strategies for social reform and visions of a new society have – almost without exception – involved an uncritical and at times idealized attitude towards the state: state ownership of the 'commanding heights' of the economy, state provision of welfare, state redistribution of resources. Conflicts between left and right within the Labour Party have typically concerned the extent to which state intervention is desirable and the pace at which it is attainable, not the underlying model of state socialism. Yet it is clear that the application of this model has in practice (and many would add, necessarily) tended to replicate the hierarchical and authoritarian character of capitalist relations of production. And these characteristics have rarely been coherently challenged on the left, precisely because they parallel the bureaucratic-hierarchical tendencies within the labour movement itself. The state functionary could be seen as analogue of the trade union representative: following the rule-book, applying specialized experience and expertise, acting beneficently *on behalf* of the working class. If the reality was rather different, this was because of particular functionaries' lack of sympathy for the state socialist ideal and not because of any fundamental flaw in the model.

Hence the experience of Thatcherism has provoked little critical debate on the *qualitative* implications of bureaucratic state intervention as a strategy for socialists. The dominant responses have involved reassertions of traditional Labour politics: cutting unemployment through a return to Keynesian demand management (or through various 'Keynes plus' packages); fighting the cuts through a defence of the 'welfare state' as it exists. This virtual fetishism of the state has inhibited attention to alternative possibilities for collective control of social relations of production; and to the need for anti-capitalist struggle within and against existing state institutions to complement any resistance to cuts and privatization.

Fetishism of the state reflects a more general vacuum of political imagination. British socialism is modest and banal in its long-term vision even when superficially radical in its short-term programme. The attack on the unions puts in question the traditional forms of institutionalized accommodation between capital and labour, suggesting the need for a more explicitly anti-capitalist reaction; but the dominant response is the call to restore 'free collective bargaining'. Mounting unemployment puts in question the traditional conception of 'work' as a five-day-a-week subordination to the will of an employer, segregated from other spheres of social and domestic life; but the dominant response is the reiteration of the demand for a 'right to work'. The eclipse of Keynesianism and the brutalities and irrationalities of monetarism put in question the viability of any solution to the crisis, short of a fundamental restructuring of social and economic relations; but the dominant response is a blueprint for an 'alternative economic strategy'. Imagination is dangerous; in particular, it threatens to disrupt established bureaucratic routines. The official labour movement still has effective reflexes to contain such disturbing possibilities, even if it has no answer to the real crisis which envelops it: hence in autumn 1983 the TUC embraced the slogan of realism, the Labour Party that of unity. Both represent a reaffirmation of the politics of tradition.

There are indeed exceptions. The idea of workers' alternative plans has sought to link the defence and creation of jobs to the demand for socially useful production. Feminist critiques have stressed the need for an attack on women's subordination – inherent in the sexual division of labour and in the relationship of waged to domestic work – as part of any viable response to the crisis. Community-based action groups – occasionally with the support of left-wing Labour municipalities – have attempted to develop collective initiatives which transcend the division between representatives and represented. And the revival of the peace movement has restored to the political agenda many of the forms of campaigning and mobilization which have atrophied within the orthodox labour movement.

Any credible response to the crisis must build on such examples. Three essential principles may be suggested. First, the 'labour movement' – today a tired epithet rather than a lived reality – must be informed by workers' current experiences and aspirations, their hopes and fears, their grievances and enthusiasms. The right has shown – cynically and manipulatively – a frightening ability to communicate with the working class. Neither the trade unions nor the political left have displayed any parallel capacity: often assuming that they *are* the working class, or at least possess exclusive authority to speak on its behalf. The notions of humanity, of solidarity, of conscious collective determination of social existence, have become empty slogans which can be reinvigorated only when inspired by a social vision which connects with (even as it seeks to enlarge) people's own understanding for their current predicament.

Secondly, it follows that any strategy to unify existing disparate and fragmented struggles must proceed from the grassroots upwards. Sectionalism, it was suggested previously, is a source of both material and ideological weakness. Yet the decentralized character of British trade unionism, its traditions of extensive lay involvement, provide a vital counterpoint to the bureaucratic tendencies which have been emphasized; thus centralization at the *expense* of grassroots democracy is no solution to the problem, but would rather accentuate the alienation of the ordinary membership from the institutions of the labour movement. It is essential to co-ordinate activity; to avoid divisive demands and strategies; to relate particularistic interests to broader class interests; to show special concern for those sections of the class whose oppression by capital is matched by subordination within trade unionism itself. But such solidarity cannot be artificially imposed: it must derive from commitment and conviction which in turn presuppose a process of internal education and argument of major extent and intensity. Such a process would represent a radical innovation: an initiative which can come only from the broad cadre of activists already identified, many of them indeed anxious for new forms of response and receptive to new definitions of socialist trade unionism.

Thirdly, trade union activities must connect far more directly with wider social movements and social struggles. Trade unionists – and the majority of the socialist left – have traditionally accepted, by default it not through conviction, the capitalist fragmentation of social identity. 'Work' – identified with wage-labour, and often also with the stereotype of a muscular male hammering metal – is separate from home, from community, from culture, and has priority over all of these. Accordingly, the trade union struggle is the organizing centre of the class struggle; 'peripheral' activities are at best a reinforcement and at worst a distraction. Always disabling, such a conception is suicidal when so many workers – and so many who are at most marginally integrated within the realm of wage-labour – place high priority on problems and commitments outside employment, and are willing to act collectively in such contexts.

These points provide a sharper focus for the subject of this book. Cronin has insisted (1979: 9) that we must 'look upon the act of striking as a positive statement by working people. Strikes are not the defensive actions of desperate and downtrodden men and women. . . . Most strikes are essentially creative acts of an offensive kind, signs not of weakness but of collective resources, not of resignation but of an often hopeful and heightened sense of self-worth. . . .' Perhaps this is to glamorize and romanticize the aims and attitudes of most strikers. But it captures an essential point: that strikes, at least potentially, are vehicles of people striving to make their own history. We live in times when the brutality and irrationality which underlie the strategies of the powerful – and which are embedded in seemingly undirected and uncontrollable structural forces – not only constrain our humanity but threaten our very existence. The obstacles to attempts to make our own history are more momentous than at any previous time.

Any effective opposition to these obstacles must involve a constant broadening of the constituencies of people's self-assertiveness. As part of such a process it is essential that the positive statement implicit in the act of striking should be amplified, its perspectives enlarged, the connections with other social movements outside the narrow relationship of worker and employer extended. A humane society can be built only on the collective initiative manifest, at present, in merely fragmented revolts; but such revolts will remain erratic and ineffectual unless guided by a vision of an alternative order.

The 1980s have seen major extensions in the control of the state over our everyday lives (inspired by a government whose slogan is to eliminate individual dependence on the state); an escalation of global conflicts (by governments each of which profess peace, and all of which exploit the spectre of external threat to legitimize constraints on internal dissidence); and the elaboration of the media

Guide to Further Reading

'The striker is unloved, unhonoured and unsung; above all, he is largely unstudied' (Knowles, 1952: xi). After three decades, and the development of industrial sociology and industrial relations as major areas of study, this verdict is no longer true. Knowles' own book continues to offer the most extensive general discussion of strikes. The multi-disciplinary collection of essays edited by Kornhauser *et al*. (1954) is also of considerable importance. Additional reading relevant to the subject matter of each chapter of this book is suggested below. Details of these and all other publications cited in the text are listed at the end.

1. The Anatomy of the Strike
Numerous descriptions of strikes have been published, but most of these are journalistic accounts accompanied by little serious analysis. Frow and Katanka (1971) provide an interesting collection of contemporary documentation on significant stoppages in British labour history; while Brecher (1972) is an important historical analysis of strikes in America. Two of the most famous sociological studies of disputes are Warner and Low (1947) and Gouldner (1955). Analyses of three important national stoppages in Britain can be found in Clegg and Adams (1957) and Foot (1967 and 1971). At the other end of the spectrum, Clack (1967) discusses his experience of 'downers' in a car factory. Notable stoppages at individual companies are examined by Arnison (1971) on the Roberts-Arundel dispute, and Lane and Roberts (1971) on the Pilkington strike; while Beynon (1975) offers important insights into conflict at Ford's Halewood factory.

Among more recent studies are Allen (1981) on the miners, Hartley *et al*. (1983) on the steel strike, and Neale (1983) on the 1982 hospital dispute. Kahn *et al*. (1983) discuss a number of key conflicts in the early 1980s. The 1984–5 miners' strike is the subject of a considerable literature; Beynon (1985) is one of the best studies. I have recorded my own views of aspects of the dispute in Hyman (1986). Important plant-level studies are Batstone *et al.* (1978) and Edwards and Scullion (1982).

Several practical guides to strike action have recently appeared: Johnston (1975), Montague (1979), Campbell and McIlroy (1981: Ch. 8) and McIlroy (1984).

For an informative discussion of women's record as strikers see Purcell (1979).

2. Strikes and British Industrial Relations

Statistics of British strikes are published monthly in the *Employment Gazette* (HMSO), with analyses of the previous year's figures in the January and July issues. The standard textbook on British industrial relations is Clegg (1979); the role of shop stewards has been analysed in general terms by Goodman and Whittingham (1973); while Brown (1973) and Batstone *et al.* (1977) examine the detailed operation of workplace organization. The Donovan Report (1968) provides a much noted interpretation of strikes in Britain; its conclusions have been in part assailed by Turner (1969) and defended by McCarthy (1970). The reader should be warned, however, that many of the above works adopt a largely managerial standpoint; a useful corrective is Cliff (1970).

3. The Sociology of Industrial Conflict

An exposition and critique of sociological theories of industrial conflict can be found in Eldridge (1968); some of these theories are also briefly summarized by Fox (1966). Works which apply such theories to individual British industries include Scott *et al.* (1956 and 1963), Liverpool University (1954) and Turner *et al.* (1967). The concept of an industrial relations system is elaborated and applied by Dunlop (1958) and criticized in Hyman (1975).

In Britain, an 'action frame of reference' has recently become popular. Its theoretical implications are expounded with great clarity by Silverman (1970), while its best-known application to industrial relations is Goldthorpe *et al.* (1968). For an incisive critique of a number of aspects of this approach see Westergaard (1970).

4. *The Institutionalization of Industrial Conflict*

The thesis that conflict normally tends to become institutionalized is argued in general terms by Coser (1956); a number of its implications in the industrial relations context are discussed by Flanders (1970). Some aspects of this theory are criticized in detail in Hyman (1971b). The continuing importance of class in our society – and the fact that this society is still capitalist – is clearly demonstrated in several recent works; see, for example, Blackburn (1965), Westergaard (1965), or Miliband (1969). Useful accounts of the basic causes of industrial conflict are given by Allen (1966), Blackburn (1967), and Coates (1967). Gouldner (1969) provides a particularly sensitive analysis of the deprivations inherent in the worker's role within capitalist society. Fox (1971) offers an important but complex analysis of the interaction of pressures towards peace and conflict in industry. Workers' own statements of their experience off work are compiled in Fraser (1968 and 1969).

5. *The Rationale of Industrial Conflict*

An influential, though complex examination of the problems of analysing rationality in social life is provided by Schutz (1964); a number of the essays in Wilson (1970) are also important, but again somewhat difficult for the beginner. Coser (1956) and Eldridge (1968) both consider the rationale of conflict in industry; while the analysis of sabotage by Taylor and Walton (1971) has interesting implications for the study of strikes. The sophisticated model of collective bargaining constructed by Walton and McKersie (1965) is of great value for the understanding of the motivation of many of the processes of industrial relations. Gouldner (1955) is the classic example of a study of industrial conflict illuminated by analysis of the participants' own motives and definitions; the same approach has been followed in the more journalistic study of Lane and Roberts (1971). More recently, Crouch (1982: Ch. 3) has offered a 'rational-action' analysis of strikes in general. The points raised in the present book in respect of levels of rationality are also discussed by Coulson and Riddell (1970) under the heading 'false consciousness' (in some ways an over-simple label).

6. Strikes and Society

The thesis that 'social problems' are socially defined is clearly stated by Blumer (1971) and Cohen (1971). Bell (1954) and Lane and Roberts (1971) both examine the social production of attitudes to strikes. On managers' ideologies, see Fox (1966 and 1971) and Nichols (1969). For a simple analysis of the importance of the ruling ideology in accommodating workers to the existing system of society, Hallas (1971) will be found useful.

Many of the economic assumptions underlying this chapter are expounded in detail by Kidron (1970); while the discussion of the role of the state follows the lucid analysis of Miliband (1969). Treatment of strikes on the basis of very different assumptions can be found in any of the orthodox texts cited with reference to Chapter 2. One account which makes its theoretical and ideological assumptions explicit is Fox and Flanders (1969); they follow Durkheim, while the present writer adopts in general the Marxist perspective. The reader who wishes to compare the approaches of Durkheim and Marx should see Horton (1964). In the concluding pages of this book it was suggested that a radical solution to the strike 'problem' would be the creation of an alternative form of social and industrial organization to that of capitalism. An extensive selection of readings on the meaning and possibilities of workers' control of industry, together with a discussion of the implications of strikes for its attainment, can be found in Coates and Topham (1970).

7. Strikes in the 1980s – and Beyond

Many of the issues discussed in the introductory section of this chapter are surveyed in a valuable assessment of 'structuralism' and 'humanism' in contemporary Marxism: see Anderson (1980). For an ambitious attempt to link recent developments in sociological analysis to the theme of industrial conflict, see Edwards (1986).

Various studies have discussed trends in British strikes since this book first appeared and have proposed a range of explanations; these include Silver (1973), Hyman (1973), Smith *et al.* (1978), Edwards (1982 and 1983), and Durcan *et al.* (1983). The specific controversy over strike ballots has been cogently examined by Fairbrother (1984).

The broader implications of the post-1979 government for trade unions and industrial relations are surveyed by MacInnes (1987).

The economic sources of the developments considered in this chapter have stimulated extensive debate. Detailed analyses by socialists of varying positions include Glyn and Harrison (1980), Gamble (1981), Hodgson (1981), and Sutcliffe (1983).

The crisis of British industrial relations has shaken the confidence with which pluralist interpretations are presented; see for example Clegg (1979), Ch. 11. Fox (1973 and 1974) are important revisions of the position of a former leading exponent of the pluralist approach. The present author has attempted to develop in greater detail than is possible here a Marxist analysis of recent trends in British industrial relations: see Hyman (1975 and 1988).

Bibliography

Allen, V. L. (1966) *Militant Trade Unionism*. London: Merlin Press.

Allen, V. L. (1981) *The Militancy of British Miners*. Shipley: Moor Press.

Anderson, P. (1967) 'The Limits and Possibilities of Trade Union Action' in Blackburn and Cockburn (1967), pp. 263–80.

Anderson, P. (1980) *Arguments Within English Marxism*. London: NLB/Verso.

Anderson, P. and Blackburn, R. (eds) (1965) *Towards Socialism*. London: Fontana.

Argyris, C. (1967) 'Individual Actualization in Complex Organizations' in Bell, G. D., *Organizations and Human Behaviour*. Englewood Cliffs: Prentice-Hall.

Arnison, J. (1970) *The Million Pound Strike*. London: Lawrence and Wishart.

Bain, G. S. (1970) *The Growth of White-Collar Unionism*. Oxford: Clarendon Press.

Bain, G. S. (ed) (1983) *Industrial Relations in Britain*. Oxford: Blackwell.

Baldamus, W. (1961) *Efficiency and Effort*. London: Tavistock.

Batstone, E. V., Boraston, I. and Frenkel, S. J. (1977) *Shop Stewards in Action*. Oxford: Blackwell.

Batstone, E. V., Boraston, I. and Frenkel, S. J. (1978) *The Social Organization of Strikes*. Oxford: Blackwell.

Behrend, H. (1957) 'The Effort Bargain'. *Industrial and Labor Relations Review*, 10, pp. 503–15.

Bell, D. (1954) 'Industrial Conflict and Public Opinion' in Kornhauser *et al.* (1954), pp. 240–56.

Berger, P. L. (1966) *Invitation to Sociology*. Harmondsworth: Penguin. (First published 1963.)

Beynon, H. (1975) *Working for Ford*. Wakefield: EP Publishers. (Originally published 1973: Penguin.)

Beynon, H. (ed) (1985) *Digging Deeper: Issues in the Miners' Strike.* London: Verso.

Blackburn, R. (1965) 'The New Capitalism' in Anderson and Blackburn (1965), pp. 114–45.

Blackburn, R. (1967) 'The Unequal Society' in Blackburn and Cockburn (1967), pp. 15–55.

Blackburn, R. and Cockburn, A. (eds) (1967) *The Incompatibles: Trade Union Militancy and the Consensus.* Harmondsworth: Penguin.

Blumer, H. (1971) 'Social Problems as Collective Behaviour'. *Social Problems*, 18, pp. 298–306.

Blumler, J. G. and Ewbank, A. J. (1970) 'Trade Unionists, the Mass Media and Unofficial Strikes'. *British Journal of Industrial Relations*, 8, pp. 32–54.

Boulding, K. E. (1963) *Conflict and Defense.* New York: Harper.

Brecher, J. (1972) *Strike!* San Francisco: Straight Arrow.

Brown, W. A. (1973) *Piecework Bargaining.* London: Heinemann.

Brown, W. A. (ed) (1981) *The Changing Contours of British Industrial Relations.* Oxford: Blackwell.

Burawoy, M. (1979) *Manufacturing Consent.* Chicago: University of Chicago Press.

Campbell, A. and McIlroy, J. (1981) *Getting Organized.* London: Pan.

Carchedi, G. (1975) 'On the Economic Identification of the New Middle Class'. *Economy and Society*, 4, pp. 1–86.

Chinoy, E. (1955) *Automobile Workers and the American Dream.* New York: Doubleday.

Clack, G. (1967) *Industrial Relations in a British Car Factory.* Cambridge: Cambridge University Press.

Clay, H. (1928) *The Problem of Industrial Relations.* London: Macmillan.

Clegg, H. A. (1956) 'Strikes'. *Political Quarterly*, 27, pp. 31–43.

Clegg, H. A. (1970 and 1976) *The System of Industrial Relations in Great Britain* (1st and 3rd editions). Oxford: Blackwell.

Clegg, H. A. (1979) *The Changing System of Industrial Relations in Great Britain.* Oxford: Blackwell.

Clegg, H. A. and Adams, R. (1957) *The Employers' Challenge.* Oxford: Blackwell.

Cliff, T. (1970) *The Employers' Offensive*. London: Pluto Press.

Coates, K. (1967) 'Wage Slaves' in Blackburn and Cockburn (1967), pp. 56–92.

Coates, K. and Topham, A. (1970) *Workers' Control*. London: Panther.

Cohen, P. S. (1968) *Modern Social Theory*. London: Heinemann.

Cohen, S. (ed) (1971) *Images of Deviance*. Harmondsworth: Penguin.

Cole, G. D. H. (1913) *The World of Labour*. London: Bell.

Cole, G. D. H. (1920) *Chaos and Order in Industry*. London: Methuen.

Cole, G. D. H. (1939) *British Trade Unionism Today*. London: Gollancz.

Coser, L. A. (1956) *The Functions of Social Conflict*. London: Routledge and Kegan Paul.

Coulson, M. A. and Riddell, D. S. (1970) *Approaching Sociology: a Critical Introduction*. London: Routledge and Kegan Paul.

Cronin, J. E. (1979) *Industrial Conflict in Modern Britain*. London: Croom Helm.

Crouch, C. (1982) *Trade Unions: the Logic of Collective Action*. London: Fontana.

Dahrendorf, R. (1959) *Class and Class Conflict in Industrial Society*. London: Routledge and Kegan Paul.

Dahrendorf, R. (1968) *Society and Democracy in Germany*. London: Weidenfeld and Nicolson.

Daniel, W. W. and Millward, N. (1983) *Workplace Industrial Relations in Britain*. London: Heinemann.

Davies, R. J. (1983) 'Incomes and Anti-Inflation Policy' in Bain (1983), pp. 419–52.

Dennis, H., Henriques, F. and Slaughter, C. (1957) *Coal is Our Life*. London: Eyre and Spottiswoode. (Republished 1969: Tavistock.)

Devlin, Lord (1965) Chairman, Committee of Inquiry, Port Transport Industry. *Final Report*. London: HMSO, Cmnd. 2734.

Donovan, Lord (1968) Chairman, Royal Commission on Trade Unions and Employers' Associations. *Report*. London: HMSO.

Dubin, R. (1954) 'Constructive Aspects of Industrial Conflict' in Kornhauser *et al.* (1954), pp. 37–47.

Dunlop, J. T. (1958) *Industrial Relations Systems*. New York: Holt.

Durcan, J. and McCarthy, W. E. J. (1972) 'What is Happening to Strikes?' *New Society*, 22, pp. 267–9.

Durcan, J., McCarthy, W. E. J. and Redman, G. P. (1983) *Strikes in Post-War Britain*. London: Allen and Unwin.

Durkheim, E. (1933) *The Division of Labour in Society*. London: Macmillan. (Original French edition 1893.)

Edwards, P. K. (1979) 'The "Social" Determination of Strike Activity', *Journal of Industrial Relations*, 21, pp. 198–216.

Edwards, P. K. (1982) 'Britain's Changing Strike Problem?' *Industrial Relations Journal*, 13, pp. 5–20.

Edwards, P. K. (1983) 'The Pattern of Collective Industrial Action' in Bain (1983), pp. 209–34.

Edwards, P. K. (1986) *Conflict at Work*. Oxford: Blackwell.

Edwards, P. K. and Scullion, H. (1982) *The Social Organization of Industrial Conflict*. Oxford: Blackwell.

Eldridge, J. E. T. (1968) *Industrial Disputes*. London: Routledge and Kegan Paul.

Fairbrother, P. (1984) *All Those in Favour*. London: Pluto Press.

Flanders, A. (1964) *The Fawley Productivity Agreements*. London: Faber and Faber.

Flanders, A. (1968) *Trade Unions*, 7th edn. London: Hutchinson. (First published 1952.)

Flanders, A. (1970) *Management and Unions*. London: Faber and Faber.

Foot, P. (1967) 'The Seamen's Struggle' in Blackburn and Cockburn (1967), pp. 169–209.

Foot, P. (1971) *The Postal Workers and the Tory Offensive*. London: Socialist Worker.

Fox, A. (1966) *Industrial Sociology and Industrial Relations*. Royal Commission Research Paper 3. London: HMSO.

Fox, A. (1971) *A Sociology of Work in Industry*. London: Collier Macmillan.

Fox, A. (1972) 'Industrial Relations and Pluralist Ideology'. (Draft of Fox 1973.)

Fox, A. (1973) 'Industrial Relations: a Social Critique of Pluralist Ideology' in Child, J., *Man and Organization*. London: Allen and Unwin.

Fox, A. (1974) *Man Mismanagement*. London: Hutchinson.

Fox, A. and Flanders, A. (1969) 'The Reform of Collective Bargaining: from Donovan to Durkheim'. *British Journal of Industrial Relations*, 7, pp. 151–80.

Fraser, R. (ed) (1968) *Work: Twenty Personal Accounts*. Harmondsworth: Penguin.

Fraser, R. (ed) (1969) *Work 2: Twenty Personal Accounts*. Harmondsworth: Penguin.

Frayn, M. (1967) 'A Perfect Strike' in Blackburn and Cockburn (1967), pp. 160–6.

Frow, R., Frow, E. and Katanka, M. (1971) *Strikes: a Documentary History*. London: Charles Knight.

Gamble, A. (1981) *Britain in Decline*. London: Macmillan.

Gamble, A. and Walton, P. (1976) *Capitalism in Crisis*. London: Macmillan.

Glyn, A. and Harrison, J. (1980) *The British Economic Disaster*. London: Pluto Press.

Glyn, A. and Sutcliffe, B. (1972) *British Capitalism, Workers and the Profits Squeeze*. Harmondsworth: Penguin.

Goldthorpe, J. H., Lockwood, D., Bechhofer, F. and Platt, J. (1968) *The Affluent Worker: Industrial Attitudes and Behaviour*. Cambridge: Cambridge University Press.

Goodman, J. F. B. (1967) 'Strikes in the United Kingdom'. *International Labour Review*, 95, pp. 465–81.

Goodman, J. F. B. and Whittingham, T. G. (1973) *Shop Stewards*. London: Pan.

Goodrich, C. L. (1920) *The Frontier of Control*. London: Bell. (Republished 1975: Pluto Press.)

Gorz, A. (1965) 'Work and Consumption' in Anderson and Blackburn (1965), pp. 317–53. (First published 1964 as 'Trade Unionism on the Attack': *International Socialist Journal*.)

Gouldner, A. W. (1955) *Wildcat Strike*. London: Routledge and Kegan Paul.

Gouldner, A. W. (1969) 'The Unemployed Self' in Fraser (1969), pp. 346–65.

Gouldner, A. W. (1970) *The Coming Crisis of Western Sociology*. New York: Basic Books.

Government Social Survey (1968) *Workplace Industrial Relations*. London: HMSO.

Griffin, J. I. (1939) *Strikes: a Study in Quantitative Economics*. New York: Columbia University Press.

Hallas, D. (1971) *The Meaning of Marxism*. London: Pluto Press.

Halloran, J. D., Elliott, P. and Murdock, G. (1970) *Demonstrations and Communications: a Case Study*. Harmondsworth: Penguin.

Handy, L. J. (1968) 'Absenteeism and Attendance in the British Coal-Mining Industry'. *British Journal of Industrial Relations*, 6, pp. 37–50.

Handy, L. J. (1981) *Wages Policy in the British Coalmining Industry*. Cambridge: Cambridge University Press.

Harbison, F. H. (1954) 'Collective Bargaining and American Capitalism' in Kornhauser *et al.* (1954), pp. 270–9.

Harris, N. (1972) *Competition and the Corporate Society*. London: Methuen.

Hartley, J., Kelly, J. and Nicholson, N. (1983) *Steel Strike*. London: Batsford.

Herberg, W. (1943) 'Bureaucracy and Democracy in Labor Unions'. *Antioch Review*, 3, pp. 405–17. (Reprinted in Rowan, R. L. and Northrup, H. R., *Readings in Labor Economics and Labor Relations*, 1968.)

Hicks, J. R. (1932) *The Theory of Wages*. London: Macmillan.

Hill, J. M. M. and Trist, E. L. (1955) 'Changes in Accidents and Other Absences with Length of Service'. *Human Relations*, 8, pp. 121–52.

Hodgson, G. (1981) *Labour at the Crossroads*. Oxford: Blackwell.

Holland, S. (1975) *The Socialist Challenge*. London: Quartet.

Horton, J. (1964) 'Alienation and Anomie'. *British Journal of Sociology*, 15, pp. 283–300.

Hyman, R. (1970) 'Economic Motivation and Labour Stability'. *British Journal of Industrial Relations*, 9, pp. 159–78.

Hyman, R. (1971a) *The Workers' Union*. Oxford: Clarendon Press.

Hyman, R. (1971b) *Marxism and the Sociology of Trade Unionism*. London: Pluto Press.

Hyman, R. (1972) *Disputes Procedure in Action*. London: Heinemann.

Hyman, R. (1973) 'Industrial Conflict and the Political Economy' in Miliband, R. and Saville, J., *Socialist Register (1973)*. London: Merlin Press.

Hyman, R. (1975) *Industrial Relations: a Marxist Introduction.* London: Macmillan.

Hyman, R. (1979) 'The Politics of Workplace Trade Unionism'. *Capital and Class*, 8, pp. 54–67.

Hyman, R. (1980) 'Trade Unions, Control and Resistance' in Esland, G. and Salaman, G. (eds), *The Politics of Work and Occupations*, pp. 303–34. Milton Keynes: Open University Press.

Hyman, R. (1982) 'Pressure, Protest and Struggle' in Bomers, G. B. J. and Peterson, R. B. (eds), *Conflict Management and Industrial Relations*, pp. 401–22. Boston: Kluwer-Nijhoff.

Hyman, R. (1986) 'Reflections on the Mining Strike' in Miliband, R. *et al.*, *Socialist Register 1985/86.* London: Merlin Press.

Hyman, R. (1988) *The Political Economy of Industrial Relations.* London: Macmillan.

Johnson, D. (1968) 'Factory Time' in Fraser (1968), pp. 11–21.

Johnston, E. (1975) *Industrial Action.* London: Arrow Books.

Kahn, P., Lewis, N., Livock, R. and Wiles, P. (1983) *Picketing.* London: Routledge and Kegan Paul.

Katz, D. (1954) 'Satisfactions and Deprivations in Industrial Life' in Kornhauser *et al.* (1954), pp. 86–101.

Kelly, J. and Nicholson, N. (1980) 'Strikes and Other Forms of Industrial Action'. *Industrial Relations Journal*, 11, pp. 20–31.

Kerr, C. (1964) *Labor and Management in Industrial Society.* New York: Doubleday. (References are to the article 'Industrial Conflict and its Mediation', first published 1954 in *American Journal of Sociology*.)

Kidron, M. (1970) *Western Capitalism Since the War.* Harmondsworth: Penguin. (First published 1968.)

Knowles, K. G. J. C. (1952) *Strikes: a Study in Industrial Conflict.* Oxford: Blackwell.

Kornhauser, A. (1954) 'Human Motivations Underlying Industrial Conflict' in Kornhauser *et al.* (1954), pp. 62–85.

Kornhauser, A., Dubin, R. and Ross, A. M. (eds) (1954) *Industrial Conflict.* New York: McGraw-Hill.

Kuhn, J. W. (1961) *Bargaining in Grievance Settlement.* New York: Columbia University Press.

Lane, T. (1974) *The Union Makes Us Strong.* London: Arrow Books.

Lane, T. and Roberts, K. (1971) *Strike at Pilkingtons*. London: Fontana.

Lipset, S. M. (1959) 'Political Sociology' in Merton, R. K. *et al.*, *Sociology Today*, pp. 81–114. New York: Basic Books.

Liverpool University (1955) *The Dock Worker*. Liverpool: Liverpool University Press.

Lockwood, D. (1955) 'Arbitration and Industrial Conflict'. *British Journal of Sociology*, 6, pp. 335–47.

Lockwood, D. (1958) *The Blackcoated Worker*. London: Allen and Unwin.

Macpherson, C. B. (1962) *The Political Theory of Possessive Individualism*. Oxford: Clarendon Press.

McCarthy, W. E. J. (1959) 'The Reasons Given for Striking'. *Bulletin of the Oxford University Institute of Statistics*, 21, pp. 17–29.

McCarthy, W. E. J. (1966) *The Role of Shop Stewards in British Industrial Relations*. Royal Commission Research Paper 1. London HMSO.

McCarthy, W. E. J. (1970) 'The Nature of Britain's Strike Problem'. *British Journal of Industrial Relations*, 8, pp. 224–36.

McCarthy, W. E. J. and Parker, S. R. (1968) *Shop Stewards and Workshop Relations*. Royal Commission Research Paper 10. London: HMSO.

McIlroy, J. (1984) *Strike!* London: Pluto Press.

McInnes, J. (1987) *Thatcherism at Work*. Milton Keynes: Open University Press.

Magrath, C. P. (1959) 'Democracy in Overalls'. *Industrial and Labor Relations Review*, 12, pp. 503–25.

Marshall, A. (1899) *Economics of Industry*, 3rd edn. London: Macmillan.

Marx, K. (1961) *Economic and Philosophic Manuscripts of 1844*. Moscow: Foreign Languages Publishing House.

Merton, R. K. (1968) *Social Theory and Social Structure*, 3rd edn. New York: Free Press. (First published 1949.)

Michels, R. W. E. (1915) *Political Parties*. New York: Hearst's. (Original German edition 1911; republished 1959: Dover Publications.)

Miliband, R. (1969) *The State in Capitalist Society*. London: Weidenfeld and Nicolson.

Mills, C. Wright (1948) *The New Men of Power*. New York: Harcourt Brace.

Mills, C. Wright (1959) *The Sociological Imagination*. New York: Oxford University Press. (Republished 1970: Penguin.)

Millward, N. and Stevens, M. (1986) *British Workplace Industrial Relations, 1980–1984*. Aldershot: Gower.

Ministry of Labour (1965) *Written Evidence to the Royal Commission*. London: HMSO.

Montague, K. (1979) *Going on Strike*. London: Rank and File.

Neale, J. (1983) *Memoirs of a Callous Picket*. London: Pluto Press.

Nichols, T. (1969) *Ownership, Control and Ideology*. London: Allen and Unwin.

Parkin, F. (1971) *Class Inequality and Political Order*. London: Paladin.

Parsons, T. (1937) *The Structure of Social Action*. New York: McGraw-Hill.

Phelps Brown, E. H. (1960) *The Growth of British Industrial Relations*. London: Macmillan.

Purcell, K. (1979) 'Militancy and Acquiescence Amongst Women Workers' in Burman, S. (ed), *Fit Work for Women*, pp. 112–33. London: Croom Helm.

Rickman, H. P. (1967) *Understanding and the Human Studies*. London: Heinemann.

Ross, A. M. (1948) *Trade Union Wage Policy*. Berkeley: University of California Press.

Ross, A. M. (1954) 'The Natural History of the Strike' in Kornhauser *et al.* (1954), pp. 23–36.

Ross, A. M. and Hartman, P. T. (1960) *Changing Patterns of Industrial Conflict*. New York: Wiley.

Roy, D. (1960) '"Banana Time": Job Satisfaction and Informal Interaction'. *Human Organization*, 18, pp. 158–68.

Runciman, W. G. (1966) *Relative Deprivation and Social Justice*. London: Routledge and Kegan Paul.

Sayles, L. R. (1958) *The Behavior of Industrial Work Groups*. New York: Wiley.

Schneider, E. V. (1969) *Industrial Sociology*, 2nd edn. New York: McGraw-Hill. (First published 1957.)

Schutz, A. (1964) 'The Problem of Rationality in the Social World' in *Collected Papers*, Vol. 2, pp. 64–88. The Hague: Nijhoff. (First published 1943: reprinted in Emmett, D. and MacIntyre, A., *Sociological Theory and Philosophical Analysis*, 1970.)

Scott, J. F and Homans, G. C. (1947) 'Reflections on the Wildcat Strikes'. *American Sociological Review*, 12, pp. 278–87.

Scott, W. H., Banks, J. A., Halsey, A. H. and Lupton, T. (1956) *Technical Change and Industrial Relations*. Liverpool: Liverpool University Press.

Scott, W. H., Mumford, E., McGivering, I. C. and Kirkby, J. M. (1963) *Coal and Conflict*. Liverpool: Liverpool University Press.

Silver, M. (1973) 'Recent Strike Trends: a Factual Analysis'. *British Journal of Industrial Relations*, 11, pp. 66–104.

Silverman, D. (1970) *The Theory of Organizations*. London: Heinemann.

Simon, H. A. (1957) 'Authority' in Arensberg, C. M. (ed), *Research in Industrial Human Relations*, pp. 103–15. New York: Harper and Row.

Slichter, S. H., Healy, J. J. and Livernash, E. R. (1960) *The Impact of Collective Bargaining on Management*. Washington: Brookings.

Smelser, N. (1963) *The Sociology of Economic Life*. New York: Prentice-Hall.

Smith, C. T. B., Clifton, R., Makeham, P., Creigh, S. W. and Burn, R. V. (1978) *Strikes in Britain*. London: HMSO.

Steuben, J. (1950) *Strike Strategy*. New York: Gaer.

Sutcliffe, B. (1983) *Hard Times*. London: Pluto Press.

Tannenbaum, A. S. and Kahn, R. L. (1958) *Participation in Union Locals*. New York: Harper and Row.

Tawney, R. H. (1921) *The Acquisitive Society*. London: Bell. (Republished 1961: Fontana.)

Taylor, L. and Walton, P. (1971) 'Industrial Sabotage' in Cohen (1971), pp. 219–45.

Thompson, P. (1983) *The Meaning of Work*. London: Macmillan.

Topham, A. (1967) 'New Types of Bargaining' in Blackburn and Cockburn (1967), pp. 133–59.

Touraine, A. (1965) *Workers' Attitudes to Technical Change*. Paris: OECD.

Toynbee, P. (1967) 'The Language of Inequality' in Blackburn and Cockburn (1967), pp. 95–102.

Trist, E. L., Higgin, G. W., Murray, H. and Pollock, A. B. (1963) *Organizational Choice*. London: Tavistock.

Turner, H. A. (1963) *The Trend of Strikes*. Leeds: Leeds University Press.

Turner, H. A. (1969) *Is Britain Really Strike-Prone?* Cambridge: Cambridge University Press.

Turner, H. A., Clark, G. and Roberts, G. (1967) *Labour Relations in the Motor Industry*. London: Allen and Unwin.

Turner, H. A. and Wilkinson, F. (1971) 'Real Net Income and the Wage Explosion'. *New Society*, 17, pp. 309–10.

Walker, C. R. and Guest, R. H. (1957) *The Man on the Assembly Line*. New Haven: Yale University Press.

Walton, R. E. and McKersie, R. B. (1965) *A Behavioral Theory of Labor Negotiations*. New York: McGraw-Hill.

Warner, W. L. and Low, J. O. (1947) *The Social System of the Modern Factory*. New Haven: Yale University Press.

Webb, S. and Webb, B. (1897) *Industrial Democracy*. London: Longmans.

Wellisz, S. (1953) 'Strikes in Coal-Mining'. *British Journal of Sociology*, 3, pp. 346–66.

Westergaard, J. H. (1965) 'The Withering Away of Class: a Contemporary Myth' in Anderson and Blackburn (1965), pp. 77–113.

Westergaard, J. H. (1970) 'The Rediscovery of the Cash Nexus' in Miliband, R. and Saville, J., *Socialist Register (1970)*, pp. 111–38. London: Merlin Press.

Whyte, W. F. (1951) *Pattern for Industrial Peace*. New York: Harper and Row.

Whyte, W. F. (1955) *Money and Motivation*. New York: Harper and Row.

Wigham, E. L. (1961) *What's Wrong with the Unions?* Harmondsworth: Penguin.

Williams, R. (1968) 'The Meanings of Work' in Fraser (1968), pp. 280–98.

Wilson, B. R. (ed) (1970) *Rationality*. Oxford: Blackwell.

Woodward, J. (1958) *Management and Technology*. London: HMSO.

Worsley, P. (1964) 'The Distribution of Power in Industrial Society' in Halmos, P., *The Development of Industrial Societies*, Sociological Review Monograph 8, pp. 15–34. Keele: University of Keele Press.

Young, J. (1971) 'The Role of the Police as Amplifiers of Deviancy' in Cohen (1971), pp. 27–61.

Index